The Dynamics of Social Exclusion in Europe

The Dynamics of Social Exclusion in Europe

Comparing Austria, Germany, Greece, Portugal and the UK

Edited by

Eleni Apospori

Visiting Lecturer, Athens University of Economics and Business, Greece

and

Jane Millar

Professor of Social Policy and Director, Centre for the Analysis of Social Policy, University of Bath, UK

Edward Elgar
Cheltenham, UK • Northampton, MA, USA

Published by
Edward Elgar Publishing Limited
Glensanda House
Montpellier Parade
Cheltenham
Glos GL50 1UA
UK

Edward Elgar Publishing, Inc.
136 West Street
Suite 202
Northampton
Massachusetts 01060
USA

A catalogue record for this book
is available from the British Library

Library of Congress Cataloguing in Publication Data
The dynamics of social exclusion in Europe : comparing Austria, Germany, Greece, Portugal and the UK / edited by Eleni Apospori and Jane Millar.
    p. cm.
    1. Marginality, Social—Europe. 2. Poverty—Europe. I. Apospori, Eleni, 1956– II. Millar, J.

HN380.Z9 M263 2003
305.5′68′094—dc21

2002037948

ISBN 1 84064 893 7

Printed and bound in Great Britain by MPG Books Ltd, Bodmin, Cornwall

Contents

Figures

Tables

Acknowledgments

This book reports on an analysis of European Community Household Panel data, using the panel data over two (and sometimes, three) years. It is a companion to a previous book that reported the cross-sectional analysis (Barnes *et al.*, 2002). The focus is on four 'risk' groups: young adults, sick or disabled people, lone parents and retired people. The project was part of the Targeted Socio-Economic Research Programme (TSER) under Framework 1V (project reference number PL95 3229). We are grateful to the European Commission for funding.

Thanks to Camilla Lucas and Faith Howard at the University of Bath for their work on preparing the manuscript.

Abbreviations

ATS	Austrian shillings
CHAID	Chi-square automatic interaction detection
€	Euro
EC	European Commission
ECHP	European Community Household Panel
EMU	Economic and monetary union
EU	European Union
GDP	Gross Domestic Product
GDR	German Democratic Republic
GSOEP	German Socio-Economic Panel
LSA	German Longitudinal Social Assistance Panel
PTE	Portuguese Escudos
SAA	German Social Assistance Act
SILC	Survey of Income and Living Conditions (EU)
TSER	Targeted Socio-Economic Research Programme
UK	United Kingdom

Contributors

Laura Adelman is a research associate at the Centre for Research in Social Policy at Loughborough University. Her main research interests are the definition and measurement of poverty and social exclusion, and the living standards of children. Recent publications include, with D. Gordon *et al.*, *Poverty and Social Exclusion in Britain* (2000).

Eleni Apospori is a sociologist and visiting lecturer at the Department of Marketing and Communication at the Athens Universty of Economics and Business. Women's issues, youth, social control and marginalization are among her research interests. Related publications include *Gender Differences on Socioeconomic Status, First Report Based on the Analysis of Data of 1996 Labour Force Survey and 1991 Census, TSER* (1998, Athens: Diotima); *Longitudinal Comparisons on Gender Differences, Second Report Based on the Secondary Analysis of 1987–1997 Labour Force Surveys, TSER* (1998, Athens: Diotima); 'Mother's Work outside the Home and Children's Deviant Behaviour' in C.D. Spinellis, *Crime in Greece in Perspective* (1999, Athens: Sakkoulas).

Isabel Baptista is senior researcher at CESIS – Centro de Estudos para a Intervenção Social – with coordination responsibilities. Her main research interests are poverty, and social exclusion, ageing and urban poverty, especially extreme urban marginalization. Recent publications in the fields of ageing and urban poverty include *(Re)inventar solidariedades. O Local como eixo dinamizador do apoio social às pessoas idosas. Que inovação possível?* (with Heloísa Perista *et al.*, 2000), and *Women, Homelessness and Access to Services – Portugal* (with Alfredo Bruto da Costa).

Matt Barnes is a senior researcher at the National Centre for Social Research, London. His main research interest is the quantitative measurement of poverty and social exclusion. He has recently completed a doctorate investigating the multidimensional and longitudinal nature of social exclusion in the UK and comparisons with other EU countries, using data from the British Household Panel Survey and the European Community Household Panel survey.

Alfredo Bruto da Costa is Assistant Professor at the Portuguese Catholic University and research coordinator at CESIS – Centro de Estudos para a Intervenção Social. His main research interests are poverty, social exclusion and social policy. He is a member of the European Committee of Social Rights, of the Council of Europe. Recently, he was consultant to the European Commission for the evaluation of the Portuguese National Action Plan for Social Inclusion.

Ana Cardoso is a senior researcher at CESIS – Centro de Estudos para a Intervenção Social with coordination responsibilities. Her main research interests are poverty, social exclusion, young people and social policy, especially activation policies. Recent publications in the fields of urban poverty and activation policies include *Pobreza e Exclusão Social em Portugal: Região de Lisboa e Vale do Tejo e Área Metropolitana do Porto* (with Alfredo Bruto da Costa *et al.*, 1999) and 'Coordination in Activation Policies for Minimum Income Recipients: the case of Portugal' (in *Journal Assistenza Sociale*).

Andreas Cebulla is Assistant Director, Lifestyles and Living Standards, at the Centre for Research in Social Policy, Loughborough University, UK. His work includes research in urban social and economic development, in risk perceptions and assessments in social policy, and the study of the evidence basis of welfare-to-work programmes in the United States and of job retention policies. Recent publications include *Unemployment and the Insurance Compensation Principle in Britain and Germany* (with R. Walker and H. Heinelt, 2001).

Christopher Heady is Head of the Tax Policy and Statistics Division of the OECD and a Visiting Professor of Economics at the University of Bath. His interests include public economics, development economics and the economics of the environment and natural resources. Within public economics, he has published a number of papers on the design and distributional effects of tax and social transfer systems in developed, developing and transitional economies.

Karin Heitzmann is Assistant Professor at the Department of Social Policy of the Vienna University of Economics and Business Administration, and consultant of the Human Development Network, Social Protection Department, of the World Bank. Her research interests include poverty and social exclusion, non-profit organizations, and comparative social policy.

Olaf Jürgens is a Research Fellow at the Centre for Social Policy Research in Bremen. He was a Visiting Fellow at the University of Milan I (Università degli Studi di Milano) in Milan, Italy and worked also for the EU project, 'Social Integration through Obligations to Work? Current European "Workfare" Initiatives and Future Directions'. Currently he is participating in the project, 'Grundlagen und Methoden des Lebenslagenansatzes', which provides an expert's report for the annual poverty report of the German government. His PhD thesis will be an empirical analysis of social security and social justice. Recent publications include *Sozialhilfebezug erwerbsfähiger Armer. Drei europäische Städte im Vergleich* (2001).

Sue Middleton is Co-Director of the Centre for Research in Social Policy (CRSP) at the University of Loughborough. She has over 25 years of research experience in a range of academic, commercial, government and voluntary sector settings. She currently leads programmes of national and international work on poverty and social exclusion and young people's transitions to adulthood. Her main research interests are in social policy for children, young people and families, and in the definition and measurement of poverty and social exclusion.

Jane Millar is Professor of Social Policy and Director of the Centre for the Analysis of Social Policy at the University of Bath. Her main research interests are social security and family policy, especially lone parenthood, poverty and support for children. Recent publications include *Lone parents, employment and social policy: cross-national comparisons* (editor with K. Rowlingson, 2001) and *Families, poverty, work and care: a review of the literature on lone parents and low-income couple families with children* (with T. Ridge, 2001).

Pedro Perista is a junior researcher at CESIS – Centro de Estudos para a Intervenção Social. His main research interests are poverty and social exclusion, ageing, social policies, migrations and ethnic minorities. Recent publications in the fields of ageing and social policies and social exclusion dynamics include (*Re*)*inventar solidariedades. O Local como eixo dinamizador do apoio social às pessoas idosas. Que inovação possível?* (with Heloísa Perista *et al.*, 2000) and 'Pobreza, exclusão social e transições em ciclo de vida' (with Ana Cardoso *et al.*, 2001, in *Cidades, Comunidades e Territórios, n.° 2*).

Graham Room is Professor of European Social Policy at the University of Bath. He has acted as a consultant to the European Commission on the development of its programmes in the field of poverty and social exclusion. He was founding editor of the *Journal of European Social Policy, 1990–2000*. Relevant publications include *Europe Against Poverty: The European Poverty Programme 1975–80* (1982), *New Poverty in the European Community* (1990), *Towards a European Welfare State?* (1991), *Anti-Poverty Action-Research in Europe* (1993) and *Beyond the Threshold: The Measurement and Analysis of Social Exclusion* (1995).

Panos Tsakloglou is Associate Professor at the Department of International and European Economic Studies (DIEES) of the Athens University of Economics and Business and Research Fellow of IZA (Bonn) and IMOP (Athens). He has written a large number of articles in academic journals and contributions to collective volumes on issues of poverty, inequality, social exclusion and social policy. Recent publications include *Poverty and Social Exclusion in Europe* (with M. Barnes, C. Heady, S. Middleton, J. Millar, F. Papadopoulos and G. Room, 2002), and *Social Exclusion in European Welfare States* (editor with R. Muffels and D. Mayes, 2003), both published by Edward Elgar.

Wolfgang Voges is Professor at the Institute for Sociology and the Centre for Social Policy Research of the University of Bremen. His major research interests are social structure analysis and social policy, health and social inequality, and methods and techniques of international comparative empirical research. He directed the German part of several projects of the EC-Program TSER and co-directed the 'Social Assistance Dynamics' project of the Special Research Center 186 of the German National Science Foundation. Currently he is directing a project on 'Foundations and Methods for the Way of Living Approach' for the German government. Voges has been Visiting Fellow at the University of Wisconsin, Madison, University of Michigan, Ann Arbor, Northwestern University, Evanston, University of Gothenburg and CEPS/INSTEAD in Luxembourg. He is the co-editor of a book series on social policy research. Recent publications include *Pflege alter Menschen als Beruf. Soziologie eines Tätigkeitsfeldes* (Sociology of Occupation and Skills exemplified at the Labour Market Area Taking Care for the Elderly) and an edited methodological volume, *Dynamic Approaches to Comparative Social Research*. Recent articles and book chapters include 'Social Policy towards Poverty', 'Material hardships and social justice' and 'Social Inclusion or Exclusion by Minimum Income Support Programmes in Europe'.

1. Introduction: the dynamic analysis of poverty and social exclusion

Sue Middleton, Matt Barnes and Jane Millar

Poverty and social exclusion have never been higher on the agenda of the European Union (EU). At the conclusion of the European Summit held in Lisbon in March 2000, the European Council stated that 'steps must be taken to make a decisive impact on the eradication of poverty by setting adequate targets to be agreed by the Council by the end of the year'. Following the Summit and the European Council in Nice in November 2000, each member state was required to draw up biannual National Implementation Plans for Social Inclusion, including specific indicators and monitoring mechanisms capable of measuring progress. The first set of plans were delivered to the Commission in May 2001 and have been summarized in the European Commission report, *Joint Report on Social Inclusion*, this being the 'first time that the European Union endorses a policy document on poverty and social exclusion' (European Commission, 2002, p. 9).

This represents a significant shift in policy emphasis. Prior to the Lisbon Summit of March 2000, the focus of EU concern was unemployment, and particularly long-term unemployment, as the manifestation of poverty and social exclusion with which policy should concern itself. The Lisbon summit, which emphasized the role of social policy, alongside employment and economic policies, in combating poverty and social exclusion, re-focused the European policy agenda, recognizing the multi-dimensionality of poverty and social exclusion. While unemployment remains a central concern, policy should no longer confine itself to labour market issues but should tackle poverty and social exclusion in all its manifestations. In addition to long-term unemployment, recognized risk factors for poverty and social inclusion include low education level, growing up in a vulnerable family, disability, poor health, multiple disadvantage in the area of residence, homelessness and ethnicity (ibid., 2002, pp.24–6). The existence of an intergenerational cycle of poverty and disadvantage is also recognized.

The requirement for indicators that will allow international comparison of the success, or otherwise, of national policies to address poverty and social exclusion has been addressed by the development of a set of common indicators, agreed at the Laeken Summit of December 2001. The intention is that each country will use a common set of first- and second-level indicators in collecting and analysing national data on poverty and social inclusion (Atkinson *et al.*, 2002). These indicators include measures of the persistence of poverty over time, as well as a range of indicators of non-monetary poverty such as poor education, housing and health. With the exception of housing amenities and problems, non-monetary indicators of deprivation are not included in the set of first- and second-level indicators, but are left to member states to develop at a national level if they so choose. Two points should be noted here. First, and rather obviously, the measurement of poverty persistence among the same individuals over time, and the ability to make international comparisons of this, requires that internationally comparable data be collected and analysed from the same individuals over time. Yet the European Community Household Panel (ECHP), which is at present the only source of data that allows such comparisons of income movements over time to be made among the member nations of the EU, is to be replaced by an annual cross-sectional survey (Survey of Income and Living Conditions, or SILC). Member states are simply encouraged to collect longitudinal panel data. Secondly, the failure to include non-monetary indicators of deprivation, such as lack of ownership of consumer durables, access to commonly accepted necessities of life, or social relationships, as first- or second-level indicators, will limit the extent to which the material circumstances of the potentially poor and socially excluded population can be properly investigated and understood. Such indicators are also included in the ECHP.

The aim of this book, therefore, is to exploit the potential of the ECHP, both to understand and compare the dynamics of income poverty, as well as of non-monetary deprivation, while the opportunity still exists. In doing so, the book explores the dynamics of poverty and social exclusion in five European countries: Austria, Germany, Greece, Portugal and the UK. It thus provides a unique opportunity, not only to compare the extent of social exclusion across countries, but also to compare different trajectories of change over time. In the book we analyse the dynamics of social exclusion in each of the five countries, and place the results within a wider discussion of the different national policy contexts. We also compare across the countries and consider the implications for policy at the European level.

The five countries represent a range of economic and social conditions, differing in respect of levels of poverty and wealth, demographic patterns, institutional arrangements, values and social attitudes. They are countries with different types of welfare states in term of levels of spending, types and coverage of state provision, and philosophies of state involvement in welfare. Table 1.1 provides a snapshot of the five countries in the mid-1990s, and shows the variation in size, GDP, employment and unemployment, family structures and welfare spending. Among these countries, Austria has the smallest population, has high levels of GDP per head, high male employment participation rates, low unemployment rates and high social spending. Germany is the largest country in population, with high GDP per head, fairly low employment participation rates and high unemployment rates for women, a lower proportion of young people, and high social spending. Greece has the lowest GDP per head, low employment participation rates and high unemployment rates for women, high youth unemployment, relatively few people living alone and few lone parents, low social spending and high rates of poverty. Portugal is similar to Greece in respect of GDP per head, social spending, poverty and family structures, but has a higher employment participation rate for women. The UK has relatively high unemployment rates, high rates of lone parenthood, and falls between Austria and Germany on the one hand and Greece and Portugal on the other in terms of poverty rates and social spending.

Policy approaches to poverty also differ. Germany and Austria have long-established and well developed systems of social insurance at the centre of their social security systems, with social assistance acting as a last-resort safety net. The UK has increasingly moved away from social insurance towards a greater emphasis on means-tested benefits, including wage supplements for those in work in the form of tax credits. Portugal and Greece have much less well-developed and resourced systems of social protection, with much less comprehensive coverage within social insurance schemes and more reliance upon family support and solidarity.

These countries also have somewhat different priorities in respect of tackling social exclusion, reflected in their first National Implementation Plans for Social Inclusion. The Austrian plan notes that there is already comprehensive coverage of social assistance and so does not propose many new initiatives, focusing instead on evaluation and monitoring of existing measures. The German plan emphasizes the multidimensional nature of social exclusion and identifies four priorities: integration into the labour market, reconciliation of work and family life, assistance for the most vulnerable and better allocation of social assistance. The Greek plan highlights the need for macroeconomic expansion, reductions in unemployment and greater flexibility in the labour market, reforms to welfare services, and specific support for the most vulnerable groups. The Portuguese plan emphasizes integration into the labour market, the need to develop social protection systems, and the need for the reintegration of excluded groups into society. It also sets some specific targets, including anti-poverty goals to eradicate child poverty by 2010 and to reduce absolute poverty by half

Table 1.1 *Economic and social indicators, mid-1990s*

	Austria	Germany	Greece	Portugal	UK
Total population (000s)[1]	8020	81422	10426	9902	58395
Population of working age (15–64 years) (000s)[1]	5306	54936	6769	6750	37286
GDP (million US$)[2]	168411	1669802	122620	128171	1078906
GDP per head (US$)[2]	20999	20508	11761	12944	18476
Male employment participation rate[1]	81.0	72.9	74.9	76.6	76.1
Female employment participation rate[1]	60.0	54.1	38.2	55.7	62.5
Unemployment rates men[1]	2.9	7.2	6.0	6.1	11.3
Unemployment rates women[1]	5.0	10.1	13.7	8.0	7.5
Youth unemployment rate (15–24 years)[1]	5.7	8.7	27.7	15.1	17.0
% of pop under 24[3]	30.1	26.5	30.1	33.1	32.3
% of pop over 65[3]	14.8	16.4	17.2	14.8	15.2
% of people living alone[3]	11.0	15	7.0	4.0	11.0
Lone-parent families as % of all h/holds[3]	3.0	2.0	2.0	2.0	5.0
% of GDP spent on social security[4]	25.8	28.3	17.2	16.4	21.6
% of persons in poor households[3]	17.0	18.0	21.0	24.0	20.0

Notes:
[1] European Commission (1996).
[2] OECD (1995a).
[3] European Commission (1999a); poverty is defined as households below 60 per cent of median total equivalized income.
[4] OECD (1996).

by 2005. The UK plan also includes a commitment to the abolition of child poverty (within 20 years). For working age people the main focus of the UK plan is on providing opportunities and support for employment, as the main route to social inclusion. There is also a commitment to tackling pensioner poverty, and to narrowing the gap between the richest and the poorest neighbourhoods.

It is clear, therefore, that despite the changing focus of the EU policy agenda described above, these plans continue to emphasize the importance of employment and labour market issues, although locating these within different contexts.

One of the main aims of this book is to contribute to policy development through an analysis that develops knowledge about the nature and persistence of social exclusion in different national contexts. In the next part of this chapter, therefore, previous research in this area is briefly reviewed and further consideration given to the importance of a dynamic approach to the definition and proposed measurement of poverty and social exclusion within the EU, before we give a more detailed introduction to the ECHP and to our particular approach to analysing the dynamics of social exclusion.

THE DYNAMICS AND MULTI-DIMENSIONALITY OF POVERTY AND SOCIAL EXCLUSION

The standard definition of poverty used by the EU is that 'the poor shall be taken to mean persons, families and groups of persons where resources (material, cultural and social) are so limited as to exclude them from a minimum acceptable way of life in Member States in which they live' (European Commission, 1984). The standard way of measuring poverty is to count 'individuals living in households where the household income is below 60 per cent of national equivalized median income'. While there is widespread, if by no means unanimous, agreement about this way of defining and measuring poverty, the definition of social exclusion remains a contested term and one which is phrased in different ways by different authors (for example, Paugam, 1996; Room, 1995, 1999; Berghman, 1995; Atkinson, 1998; Levitas, 1998; Hills, 1999; Hills *et al.*, 2002; Micklewright, 2002). However, all these definitions have in common an approach that defines social exclusion not only in terms of income poverty and the lack of material resources, but also in terms of the processes by which some individuals and groups become marginalized in society. They are excluded not simply from the goods and standards of living available to the majority but also from their opportunities, choices and life chances.

Less has been said in these debates about the importance of measuring poverty and social exclusion (however defined) over time and in more than one dimension for the same individuals and families. Take, for example, two individuals of working age living in the same country. The first has been income poor for only one or two months, is in good health, has high-level educational qualifications and has no children to support. The second has been income poor for most of his adult life, suffers from a disability, has no educational qualifications and two young children. Measuring poverty only at a point in time and only according to low income will suggest that both individuals are experiencing the same circumstances and would benefit from the same (limited) policy intervention. Policy based on a static 'point-in-time', unidimensional definition of poverty is likely to compensate some individuals unnecessarily while underestimating the needs of those who are multiply deprived over a long period.

When we move from national to international comparisons, further complications are added, since the rates at which people experience income and other forms of poverty and social exclusion, however defined, vary from country to country. There are also differences in the types of families and households most at risk of poverty, and the circumstances in which poor people live. Understanding these complexities requires an approach that goes beyond income to include a wider range of indicators of multidimensional disadvantage and beyond current situation to include analysis of change over time. This sort of analysis has been made possible by the advent of panel data sets, including the ECHP, which is the basis for the analysis in this book.

ANALYSING SOCIAL EXCLUSION USING ECHP DATA

The ECHP, which started in 1994, collects a range of socioeconomic data for the same respondents on an annual basis. Eurostat has published some descriptive analysis of non-monetary deprivation across the EU12 countries using the ECHP data (European Commission, 1999a, 2000b, 2002). Gallie and Paugam (2000) have used ECHP data to examine the living standards and social participation of unemployed people. They found that living standards depend to a considerable extent on the intervention of the welfare state and that the degree of social integration depends on the type and stability of family structures. Whelan *et al.* (2001, 2002) examined the relationship between persistent income poverty and multiple deprivation and showed that only a modest proportion of the persistently poor can be characterized as being exposed to such deprivation. Barnes *et al.* (2002) summarized findings from cross-sectional analysis of the ECHP data and focused on inter-country comparisons. The present volume reports on a dynamic analysis, one that explores the dynamics of social exclusion both cross-nationally and through detailed analysis at the national level.

The approach is 'dynamic' in two main senses. First, in respect of the life course, the analysis focuses on four 'transition' or 'risk' groups who might be anticipated to be at particular risk of poverty and social exclusion:

1. young adults (who may be leaving school, entering work or further education, leaving home, forming families);
2. lone parents (who are caring for children without a partner for a period of time);
3. people experiencing sickness or disability (which may be limiting employment or other opportunities); and
4. people retiring from employment (who are becoming reliant on other sources of income apart from their own earnings).[1]

Two of these – young adulthood and retirement – are universal life course transitions that everyone experiences, wherever they live, provided, of course, that they live long enough. The other two – lone parenthood and sickness/disability – are risks faced only by some people and there are substantial differences across countries in the extent of these. Focusing upon these times of transition allowed us to consider the extent to which life course changes make people particularly vulnerable to poverty and social exclusion.

The project is also dynamic in the sense that it aims to follow individuals over time. The four risk groups identify people at different stages of the life course, but to understand how the transitions affect individuals an examination is also needed of the nature and extent of the changes they experience. In practice, for statistical reasons (see further below), we have concentrated on changes within the four risk groups over a 12-month period.

As ever with empirical work of this sort, a number of issues of definition and measurement had to be resolved. Here four key areas are discussed: the static and dynamic definition of the risk groups, the choice of data, the static and dynamic definition and measurement of income and the static and dynamic definition and measurement of non-monetary material deprivation and multidimensional disadvantage.

DEFINING THE RISK GROUPS

The project focuses upon four 'transitions' or 'risk' groups, as described above, and a detailed definition of each group is shown in Table 1.2. Each

Table 1.2 'Risk group' definitions

Risk group	Definition
Young adults	Individuals between 16 and 29 years of age.
Lone parents	Individuals 16 years and over and below state retirement age: 1. who live without a cohabiting partner but with at least one dependent child (under 16 years or in full-time education), 2. who live without a cohabiting partner but with children – all of whom are non-dependent.
Sick or disabled people	Individuals 16 years of age and over and below state retirement age, whose health in general is very bad, or who are severely hampered in daily activities.
Retired people	Adults over 45 years of age who declare themselves as retired, or adults who do not declare themselves as retired but who are over state retirement age and not working full-time (16 or more hours per week).

of these represents times of transition that may make people particularly vulnerable to poverty and social exclusion.

The complexity of the issues involved in making comparisons across countries is apparent when defining the four risk groups. Although the transition from youth to adulthood is an inevitable and universal process, the characteristics that are used to differentiate a young person from an adult vary between countries and this is reflected in the provisions made for young people, and the rights and responsibilities given to them. Each country has its own age-based definition of a 'young person'. In the countries in our study, ages range from 15 to 19 years in Greece to 15 to 30 years in Germany. These differences in definition result in variations in the proportion of each country's population that is identified as belonging to the transitional group. For the purposes of this analysis a common age-based definition was chosen – those between 16 and 29 years of age – which approximately encompasses the range found in the different countries.

Defining lone parenthood also meant creating a compromise between different national definitions. Some countries define lone parenthood according to the age of the youngest child, but the age limit varies. Austria, for example, limits the definition of lone parenthood to families where the youngest child is under 15 years old, whereas the UK age limit is under 16 years, or under 18 years if the child is not in employment. Germany,

Portugal and Greece consider any single person with never married children living in their household, whatever their age, to be a lone parent.

These patterns raise questions about the most appropriate definition of lone parenthood for cross-national comparative purposes. Often the focus of research has been on lone parents with dependent children only (for example, Hobson, 1994; Kilkey and Bradshaw, 1999). This makes sense when we are seeking to compare the circumstances of those who are solely responsible (financially and in other ways) for children. However, the focus on dependent children ignores the circumstances of quite a substantial group of lone parents, especially in the southern countries. Thus two main groups of lone parents have been chosen: those living with at least one dependent child (under 16 years or in full-time education) and those living with only non-dependent children. This allows an examination of whether these demographic differences are reflected in differences in incomes and a comparison of what may be very different experiences of lone parenthood in these countries.

The definition of ill-health and disability in respect of access to state welfare provisions varies between countries and within countries. It is sometimes based on incapacity to carry out certain activities and sometimes linked to a person's ability to participate in the labour market. The definition of sickness or disability chosen for the project is based on age and subjective assessments of individuals' health – individuals 16 years of age and over and below state retirement age, whose health in general is very bad, or who are severely hampered in daily activities. The definition is relatively strict, identifying those who believe their health to be very bad (the fifth point of a five point scale) or who feel severely hampered in their daily activities. The focus is kept on working age people in order not to conflate issues of ill-health and ageing.

Finally, at the time of the research official retirement ages varied between men and women in all countries, with women retiring at 60 in most countries – five years earlier than men. The *actual* age of retirement, however, is often much lower and with a smaller difference between men and women. Some countries make statutory provision for certain groups of workers to take earlier retirement with a pension, and workers also have the option of reaching private arrangements with their employers. Retirement may also be a tricky concept for women who have had no, or little, labour market participation and who may not, therefore, define themselves as retired. The definition chosen for the project – those over 45 years of age who say they are retired and those over state retirement age who are not working full-time even if they do not say that they are retired – is intended to pick up both early retirees and women even if they do not describe themselves as retired.

The original intention of the project was to examine what happens to individuals as they enter or leave a particular risk group: become a lone parent, for example, or take another partner, become sick or disabled, enter retirement, and so on. In practice, however, the data did not usually provide sufficient numbers of people making these transitions because, over the course of 12 months, the numbers making such changes (becoming a lone parent, for example) are relatively small. Such analyses have been made where possible but, in general, we have concentrated upon changes in employment, income and living standards within the four risk groups over a 12-month period.

In fact, small sample sizes limit the analysis in a number of ways. For the cross-sectional analysis, small sub-group sizes make it difficult to carry out detailed examination of some groups. The number of lone parents, for example, is very small in some of the countries under study. For the dynamic analysis, small numbers mean that we have been unable to analyse transitions into and out of the risk groups (as noted above) and, instead, have focused on changes within each group. Again, for lone parents, small numbers also limit what is possible. Where possible, statistical techniques based on linear models have been used, which do not require such large sample sizes.[2]

WAVES OF DATA

The panel design of the ECHP survey allows the same individuals to be followed over time by annually re-interviewing original sample members (those in households selected for inclusion in the first wave of the survey) on a yearly basis. The majority of dynamic analysis presented in this book uses data from waves 2 and 3 of the ECHP. This limited time span is less than ideal for dynamic analysis, but this was the only ECHP information available at that time. Initial analysis of the ECHP used the first wave of data (reference year 1994) but experience with wave 1 data, combined with reports from other users, suggested that data quality was not as good as for wave 2. It was therefore decided to concentrate upon wave 2 as the base for the longitudinal analysis. Cross-sectional and longitudinal sample sizes for adults aged 16 years and over for each country are presented in Table 1.3.[3]

As with all panel surveys, the ECHP suffers from non-response and attrition. The size of subsequent wave samples falls short of the original panel sample collected in the first year because of non-contact, non-response, failure to follow up sample cases for other reasons, and households ceasing to exist. Analysis of non-response shows that, on the whole, cross-sectional response rates of the ECHP are comparable to those of similar complex

Table 1.3 *Cross-sectional and longitudinal populations, adults 16 years of age and over,[1] ECHP, 1995–6*

	Cross-sectional sample		Longitudinal sample
	Wave 2	Wave 3	Wave 2–Wave 3
Austria	7437	7270	6579
Germany	9002	8744	8539
Greece	12271	11605	11125
Portugal	11858	11706	10964
UK	8386	6938	6645

Note: [1] Samples restricted to adults who completed a personal interview.

national surveys. At a longitudinal level, more than 75 per cent of all people participating in the ECHP had been interviewed in all of the first three waves of the survey (European Commission, 2000b).[4]

THE DEFINITION AND MEASUREMENT OF INCOME, POVERTY AND POVERTY MOVEMENTS

Income and income poverty are key concepts in almost all studies of deprivation, yet are extremely difficult concepts to define. In the cross-sectional analysis of the project (Barnes *et al.*, 2002) the detailed income information collected from all household members was used to measure annual equivalized net disposable household income[5] (as is standard in income analysis, income is adjusted to reflect the needs of the household).[6] The definition of income poverty used was that approved by Eurostat, the statistical arm of the European Commission. They set a poverty line at 60 per cent of the median of total net equivalized household income (for all population members, including children).

One issue that causes some difficulties for longitudinal analysis is the timing of the income data in relation to all the other data collected in the ECHP survey. The income measure used in cross-sectional analysis has the disadvantage that it refers to the calendar year before the interview and so does not relate to the same time period as the other household and individual information. This disadvantage becomes absolutely crucial in dynamic analysis because changes in the household circumstances (such as sickness of an income earner) from one year to the next are not reflected in the corresponding income data. This means that attempts to relate changes in household circumstances to changes in the detailed income data produce paradoxical results, because of the difference in the timing of the different pieces of information. To deal with this problem the question that asks the main respondent to estimate the household's current monthly income has been used.[7]

When looking at poverty dynamics, the focus of analysis is on individuals who make significant moves into or out of poverty (above or below the poverty line). Analysis is not restricted simply to crossing the poverty line, as this may mean that some individuals' income may rise, or fall, by only a few Euros per year. Poverty dynamics is therefore defined in terms of both crossing the poverty line[8] and moving a significant distance in the income distribution. There are a number of possible methods that can be used to measure significant movements into (or out of) poverty. The method adopted here states that to enter (escape from) poverty an individual must be above (below) the poverty line in wave t and below (above) the poverty line in wave $t+1$, and move at least five percentile points in the relative income distributions.

Of particular interest to poverty researchers are the rate and the magnitude of movements into and out of poverty. It is possible to distinguish between four groups of individuals according to their poverty turnover: those who have remained in poverty over the two years, those who have entered poverty, those who have exited from poverty and those never in poverty over the two years.

In addition to determining groups of individuals according to their poverty turnover status, it is also possible to identify the rates of movement between groups, or poverty transitions. These identify the likelihood of moving into (entrance rate) or out of (exit rate) poverty, given an individual's position in the previous year. The poverty entrance rate is calculated as the proportion of people not in poverty in wave t who enter poverty in wave $t+1$. The poverty exit rate is calculated as the proportion of those in poverty in wave t who escape poverty in wave $t+1$. Likewise, poverty persistence and avoidance rates can be calculated. The poverty persistence rate is calculated as the proportion of those in poverty in wave t who remain in poverty in wave $t+1$. The poverty avoidance rate is calculated as the proportion of those not in poverty in wave t who remain not in poverty in wave $t+1$.

THE DEFINITION AND MEASUREMENT OF MULTIDIMENSIONAL DISADVANTAGE, SOCIAL EXCLUSION AND RELATED TRANSITIONS

The multidimensional qualities of the ECHP mean that it is possible to explore transitions into and out of states of non-monetary deprivation (as well as combining both income and deprivation measures). The deprivation measures used include items under the headings of household amenities (items such as having a separate kitchen, hot running water and central heating); household durables (items such as a television, a telephone and access to a car or van); and household necessities (items such as being able to afford a holiday once a year, new rather than second hand clothes and to replace worn-out furniture).

As with household income, working out a summary measure of who is deprived is not straightforward. One approach when calculating deprivation rates is to construct a 'proportional deprivation index' to take account of each household's possession of such items relative to that in the population as a whole. In this method, to be without an item owned by a large proportion of the population indicates greater deprivation than to be without an item owned by a lesser proportion. To ensure relativity between countries, only items that are owned by the majority of each country's population are included in the analysis. This approach to measuring relative deprivation has not often been used before, particularly in an international context.

To calculate the index, each individual is given a score for each item of zero if they possess the item and one if they do not. This score is then multiplied by the proportion of the population that possesses the item to give an 'item deprivation score'. These scores are then aggregated to give an 'overall deprivation index' (this is done separately for amenities, durables and necessities). As with income poverty, a 'deprivation line' is then calculated at 60 per cent of the median 'overall deprivation index' (80 per cent for amenities and durables, given their high ownership in the population) and anyone who falls below this is deemed to be 'in deprivation'.

As well as looking at income poverty and material deprivation, the analysis also considers social relationships. Three indicators of social relationships are used. The first denotes whether an individual is not a member of a club or organization, the second whether an individual talks to neighbours once or twice a week or less, and the third whether an individual meets friends or relatives (who live outside the household) once or twice a week or less. Unlike income poverty, deprivation and social exclusion dynamics are not restricted to individuals who make 'significant' movements across the deprivation line. This is because the properties of the deprivation index are different to those of income: in particular, it is difficult to relate a deprivation score, and hence a change in deprivation score, to a precise level of resources as is possible with income. Therefore both deprivation and social exclusion transitions are defined according to annual changes in the binary indicator of deprivation (1 if in deprivation and 0 if not in deprivation).

BOOK CONTENTS

Chapter 2 contains an inter-country comparison of the dynamic analysis of poverty and social exclusion for each of the life course or 'risk' groups. Chapters 3 to 7 place these findings in a national context. Results relating to the life course or 'risk' groups for each country are described in the context of welfare policies affecting each group at the time the data were collected. Finally, Chapter 8 provides a synthesis of the cross-national comparisons in the individual country chapters and considers their policy implications at both national and European levels. It also raises methodological issues that have arisen in the research and that have implications for future analysis and data collection.

NOTES

1. Note that unemployment has been analysed, not as a transition in itself, but as an event that can face people in any of these transitions. This was done in order to be able to analyse how unemployment, and labour market exit more widely, affect each of the groups. For a detailed analysis of unemployment using ECHP data, see Gallie and Paugam (2000).
2. The analysis presented in this book conforms to the Eurostat requirements in respect of sample sizes. These requirements are set up to prevent inaccurate reporting of results due to small sample size. The thresholds for longitudinal analysis are (a) below 10 observations (unweighted sample), base too small, results not published (shown in tables by *); (b) from 10 to 29 observations (unweighted sample), small base, so analysis must be read with caution; results may be published but are to be individually identified (shown in tables in brackets). Exactly the same rule applies for cross-sectional analysis, except that the thresholds are put respectively at 20 and 49 observations.
3. The majority of analysis focused on adults of 16 years of age and over, as they qualified to answer the individual interview, containing such information as health, social relations and labour-market activity. Those under 16 years of age were included in some analysis, as household characteristics (income, deprivation and so on) could be attributed to them.
4. As with all surveys, non-response bias can occur when households and individuals that failed to respond to the survey are systematically different from those who do respond. This can result in biased estimates when the survey results are used to make generalizations regarding the whole population. The normal method of compensating for survey non-response is to use weights that adjust the responding survey units for those that fail to respond. The ECHP applied this method in formulating both cross-sectional and longitudinal non-response rates, which were combined with weights to account for design effect and to correct the distribution of households and individuals on variables such as age, sex, main activity status and other relevant characteristics. Appropriate weights are used in all analysis presented in this book.
5. Net disposable income covers all market incomes (including wages, self-employment income, investment income, rent received) plus social transfers received, including all types of pensions plus private transfers, minus income taxes and social insurance contributions.
6. This assumes that there is considerable sharing between household members that allows for the reasonable supposition that children benefit from the income of their parents and that non-working adults benefit at least in part from the income of their working partner.

The equivalence scale used in the ECHP survey is the modified OECD scale. The modified OECD scale adopts a multiplier of 1.0 for the first adult, 0.5 for every other adult and 0.3 for every child under 14.

7. This question relies on the competence of the main respondent to estimate the household's monthly income. An alternative option would be to use the detailed income data from the next wave to represent household income for the current wave. Although probably a more reliable approach, this was impossible within the time scale of this project.

8. The poverty line for each wave is calculated using each cross-sectional population (adults and children) sample.

2. The risk of multidimensional disadvantage and social exclusion during four life stages in a dynamic perspective

Panos Tsakloglou

INTRODUCTION

Tsakloglou and Papadopoulos (2002) analysed the risk of multidimensional disadvantage and social exclusion of four risk groups – retired persons, sick or disabled persons, young adults and lone parents – in comparison with the living standards of the entire population from a static point of view in five EU member states (Austria, Germany, Greece, Portugal and the UK) using the micro data of the second wave of the European Community Household Panel (ECHP). The purpose of this analysis is to repeat this exercise in a dynamic framework, using the data of the first three waves of the ECHP, which cover the period 1994–6. Naturally, this limited time span is less than ideal for a dynamic analysis, but this was the only ECHP information available during the implementation of our project. For the purposes of the main part of the analysis, comparisons are performed in terms of low income (poverty), and relative deprivation in the fields of housing amenities, ability to afford particular durable goods and household necessities.

In broad terms, the results of the static analysis show that a number of similarities and differences can be identified in these five countries with respect to the relative welfare position of the four risk groups under examination. According to most of the indices used, two of these groups – members of lone-parent households and sick or disabled persons – face a substantially higher risk of poverty, non-monetary material deprivation and multidimensional disadvantage than the average population member in all five countries. Retired persons were found to enjoy a considerably lower standard of living than the rest of the population in the southern countries (Greece and Portugal) and the UK. In contrast, with the possible exceptions of Germany and the UK, young adults did not seem to face particularly high risks of poverty and non-monetary material deprivation.[1]

The rest of the chapter is organized as follows. The second section deals with dynamic aspects of monetary and non-monetary deprivation of the four groups under consideration. The third section examines the impact of particular transitions on the probability of moving into or out of poverty in the case of two groups (young adults and retired persons). The analysis in these two sections makes use of the information of two waves of the ECHP for all five countries. The fourth section presents results derived from all three ECHP waves and uses a slightly different concept of multidimensional disadvantage than that used in the rest of the analysis, but for four countries only. The final section provides the conclusions and highlights similarities and differences between the results of static and dynamic analysis.

DYNAMIC ASPECTS OF MONETARY AND NON-MONETARY DEPRIVATION

The concepts used in this section, such as the definitions of risk groups, income, deprivation indicators and cut-off points, are as described in Chapter 1. Naturally, for the purposes of the dynamic analysis, we restrict our focus to the longitudinal (balanced) sample, that is, the members of the population who were present in the samples of both the second and the third wave of the ECHP.

We start by looking at the aggregate picture. Table 2.1 reports for each country the proportion of the population falling below the relevant thresholds[2] in waves two and three, as well as the corresponding persistence rates.[3] The latter is the share of those who were classified as deprived in both waves among those classified as deprived only in the first wave. Persistence rates convey important information both for the purposes of our analysis and for the design of policies aimed at fighting poverty and social exclusion. This can be highlighted with a hypothetical example (Heady, 1997). Suppose that, in two countries, the poverty rate remains at 20 per cent for five consecutive years. However, in the first country the 20 per cent of the population in poverty consists always of the same individuals, whereas in the second country each year a different fifth of the population falls below the poverty line. Apparently, social exclusion is likely to be more of a problem in the first rather than the second country and, furthermore, different types of policies may be needed in order to deal with the problem in each case. For example, in the case of the second country a monetary temporary relief programme may be sufficient, whereas in the first country more structural measures may be required.

Table 2.1 Deprivation dynamics: aggregate picture, ECHP, 1995–6

Country	Poverty			Amenities deprivation			Durables deprivation			Necessities		
	Wave 2	Wave 3	Persist. rate	Wave 2	Wave 3	Persist. rate	Wave 2	Wave 3	Persist. rate	Wave 2	Wave 3	Persist. rate
Austria	10.3	11.0	64	11.5	10.0	66	9.0	9.1	46	7.8	11.3	62
Germany	10.3	9.9	63	6.3	5.0	61	9.3	10.3	31	10.8	10.7	56
Greece	19.9	20.7	82	14.6	11.2	54	17.9	17.6	63	26.8	15.9	39
Portugal	20.6	23.2	72	15.3	13.3	78	30.5	32.3	74	18.5	15.6	61
UK	23.2	22.3	78	1.2	1.0	34	9.5	7.0	48	19.6	17.7	65

The estimates in Table 2.1 suggest that between the second and the third wave the poverty rates remained quite stable (changed by less than one percentage point) in all countries apart from Portugal, where it rose substantially. Deprivation in the field of housing amenities declined in all countries under examination – relatively more so in the countries with the highest deprivation scores (Greece and Portugal). With respect to aggregate relative deprivation in the field of durable goods, the picture is mixed, with considerable changes recorded only in the UK (decline) and Portugal (increase). Finally, in the field of household necessities, all countries apart from Austria recorded declines in aggregate relative deprivation (in the case of Greece the decline is spectacular).[4] Regarding the persistence rates, with few exceptions, over half of those classified as deprived in the second wave were also classified as deprived in the third wave. As a rule of thumb, it can be noted that, as anticipated, these rates tended to be higher when the deprivation rates were relatively high in both waves.

Tables 2.2 to 2.5 report the main results of the analysis of deprivation dynamics for the four risk groups. Each of these tables is divided into four panels examining, respectively, dynamic aspects of relative deprivation in the fields of income (poverty), housing amenities, consumer durable goods and household necessities. In every panel, the members of each risk group are compared with both the entire population aged 16 plus[5] and with population members aged 16 plus with similar characteristics apart from the risk factor[6] with respect to two attributes: their probability of remaining in deprivation in both waves and their deprivation persistence rate. Since these tables report ratios, values higher (lower) than 1 denote higher (lower) than average risk of deprivation with respect to the particular attribute in the relevant field. It should be noted also, that under normal circumstances, the relative persistence rate is not likely to take values substantially different from 1, whereas this is not the case with respect to the relative probability of remaining in deprivation.[7]

The interpretation that should be given to the two sets of estimates reported in Tables 2.2 to 2.5 – comparisons of the risk groups with the entire population aged 16 plus and comparisons of the risk groups with their 'reference groups' – is the following. Comparisons with all individuals aged 16 plus provide an indication of the average dynamic risk of deprivation in comparison with the entire population. If the corresponding estimates are substantially higher (lower) than 1, it can be argued that the members of the risk group face a high (low) probability of deprivation from a dynamic point of view in comparison with the average population member. Comparisons of the risk groups with their reference groups provide a rough indication of the marginal effect of the risk factor on dynamic deprivation. In other words, if the risk factor (sickness, young age, retirement, lone parenthood) did not have any effect on dynamic deprivation, the corresponding ratios should be around 1. Values of the ratios substantially higher (lower) than 1 in the relevant rows imply that, *ceteris paribus*, the risk factor is associated with a high (low) risk of deprivation from a dynamic point of view.

Sick or Disabled Persons

Table 2.2 reports deprivation dynamics for the group of persons who were classified as sick or disabled in both waves. The estimates of the first panel show that, when the members of this group are compared with all persons aged 16 plus in the longitudinal sample with respect to their poverty situation, their poverty persistence rate appeared to be higher than average in all countries apart from Portugal (very marginally, though). Further, their relative probability of remaining in poverty in both waves was considerably higher than that of the entire population aged 16 plus in all countries under examination, especially in Germany, where the probability of remaining in poverty in both waves was almost three times higher than that for the entire population aged 16 plus. In the last two rows of each panel of Table 2.2, comparisons are performed between the members of the sick or disabled group and their reference group; that is, all persons aged 16 plus and under state retirement age who were not members of the sick or disabled group in either wave. When the sick or disabled persons are compared with their reference group, their relative position appears even more disadvantaged. In all countries their relative probabilities of remaining below the poverty line in both waves as well as their relative persistence rates were considerably higher than when the members of the group are compared with the entire population aged 16 plus.

The second panel, which examines the relative position of the members of the group in terms of their dynamic relative deprivation in the field of housing amenities, reveals that the corresponding relative persistence rates were not substantially different from those of either the entire population aged 16 plus or the members of the reference group. However, when we turn to the relative probability of remaining in deprivation, the ratios were much higher than 1 – especially when the risk group is compared with the reference group – in all countries apart from Austria.

When we examine the group's dynamic relative deprivation in terms of durable goods in the third panel of Table 2.2, persistence rates were lower than average in two countries (Austria and, especially, the UK) and higher in three (Portugal, Greece and, especially, Germany). Irrespective of whether the comparisons are made with the entire population aged 16 plus or the members of the reference group, the group's probability of remaining

Table 2.2 Deprivation dynamics: sick or disabled persons, ECHP, 1995–6

	Austria	Germany	Greece	Portugal	UK
Poverty					
Relative probability of remaining in deprivation (without controls)[1]	1.50	2.83	1.35	1.80	1.73
Relative persistence rate (without controls)[1]	1.31	1.19	1.02	0.99	1.09
Relative probability of remaining in deprivation (with controls)[2]	2.25	3.40	1.92	3.00	2.17
Relative persistence rate (with controls)[2]	1.47	1.36	1.02	1.03	1.12
Amenities deprivation					
Relative probability of remaining in deprivation (without controls)[1]	0.71	1.75	1.25	1.67	—
Relative persistence rate (without controls)[1]	1.00	0.92	1.05	1.07	—
Relative probability of remaining in deprivation (with controls)[2]	0.71	2.33	1.67	2.50	—
Relative persistence rate (with controls)[2]	0.96	0.95	1.21	1.15	—
Durables deprivation					
Relative probability of remaining in deprivation (without controls)[1]	1.25	1.67	1.33	1.71	1.25
Relative persistence rate (without controls)[1]	0.91	1.40	1.21	1.11	0.54
Relative probability of remaining in deprivation (with controls)[2]	1.25	2.50	1.45	2.00	1.25
Relative persistence rate (with controls)[2]	0.85	1.56	1.19	1.07	0.53
Necessities deprivation					
Relative probability of remaining in deprivation (without controls)[1]	2.75	3.60	2.22	1.91	3.82
Relative persistence rate (without controls)[1]	1.21	1.31	1.23	1.18	1.30
Relative probability of remaining in deprivation (with controls)[2]	3.67	4.50	3.43	2.63	4.67
Relative persistence rate (with controls)[2]	1.32	1.39	1.53	1.29	1.38

Notes:
[1] Probability of remaining in deprivation in both waves (persistence rate) for the members of the life course group over probability of remaining in deprivation in both waves (persistence rate) for all persons aged 16 plus.
[2] Probability of remaining in deprivation in both waves (persistence rate) for the members of the life course group over probability of remaining in deprivation in both waves (persistence rate) for all persons aged 16 plus and under state retirement age, who were never in the life course group.
All ECHP tables based on weighted sample; see Chapter 1.

in deprivation in both waves was higher than average in all countries (again, especially in Germany).

In the last panel of Table 2.2, which examines the group's dynamic relative deprivation in terms of household necessities, the picture is very clear. In all countries, the risk group's deprivation persistence rates were higher than those in the entire longitudinal sample of those aged 16 plus and become even higher when comparisons are restricted between the members of the risk group and the members of the reference group. When we turn to the probability of remaining in deprivation in the field of household necessities in both waves, the results of Table 2.2 are even more revealing. In all countries under consideration, the probability of remaining in deprivation among the members of the risk group was considerably higher (between 1.91 and 3.82 times) than among all population members aged 16 plus and, especially, than among the members of the reference group (between 2.63 and 4.67 times). In both cases, the highest ratios were recorded in the UK and Germany.

Young Adults

Table 2.3 is devoted to the examination of dynamic aspects of relative deprivation of the group of young adults. Since this group was defined in a purely demographic way, it was decided to present comparisons with the entire population only (in other words, we did not compare the group's situation with that of a reference group). With respect to poverty dynamics, only in Germany was the relative probability of the group's members remaining in poverty higher than that of all population members aged 16 plus. When we turn to the examination of the relative poverty persistence rates, the estimates of Table 2.3 suggest that in all countries under examination these rates were lower than average. In other words, the average poor member of the risk group in wave 2 was less likely to remain in poverty in wave 3 than the average poor population member aged 16 plus.

Unlike poverty, the situation is not that clear-cut when we turn our focus to deprivation in the fields of housing amenities and, especially, durable goods. In the field of housing amenities, a north/south divide becomes apparent. In both Greece and Portugal young adults face a substantially lower probability of remaining in deprivation as well as a lower persistence rate than the entire population, whereas in Austria and Germany these probabilities and rates were approximately equal to or higher than those faced by the average population member. Likewise, comparisons in the field of durable goods show that, with the exceptions of Portugal in the case of relative probability of remaining in deprivation in both waves and Greece

Table 2.3   Deprivation dynamics: young adults, ECHP, 1995–6

	Austria	Germany	Greece	Portugal	UK
Poverty					
Relative probability of remaining in deprivation (without controls)[1]	0.67	1.33	0.76	0.60	0.93
Relative persistence rate (without controls)[1]	0.83	0.86	0.96	0.97	0.97
Amenities deprivation					
Relative probability of remaining in deprivation (without controls)[1]	1.00	1.25	0.63	0.67	—
Relative persistence rate (without controls)[1]	1.04	0.98	0.78	0.88	—
Durables deprivation					
Relative probability of remaining in deprivation (without controls)[1]	1.25	1.33	1.05	0.95	1.50
Relative persistence rate (without controls)[1]	1.09	1.13	0.78	1.01	0.96
Necessities deprivation					
Relative probability of remaining in deprivation (without controls)[1]	1.25	1.00	0.73	0.73	3.00
Relative persistence rate (without controls)[1]	0.94	0.93	0.78	0.95	1.33

Note:
[1] Probability of remaining in deprivation in both waves (persistence rate) for the members of the life course group over probability of remaining in deprivation in both waves (persistence rate) for all persons aged 16 plus.

and the UK in the case of relative persistence rates, all other probabilities and rates reported in the third panel of Table 2.3 are higher for the group of young adults than for the entire population aged 16 plus.

The picture is also mixed in the last panel of Table 2.3, which focuses on deprivation in terms of household necessities. In the two southern countries (Greece and Portugal), both the probability of remaining in deprivation in both waves and the deprivation persistence rate of the young adults were considerably lower than those of all persons aged 16 plus. Likewise, from this point of view, young adults also appear to fare marginally better than the average population member in Germany. However, in the UK the deprivation persistence rate of young adults was higher than the population average and in both Austria and the UK the probability of remaining in deprivation in both waves was higher than the national average (particularly in the UK, where the relevant figure among young adults was three times higher than that for all persons aged 16 plus).

Retired Persons

The estimates reported in the first panel of Table 2.4 show that in all countries under examination the dynamic poverty risks of retired persons were higher than those faced both by all those aged 16 plus and by the relevant reference group (that is, persons aged over 45 who did not belong to the group of retired persons in either wave). This holds for both the poverty persistence rates (with the partial exception of Portugal) and the probability of remaining below the poverty line. In particular, when comparisons were made between the risk group and the reference group in terms of their probabilities of remaining below the poverty line, the probabilities of the retired appear to be over twice as high as those of the reference group in Austria and Portugal and over three times higher in the UK.

When comparisons were performed in terms of deprivation in the field of housing amenities, the retired appear to face lower risks than the average population member in Austria and Germany, but higher in Greece and Portugal. A peculiar picture appears when comparisons are made in terms of dynamic relative deprivation in the field of durable goods. In this case, the deprivation persistence rates of the retired were lower than those of both the reference group and all the people aged 16 plus in all countries apart from Germany. However, when we turn to the examination of the probability of remaining in deprivation in both waves, in almost all cases these probabilities were higher for the retired (especially so in the case of the UK and, in particular, when the risk group was compared with the reference group).

The results of the last panel of Table 2.4 on deprivation in terms of household necessities are very similar to those reported in the first panel of the table. In all countries, and irrespective of whether comparisons are made between the risk group and the reference group or between the risk group and the entire population aged 16 plus, the retired appear to face higher persistence rates as well as considerably higher probabilities of remaining in deprivation in both waves. In some cases, and especially when comparisons are performed between the risk group and the reference group, the differences in the corresponding probabilities were very large. For example, in the UK and Germany, the probability of a retired person remaining in relative deprivation in terms of household necessities in both waves was four times higher than the corresponding probability of somebody aged over 45 who was not a member of the group in either wave.

Table 2.4   Deprivation dynamics: retired persons, ECHP, 1995–6

	Austria	Germany	Greece	Portugal	UK
Poverty					
Relative probability of remaining in deprivation (without controls)[1]	1.83	1.17	1.15	1.86	1.53
Relative persistence rate (without controls)[1]	1.13	1.12	1.02	1.03	1.03
Relative probability of remaining in deprivation (with controls)[2]	2.75	1.40	1.65	2.33	3.29
Relative persistence rate (with controls)[2]	1.19	1.15	1.04	0.95	1.18
Amenities deprivation					
Relative probability of remaining in deprivation (without controls)[1]	0.71	0.25	1.13	1.25	—
Relative persistence rate (without controls)[1]	0.94	1.00	1.18	1.09	—
Relative probability of remaining in deprivation (with controls)[2]	1.00	0.50	1.50	2.14	—
Relative persistence rate (with controls)[2]	0.94	1.07	1.27	1.15	—
Durables deprivation					
Relative probability of remaining in deprivation (without controls)[1]	0.75	1.33	1.25	1.48	3.00
Relative persistence rate (without controls)[1]	0.80	1.07	0.97	0.85	0.89
Relative probability of remaining in deprivation (with controls)[2]	1.50	2.00	1.36	1.94	6.00
Relative persistence rate (with controls)[2]	1.00	1.10	0.92	0.80	0.78
Necessities deprivation					
Relative probability of remaining in deprivation (without controls)[1]	1.25	3.20	1.91	1.27	2.27
Relative persistence rate (without controls)[1]	1.11	1.07	1.18	1.08	1.03
Relative probability of remaining in deprivation (with controls)[2]	1.67	4.00	2.33	2.33	4.17
Relative persistence rate (with controls)[2]	1.25	1.00	1.24	1.30	1.03

Notes:
[1] Probability of remaining in deprivation in both waves (persistence rate) for the members of the life course group over probability of remaining in deprivation in both waves (persistence rate) for all persons aged 16 plus.
[2] Probability of remaining in deprivation in both waves (persistence rate) for the members of the life course group over probability of remaining in deprivation in both waves (persistence rate) for all persons aged over 45, who were never in the life course group.

Members of Lone-parent Households

Table 2.5 reports deprivation dynamics for the group of members of lone-parent households (hereafter, lone parents). For the purposes of our analysis we use two reference groups, instead of one. More specifically, we subdivided the group of lone parents into lone parents with some dependent children and lone parents without dependent children, and compared their living standards in a dynamic framework with partnered mothers with some dependent children, and partnered mothers without dependent children, respectively (in both cases, including the other members of their households).[8]

When lone parents are compared with the entire population in terms of poverty dynamics, the picture is mixed. In all countries the relative probability of lone parents remaining in poverty in both waves was higher than the national average. However, the relevant ratios differ considerably across countries. In Austria, Portugal and, particularly, Greece the differences were not enormous. However, in Germany and the UK the probability of a lone parent staying in poverty in both waves was found to be over three times higher than the national average. In terms of persistence, in all countries, apart from Greece, the corresponding rates were higher than 1. When comparisons are performed between the risk groups and the reference groups, it becomes clear that even though both sub-groups of lone parents fared worse than their reference groups, in all countries under examination, apart from Austria,[9] lone parents with some dependent children fared much worse than lone parents without dependent children vis-à-vis their reference groups.

Similar pictures emerge from the second and, particularly, the third panel of Table 2.5, where dynamic aspects of deprivation in terms of housing amenities and consumer durable goods are analysed. In all countries, apart from Austria, members of lone-parent households fared worse than the average population member. In fact, in Austria members of lone-parent households seemed to face a lower risk of dynamic deprivation in these fields than the rest of the population. In the rest of the countries under examination, the differences between members of lone-parent households and the rest of the population were far more pronounced in Germany and the UK than in Greece and Portugal. As in the first panel of Table 2.5, with the exception of Austria, the differences between the members of the risk group and the members of the reference group were larger when comparisons are made with members of households of partnered mothers with dependent children than with members of households of partnered mothers without dependent children.

The last panel of Table 2.5 also presents a picture relatively similar to that

Table 2.5 Deprivation dynamics: members of lone-parent households, ECHP, 1995–6

	Relative probability of remaining in deprivation (relative persistence) in comparison with:														
	Members of lone-parent households v. all population members					Lone parents v. partnered mothers with some dependent children[1]					Lone parents v. partnered mothers with no dependent children[1]				
	Austria	Germany	Greece	Portugal	UK	Austria	Germany	Greece	Portugal	UK	Austria	Germany	Greece	Portugal	UK
Poverty															
Relative probability of remaining in deprivation	1.55	3.02	1.16	1.53	3.10	2.40	3.83	2.40	2.18	5.25	3.00	1.33	1.23	1.83	2.86
Relative persistence rate	1.29	1.06	0.92	1.06	1.09	1.17	1.23	1.01	1.03	1.21	3.45	0.68	0.89	1.11	1.01
Amenities deprivation															
Relative probability of remaining in deprivation	0.81	2.09	1.00	1.32	—	1.17	5.00	2.00	1.83	—	4.00	1.25	1.17	1.25	—
Relative persistence rate	0.96	1.29	1.09	0.98	—	1.09	1.57	1.42	1.13	—	1.80	0.82	1.17	1.23	—
Durables deprivation															
Relative probability of remaining in deprivation	0.92	6.40	2.05	1.27	3.64	1.00	7.00	4.00	1.35	5.33	2.00	1.50	1.80	1.19	5.00

Table 2.5 continued

	Relative probability of remaining in deprivation (relative persistence) in comparison with:														
	Members of lone-parent households v. all population members					Lone parents v. partnered mothers with some dependent children[1]					Lone parents v. partnered mothers with no dependent children[1]				
	Austria	Germany	Greece	Portugal	UK	Austria	Germany	Greece	Portugal	UK	Austria	Germany	Greece	Portugal	UK
Relative persistence rate	0.63	0.51	1.10	1.15	1.05	0.83	2.76	1.22	1.16	1.23	0.85	1.05	1.07	1.00	1.05
Necessities deprivation Relative probability of remaining in deprivation	1.02	2.89	1.73	1.43	3.19	2.00	3.80	3.40	2.60	5.50	4.00	2.80	2.22	1.64	2.86
Relative persistence rate	0.98	1.18	1.15	1.20	1.16	0.87	1.21	1.20	1.75	1.45	3.55	1.18	1.58	0.98	1.15

Note: [1] Including other household members.

of the first panel of the table. In Austria, the risk of dynamic deprivation in the field of household necessities of the members of lone-parent households did not seem to be substantially different from that of the rest of the population. In all other countries under consideration, the deprivation persistence rates of the group were higher than those for the rest of the population and, more importantly, the probability that a member of the group remains in deprivation in both waves was higher than that for the average population member. As in the previous panels, the observed differences between the members of lone-parent households and the rest of the population were substantially higher in Germany and the UK than in Greece and Portugal. Finally, as in the rest of this table's panels, comparisons of the risk groups with their reference groups show that lone parenthood with dependent children had a stronger deprivation-inducing effect than lone parenthood without dependent children (again, with the exception of Austria).

FURTHER ANALYSIS OF POVERTY DYNAMICS IN TWO RISK GROUPS

The aim of this section is to examine the impact of factors associated with movements into and out of poverty for the two largest of the four risk groups that our project focused upon: young adults and retired persons. Owing to the small size of the two other risk groups – sick or disabled persons and members of lone-parent households – and the fact that we used only two waves of the ECHP, few transitions into and out of poverty and few changes in state variables were observed within these groups and, hence, it was difficult to employ successfully multivariate analysis techniques in them. The results for retired persons and young adults are reported in Tables 2.6 and 2.7, respectively. We focus primarily on the effects of changes in family circumstances and labour market status on the probability of moving into or out of poverty.

The estimates reported in Tables 2.6 and 2.7 are odds ratios. They should be interpreted as the expected number of retired persons (young adults) who moved from state X in wave 2 to state Y in wave 3 and into/out of poverty for every retired person (young adult) who made the same move but did not change poverty status, over the same ratio for retired persons (young adults) who remained in both waves in the households of the reference group.[10] As a consequence, odds ratios higher (lower) than one imply that the corresponding change from state X to state Y between the two waves is associated with an increased (decreased) probability of moving into or out of poverty. The estimates of the odds ratios were derived from logistic regressions. Four equations were estimated for each country: one for the probability of moving into poverty and one for the probability of moving out of poverty for retired persons and young adults. Naturally, the dependent variable was the movement into or out of poverty. The independent variables were sets of dummy variables for the family situation (living arrangements) and the employment situation of the retired person or the young adult in each wave, the employment situation of his/her household in each wave, his/her health status, age, sex and educational level. Tables 2.6 and 2.7 report selective odds ratios. Several other such ratios could be estimated using the coefficients of the estimated equations, reflecting the impact of various transitions.

For a number of reasons, these estimates should be interpreted with caution. In the logistic regression analysis we used as independent variables state variables in waves two and three (for example, employment status in wave two and employment status in wave three). In several pairs of such variables there were few changes between the two waves. As a result, the corresponding variables exhibited a high degree of correlation, thus violating one of the basic assumptions of regression analysis (non-collinearity). The consequence of this treatment is that, in many cases, several coefficients turned out to be statistically not significant (quite unjustifiably) and, further, a number of estimated coefficients appear to be implausibly large or small (as well as unstable). For this reason, we focus primarily on odds ratios derived from at least one statistically significant at the 5 per cent level coefficient (they are reported in bold characters in Tables 2.6 and 2.7) and, even in these cases, the above qualifications should be kept in mind when interpreting the results.

Table 2.6 reports the corresponding results for retired persons. The top panel deals with movements into poverty and the lower with movements out of poverty. Initially, we examine the effects of changes in family circumstances (for example, from living with partner and no children to living alone) for different sex and age groups. Then we examine the effect of moving from a situation where all other household members of working age were working to one where no such member was working, for males and females separately. In general, one would anticipate that if the odds ratio associated with a particular movement in the top panel of the table was higher than one, the corresponding figure in the lower panel of the table would be lower than one. It turns out that this is not always the case.

The first four rows of Table 2.6 show that in all countries a movement from a situation where the retired person lived with his/her partner to a situation where he/she was living alone – most probably because the partner died – was associated with an increased probability of moving into poverty, irrespective of the sex or the age of the retired person. However, the corre-

Table 2.6   Odds ratios resulting from changes in critical variables from wave 2 to wave 3 on the probability of moving into or out of poverty (retired persons), ECHP, 1995–6

	Austria	Germany	Greece	Portugal	UK
Movements into poverty					
From living with partner, no children to living alone (male, aged SRA-74)	3.54	**19.31**	1.38	**5.25**	2.75
From living with partner, no children to living alone (female, aged SRA-74)	3.29	**17.98**	1.73	**3.77**	3.63
From living with partner, no children to living alone (male, aged 75+)	2.24	n.a.	1.55	**4.39**	3.01
From living with partner, no children to living alone (female, aged 75+)	2.08	n.a.	1.94	**3.15**	4.79
From all other HH members working to no HH member working (male)	2.61	1.11	**0.16**	1.49	2.88
From all other HH members working to no HH member working (female)	2.43	1.04	**0.20**	1.07	3.80
Movements out of poverty					
From living with partner, no children to living alone (male, aged SRA-74)	n.a.	n.a.	1.86	0.34	n.a.
From living with partner, no children to living alone (female, aged SRA-74)	n.a.	n.a.	1.53	0.36	n.a.
From living with partner, no children to living alone (male, aged 75+)	n.a.	n.a.	1.69	**0.17**	n.a.
From living with partner, no children to living alone (female, aged 75+)	n.a.	n.a.	1.39	**0.19**	n.a.
From all other HH members working to no HH member working (male)	0.25	0.89	0.37	1.33	n.a.
From all other HH members working to no HH member working (female)	0.23	0.50	0.30	1.45	n.a.

Note: Bold figures imply that the odds ratio was derived from a statistically significant coefficient (at the 5% level); SRA = standard retirement age; HH = household.

sponding ratios differ very considerably across countries, with the strongest effects observed in Germany and the least strong in Greece. A movement from a situation where all other household members of working age are working to one where nobody is, does was associated with an increased probability of moving into poverty for both males and females in all countries apart from Greece (perhaps reflecting peculiarities of the Greek pension system). However, in all other countries apart from Greece the corresponding coefficients were not statistically significant. Almost all the odds ratios reported in the lower panel of Table 2.6 were derived from coefficients that were not significant at the 5 per cent level and, in fact, in many cases it was not possible to include the relevant sets of variables in the estimated equation because of the aforementioned problems of multi-collinearity. In general, movements from living with partner to living alone were negatively associated with the probability of moving out of poverty in Portugal but, surprisingly, the opposite was the case in Greece. Further, in Austria, Germany and Greece, the movement from a situation where all other household members are working to one where nobody is was nega-tively associated with the probability of moving out of poverty, but the case was the opposite in Portugal.

Table 2.7 is the counterpart of Table 2.6 for young adults. Here, too, the focus is on changes in labour market and family status. The first two rows of the table show that the movement from education or training to work among very young adults was strongly negatively associated with a move-ment into poverty in the UK and Greece and less so in Portugal and Germany. Conversely, in the same age group a movement from education or training to unemployment was strongly positively associated with a movement into poverty in the northern countries (Germany, Austria and the UK). In these rows, one can also discern considerable quantitative differences between odds ratios reported for males and females. The next two rows demonstrate that in all countries a movement from full-time work to unemployment among those aged 20–24 was strongly positively asso-ciated with a movement into poverty, especially so in the UK.[11] Differential effects by sex were evident but in opposite directions, especially in Austria and the UK). Surprisingly, in no country did any of the coefficients asso-ciated with a movement from unemployment in wave 2 to full-time work in wave 3 turn out to be statistically significant in the relevant equations.

Turning to effects associated with changes in family situations in the lower half of the top panel of Table 2.7, we observe that leaving the paren-tal household in order to live with others in the age group 16–19 was asso-ciated with a strong increase in the probability of falling below the poverty line in Germany and, to a far lesser extent, in Portugal as well as in Austria (in the latter, only among females). In contrast, such a movement seems to be associated with a declining probability of moving into poverty in Greece. The movement of a female aged 20–24 from living with parents to living with her partner was strongly associated with a movement into poverty only in Germany. Mixed results across countries were also obtained when we examined the impact of the arrival of the first child in a young couple's household. Finally, in all countries apart from Portugal, a movement from living with partner and a child to lone parenthood for a female aged 20–24 was strongly associated with a movement into poverty (especially in

Table 2.7   Odds ratios resulting from changes in critical variables from wave 2 to wave 3 on the probability of moving into or out of poverty (young adults), ECHP, 1995–6

	Austria	Germany	Greece	Portugal	UK
Movements into poverty					
From education/training to full-time work (male aged 16–19)	0.56	0.40	**0.10**	0.65	**0.09**
From education/training to full-time work (female aged 16–19)	**1.30**	0.55	**0.11**	0.63	**0.07**
From education/training to unemployment (male aged 16–19)	**2.44**	**2.97**	**0.96**	0.97	**1.93**
From education/training to unemployment (female aged 16–19)	**5.66**	**4.14**	**1.03**	0.94	**1.43**
From full-time work to unemployment (male aged 20–24)	**2.39**	**4.09**	7.17	1.32	**39.4**
From full-time work to unemployment (female aged 20–24)	**5.55**	**5.69**	7.74	1.28	**29.2**
From unemployment to full-time work (male aged 20–24)	0.65	0.69	0.30	0.75	2.99
From unemployment to full-time work (female aged 20–24)	1.50	0.97	0.32	0.72	2.21
From living with parents to living with others (male aged 16–19)	0.86	**16.90**	**0.27**	**2.00**	n.a.
From living with parents to living with others (female aged 16–19)	**1.98**	**23.52**	**0.29**	**1.93**	n.a.
From living with parents to couple, no children (female aged 20–24)	1.00	**7.55**	1.74	0.53	n.a.
From couple, no children to couple, one child (male aged 20–24)	2.32	**1.34**	0.42	0.01	n.a.
From couple, one child to lone parent (female aged 20–24)	**12.32**	**5.42**	5.19	0.26	n.a.
From couple, one child to living alone (male aged 20–24)	4.53	**1.86**	2.39	0.23	n.a.

Table 2.7 continued

	Austria	Germany	Greece	Portugal	UK
Movements out of poverty					
From education/training					
to full-time work (male aged 16–19)	16.16	3.40	0.28	1.31	0.45
From education/training					
to full-time work (female aged 16–19)	6.14	3.34	0.33	1.74	2.07
From education/training					
to unemployment (male aged 16–19)	1.65	**0.57**	**0.08**	0.48	**0.03**
From education/training					
to unemployment (female aged 16–19)	0.63	**0.56**	**0.10**	0.64	**0.13**
From full-time work					
to unemployment (male aged 20–24)	0.08	**0.12**	**0.31**	0.37	**0.03**
From full-time work					
to unemployment (female aged 20–24)	0.03	**0.12**	**0.37**	0.49	**0.14**
From unemployment					
to full-time work (male aged 20–24)	2.94	0.62	0.81	1.30	1.42
From unemployment					
to full-time work (female aged 20–24)	1.13	0.61	0.97	1.72	6.53
From living with parents					
to living with others (male aged 16–19)	n.a.	0.10	0.66	2.44	0.95
From living with parents					
to living with others (female aged 16–19)	n.a.	0.10	0.79	3.22	4.36
From living with parents					
to couple, no children (female aged 20–24)	n.a.	8.57	n.a.	n.a.	n.a.
From couple, no children					
to couple, one child (male aged 20–24)	n.a.	6.00	n.a.	n.a.	2.13
From couple, one child					
to lone parent (female aged 20–24)	n.a.	0.01	n.a.	n.a.	2.75
From couple, one child					
to living alone (male aged 20–24)	n.a.	0.01	n.a.	n.a.	n.a.

Note: Bold figures imply that the odds ratio was derived from a statistically significant coefficient (at the 5% level).

Austria). Likewise, a movement from living with partner and a child to living alone for a male aged 20–24 appears to increase the risk of falling below the poverty line in all countries apart from Portugal.

The lower panel of Table 2.7 examines the impact of various transitions on the probability of moving out of poverty in the group of young adults. Transitions from education or training to full-time work appear to be associated with large but not significant (from a statistical point of view) increases in the probability of moving out of poverty in Austria and, to a lesser extent, Germany. Irrespective of the age or the sex of the young adult, a movement from education and training or full-time employment to unemployment, in almost all cases, was strongly associated with a very considerable decline in the probability of moving out of poverty. Turning to the effects of transitions related to changes in the young adult's living arrangements, it should be noted that none of the relevant odds ratios was derived from statistically significant coefficients. Moreover, in many cases we were not able to include the relevant variables in the estimated equations owing to multicollinearity problems. Therefore the corresponding estimates should be interpreted very cautiously. The movement from the parental home to live with others was associated with a reduced probability of moving out of poverty in Greece and, especially, Germany, but not so in Portugal and the UK (in the latter, for females only). Further, according to these estimates, females aged 20–24 leaving the parental home in order to live with their partner increase considerably their chances of moving out of poverty in Germany. In the same country, the arrival of a child in a young couple seems to be associated with an increased probability of escaping poverty, while the opposite is true when the couple breaks up and the female becomes a lone mother and the father lives alone.

MULTIPLE DEPRIVATION DYNAMICS USING THREE WAVES OF THE ECHP

This section differs from the rest of the chapter in a number of respects. First, it utilizes the information of three instead of two waves of the ECHP. As a consequence of this, and since Austria joined the ECHP one year later than the other countries, it contains results for four countries only. Further, it uses a slightly different set of deprivation indicators. More specifically, instead of separate deprivation indicators for housing amenities and consumer durables, we use the methodology outlined in the second section of the chapter in order to derive a single deprivation indicator for living conditions. Along with this indicator and the deprivation indicators in the fields of disposable monthly income (poverty) and household necessities used in the second section, we also use a deprivation indicator for social relations, exploiting the relevant information of the ECHP.[12] Finally, for the purposes of the analysis, we draw a line classifying an individual as suffering from multiple deprivation – or facing a high risk of social exclusion, if we associate social exclusion with multiple deprivation – if he/she is classified as being in relative deprivation using at least two of the above four criteria. Naturally, for the purposes of the analysis, we restrict ourselves to the use of the longitudinal sample; that is, the part of the original ECHP sample that was present in all three waves.

Table 2.8 presents the aggregate picture. The first three columns of the table report the shares of the population in each of the four countries under examination that were considered to be at high risk of social exclusion according to the above definition. Substantial cross-country differences become evident. The relevant shares were substantially lower in Germany than in the two Mediterranean countries (Greece and Portugal), with the UK shares lying between them, a result confirming the results of the previous static analysis by Tsakloglou and Papadopoulos (2002). The estimates reported in the last four columns of the table show the shares of each country's population that were classified as being at high risk of social exclusion in no wave, at least one wave, at least two waves and in all three waves. The picture that emerges from these estimates is not substantially different from that of the first part of the table. For example, the proportions of the population that were classified as being at high risk of social exclusion in all three waves in Portugal (8.3 per cent) and Greece (7.6 per cent) are between three and four times higher than the corresponding proportion of Germany (2.2 per cent). Again, the UK percentage (5.5 per cent) lies between them.

Since leading authors stress the importance of the local dimension of social exclusion (Berghman, 1995; Atkinson, 1998; Room, 1999) the last table of the chapter is devoted to the examination of dynamic aspects of multiple deprivation and exclusion within particular countries. More specifically, for each country, the estimates reported in Table 2.9 are ratios of the proportion of the members of the four risk groups classified as suffering from multiple deprivation over the proportion of those suffering from multiple deprivation in the entire population in none, at least one, at least two or all three waves.[13]

The estimates of the first panel of the table suggest that in Germany sick or disabled persons and members of lone-parent households faced a substantially higher risk of dynamic multiple deprivation than the average population member. The corresponding risks for young adults and the retired do not seem to have been substantially different from those for the entire population. Conversely, the estimates reported in the second panel of

Table 2.8 Dynamic multidimensional disadvantage over three waves: share of the population classified as deprived according to at least two out of four criteria in each wave, ECHP, 1994–6

Country	Share of the population classified as suffering from multiple deprivation in:						
	Wave 1	Wave 2	Wave 3	No wave	At least one wave	At least two waves	All three waves
Germany	6.5	6.1	6.4	88.4	11.6	5.0	2.2
Greece	18.3	15.4	16.4	74.1	25.9	14.7	7.6
Portugal	19.2	15.9	14.1	74.6	25.4	14.3	8.3
UK	10.4	10.7	11.6	81.6	18.4	10.8	5.5

Note: Criteria used are disposable income, living conditions (amenities and durables), household necessities and social relations.

Table 2.9   Relative dynamic multidimensional disadvantage over three waves, ECHP, 1994–6

Country	Relative risk of being classified as suffering from multiple deprivation* in:			
	No wave	At least one wave	At least two waves	All three waves
Germany				
Sick/disabled	0.88	1.94	2.84	3.50
Young adults	0.96	1.31	1.08	0.91
Retired	1.01	0.92	1.04	1.18
Members of lone-parent households	0.84	2.25	3.04	3.45
Greece				
Sick/disabled	0.83	1.49	1.73	1.75
Young adults	1.09	0.74	0.65	0.46
Retired	0.77	1.64	1.91	2.28
Members of lone-parent households	0.95	1.14	1.05	1.17
Portugal				
Sick/disabled	0.88	1.36	1.47	1.46
Young adults	1.06	0.82	0.72	0.73
Retired	0.77	1.67	1.97	2.07
Members of lone-parent households	0.90	1.29	1.60	1.96
UK				
Sick/disabled	0.69	2.37	2.75	2.62
Young adults	0.97	1.13	1.05	1.05
Retired	0.95	1.24	1.25	1.15
Members of lone-parent households	0.64	2.61	3.02	3.55

Note: * Probability of risk group members being classified as deprived according to at least two out of four criteria over the same probability in the entire population

Table 2.9 suggest that in Greece, among the four risk groups, the retired faced the highest risk of chronic multiple deprivation and social exclusion, followed by the sick or disabled. Members of lone-parent households also appeared to face a higher risk of social exclusion than the average population member, but the differences were not large. As for the young adults, according to all the indicators reported in this table, they seem to face a substantially lower risk of chronic multiple deprivation and social exclusion than the entire population. The evidence for Portugal is not very different from that for Greece. Here, too, young adults face a low risk of social exclusion, whereas the retired, members of lone-parent households and, to a slightly lesser extent, the sick or disabled face a high risk of dynamic multiple deprivation and social exclusion. Finally, the last panel of Table 2.9 demonstrates that the UK was the only one of the four countries examined in which all four groups analysed face a higher risk of social exclusion than the national average. However, whereas for young adults and the retired the corresponding risks were not substantially higher than those for the entire population, the risks of the sick or disabled and, particularly, the members of lone-parent households appear to be considerably higher than the national average.

CONCLUSIONS

The aim of this chapter was to examine dynamic aspects of multiple deprivation of four risk groups (retired persons, sick or disabled persons, young adults and members of lone-parent households) in five EU member states (Austria, Germany, Greece, Portugal and the UK) using the data of the ECHP. The results of the empirical analysis highlighted several similarities and differences across countries. In comparisons with the average population member, in all countries the sick or disabled appear to face a higher risk of chronic multiple deprivation and social exclusion. However, this relative risk appears to be substantially higher in the north (Austria, Germany and the UK) than in the south (Greece and Portugal). Regarding the young adults, our analysis shows that, even in the countries where, according to the earlier results of the static analysis, they appear to face a high risk of deprivation, this deprivation was probably of a temporary character and does not translate into a high risk of social exclusion for the members of the group as a whole. Of course, this does not imply that within the group there are no pockets of high risk of exclusion (for example, young adults with low qualifications for a successful employment career, as the results of multivariate analysis show). Retired people appear to face a high risk of chronic deprivation and exclusion only in the southern countries (Portugal and, especially, Greece). Finally, members of lone-parent households seem to face a disproportionate risk of social exclusion within all countries under examination, especially so in the UK, Germany and Portugal.

NOTES

1. Further, it was found that social transfers make a significant contribution to poverty alleviation in the case of all risk groups under examination – in particular, retired persons and sick or disabled persons – especially in the northern countries (Austria, Germany and the UK).

2. These thresholds are 60 per cent of the median equivalent disposable income (using the modified OECD equivalence scales, which assign a weight of 1 to the household head, a weight of 0.5 to every other adult in the household and a weight of 0.3 to each child in the household (Hagenaars *et al.*, 1994), 80 per cent of the median deprivation score in the case of housing amenities and durable goods and 60 per cent of the median deprivation score in the case of household necessities. The formula for the calculation of each population member's deprivation score, μ_j, is:

$$\mu_j = \frac{\sum_{i=1}^{I} w_i X_{ij}}{\sum_{i=1}^{I} w_i},$$

where I is the total number of amenities/durables/household necessities for which information is available in the ECHP, w_i is the proportion of the population living in households reporting amenity/durable/necessity of life i, and X_{ij} a variable that takes the value of 0 (1) if individual j lives in a household with (without) amenity/durable/necessity of life i.

3. Due to the fact that the concept of income used in Table 2.1 differs from that used in the static analysis and, furthermore, that a considerable proportion of the comparisons made in the framework of the static analysis concerned only those aged 16 or more, whereas those of Table 2.1 refer to the entire population, the estimates of this table are not strictly comparable with the estimates of the static analysis.

4. This decline may be attributed to the considerable discontinuities observed in the distribution of individual deprivation scores in the field of household necessities in Greece.

5. The entire population, in the case of members of lone-parent households.

6. With the exception of the young adults who are only compared with the entire population aged 16 plus.

7. Moreover, it should be noted that, especially for the movements into and out of monetary deprivation (poverty), we adopted a stricter definition. More specifically, in order to consider that somebody had changed status, we assumed that he/she not only crossed the poverty line, but did so by moving by five or more percentile points in the income distribution (so as to avoid classifying as movements into/out of poverty marginal changes by a few income units).

8. In all countries the great majority of lone parents are lone mothers.

9. This result holds for all indicators of dynamic deprivation in Austria (lone parents with some dependent children faring better than lone parents without dependent children in comparison with the relevant reference groups). This does not imply that lone parents with dependent children fare better than lone parents without dependent children. This result is due to the unusually high living standards of the second reference group – partnered mothers without dependent children – in Austria.

10. Since in this section the analysis is performed within particular risk groups, the term 'reference group' does not denote the same thing as in the previous section.

11. Surprisingly, none of the relevant variables turned out to be significant in the Portuguese equation.

12. A population member aged 16 plus is defined as deprived if he/she 'talks to neighbours once or twice a month or less frequently' and, further, 'meets friends once or twice a month or less frequently'.

13. Since the number of population members who were classified as sick/disabled in all three waves was very small, for the purposes of Table 2.9 we classified as sick/disabled all those who were classified as such in any of the three waves. For the other three risk groups – young adults, retired persons and members of lone-parent households – participation in the risk group implies that they were members of the group in all three waves.

3. Characteristics and dynamics of income poverty and multidimensional deprivation in Austria

Karin Heitzmann

INTRODUCTION

Research on poverty, multidimensional deprivation and social exclusion in Austria is scarce, as is knowledge on the distribution of welfare and well-being within this country. The first large-scale survey on the poor was only conducted in the early 1990s (Lutz *et al.*, 1993).[1] Empirical evidence on social exclusion is still missing. Not least owing to this lack of information, public and political attitudes about the prevalence and significance of poverty and social exclusion vary. For example, the coalition government, elected in 1999 and consisting of the People's party (ÖVP) and the Freedom Party (FPÖ), insists that the generosity of the social security system handles poverty successfully. It is, however, concerned about increasing social exclusion. Along with political attitudes, public policies shape the perception, extent and characteristics of the distribution of these dimensions of welfare. For example, social insurance in Austria typically discriminates against non-working wives of breadwinners. Special family allowances encourage motherhood and exit from the labour market, while insurance benefits derived from the breadwinner's employment income (for example, survivors' pension) tend to be low (Langan and Ostner, 1991). This suggests that females are more likely to be affected by income poverty, and – to the extent that labour market participation signifies inclusion – to be excluded than men.

This chapter provides evidence on the characteristics and dynamics of income poverty and multidimensional deprivation in Austria. Some consideration is given to gender in order to assess whether the characteristics of the prevalent corporatist welfare state model in Austria (Esping-Andersen, 1991, 1996) discriminate against women in terms of income poverty, multidimensional deprivation,[2] and, indeed, social exclusion. The first section summarizes the main findings for the total population, based on the ECHP data, and then the analysis focuses on the four risk groups (young adults and retired adults, and then working-age sick or disabled adults and lone mothers).[3] This allows for a more detailed analysis of the specific risks encountered, and indeed the role of policy in alleviating these risks. In the final section the key findings are summarized and the policy implications discussed.

INCOME POVERTY AND MULTIDIMENSIONAL DEPRIVATION IN AUSTRIA

In 1996, about 11 per cent of the Austrian population had an income below the poverty threshold (see Table 3.1).[4] This signifies a rather even income distribution as compared with the other countries in this study, most notably Portugal, Greece or the UK, which is partly explained by generous social transfers and pensions in Austria. For example, annual income poverty would be almost doubled if no social transfers were paid, and more than tripled without social transfers and pensions. Private monetary transfers played only a minor role in alleviating income poverty, except for lone-parent families with dependent children. According to ECHP data their income poverty rate would have deteriorated from 21 per cent to 36 per cent without these transfers.

The types of factors associated with income poverty have been widely examined (for example, Förster, 2001; Till and Steiner, 2000; Steiner and Giorgi, 1997; Steiner and Wolf, 1996). The unemployed, low-income earners, people with low levels of education, large families, lone-parent families with young children and migrant worker families (originating outside the EU) account for large proportions of the Austrian poor. Moreover, in the ECHP data, 13 per cent of all women and 9 per cent of men were poor, which translates to a gender poverty ratio of 1.4, which means that the probability of a woman being poor was 40 per cent higher than that of a man. Also age makes a difference: rather lower rates were found for children, young and working-age adults (8 to 10 per cent) compared with a high rate for the elderly (17 per cent). Within all age cohorts women were more likely to be poor than men.

Apart from income poverty, 10 per cent of the population was deprived of amenities, 9 per cent of durables and 11 per cent of necessities. Again, this signifies a comparatively equal distribution of these dimensions of welfare, as compared, for example, with Greece or Portugal. Findings suggest that income was correlated with deprivation, most notably of necessities. Consequently, women were slightly more likely than men to lack

Table 3.1   Income poverty and multidimensional deprivation in Austria,
ECHP, 1996

Indicators	All			Poor			Non-poor		
	Total (%)	Female (%)	Male (%)	Total (%)	Female (%)	Male (%)	Total (%)	Female (%)	Male (%)
Income poverty	11	13	9	NA	NA	NA	NA	NA	NA
Amenities deprivation	10	10	10	24	23	24	8	8	8
Durables deprivation	9	10	9	22	21	24	8	8	7
Necessities deprivation	11	12	10	29	32	25	9	9	9
Talking to neighbours[1]	22	20	24	24	20	32	21	20	23
Meeting friends/relatives[2]	30	31	29	40	37	45	29	30	28

Notes:
[1] Adults only: 'talks to neighbours less than once a week'.
[2] Adults only: 'meets friends or relatives (not living with the person) at home or elsewhere, less than once a week'.
NA = not applicable; all ECHP tables based on weighted sample; see Chapter 1.

durables and necessities, with gender deprivation ratios amounting to between 1.1 and 1.2. In general, poor people were about three times more likely to be deprived of amenities, durables or necessities than non-poor people.

Low income also correlated with social isolation. About a third of all adults met their friends or relatives less than once a week, and about a fifth had limited contact with their neighbours – isolation ratios that were much higher than, for example, in Portugal or the UK. Women were more likely to talk regularly to their neighbours but less likely to meet friends or relatives frequently than men. Low income seemed to affect men and women differently: poor men were much less likely to have frequent contacts with neighbours, friends or relatives than non-poor men, while there was much less difference in this respect with regard to poor and non-poor women.

Dynamic data analysis generates results for Austria similar to those for many other countries (for example, Buhr, 1995; Walker, 1995). On the one hand, more people are affected by income poverty and multidimensional deprivation than cross-sectional data suggest. In 1995 or 1996, 13 per cent to 15 per cent of the total population suffered from income poverty, deprivation of amenities, durables or necessities. Another 30 per cent to 45 per

Table 3.2   *Dynamics of income poverty and multidimensional deprivation*
in Austria, ECHP, 1995–6

	Income poverty	Amenities deprivation	Durables deprivation	Necessities deprivation	Talking to neighbours[1]	Meeting friends/ relatives[2]
	(%)	(%)	(%)	(%)	(%)	(%)
Transitions						
Persistence rate	64	66	46	62	56	55
Exit rate	36	34	54	38	44	45
Entrance rate	5	3	6	7	12	21
Avoidance rate	95	97	94	93	88	80
Turnover						
Remained poor/ deprived	6	7	4	5	11	17
Exited poverty/ deprivation	3	4	5	3	9	14
Entered poverty/ deprivation	4	3	5	7	10	14
Never poor/ deprived[3]	86	87	86	86	71	55
Base (unweighted freq.)	8543	8514	8503	8516	6569	6625

Notes:
[1] Adults only: 'talks to neighbours less than once a week'.
[2] Adults only: 'meets friends or relatives (not living with the person) at home or elsewhere, less than once a week'.
[3] 'Never' in this and subsequent tables refers to the observation period: that is, never poor/deprived over the two years covered.

cent experienced social isolation (see Table 3.2). On the other hand, income poverty and multidimensional deprivation were largely transient. Between 34 per cent and 54 per cent of those who were income poor or deprived in 1995 had exited from income poverty or deprivation a year later. Similarly, 44 to 45 per cent of all those isolated in 1995 escaped isolation in 1996. Overall, only between 4 per cent and 7 per cent of the population were persistently poor or deprived in 1995 and 1996,[5] and another 11 per cent to 17 per cent were continually socially isolated. Sixty-one per cent of the persistently poor were women, and 45 per cent were older than 60/65, that is, the state retirement age for women/men in Austria, suggesting that females and the elderly were most likely to remain poor. Women were also more likely than men to remain deprived of amenities, durables and necessities, and isolated in terms of meeting friends and relatives.

Policy Implications of the Findings

Thus women in Austria were on average more likely to be (persistently) threatened by income poverty and – to a lesser extent – to be deprived of durables and necessities than men. This suggests that the corporatist Austrian welfare state model does indeed adversely affect the welfare of women. There are strong incentives for women (such as the parental leave allowance) to leave paid employment and take on full-time care of children or the needy elderly. While social policy provides incentives for females to leave the labour market, the incentives to re-enter employment are weak. For example, there is still a lack of child care facilities, and inflexible opening hours of many existing facilities pose additional obstacles for working mothers. Consequently, many women (and especially mothers) tend to be concentrated in low-paid, flexible working arrangements, which jeopardize their chances of more efficiently reconciling work and family obligations, and of earning higher incomes (Tálos, 1999). Not very surprisingly, therefore, women's wages are on average about a third lower than men's, and recent empirical evidence suggests a widening of this income gap (Hauptverband der Öster-reichischen Sozialversicherungsträger, 2001). Low (employment) income and an interrupted working pattern also translate into low (or no) insurance benefits, which increases the dependency of women on their partner, their family and indeed social assistance. Not least because of this, Austria has recently been criticized by the CEDAW (Convention on the Elimination of All Forms of Discrimination) committee of the United Nations for its traditional gender pattern. There is some concern that this pattern has been reinforced by the current government. For example, parental leave allowance (see also below), which is currently granted for 18 months to one parent, is to be extended to 24 months. This extension might reduce the chances of reintegration into the labour market for women even more.

It has been possible to see that public and insurance transfers play an important role in preventing income poverty in Austria. These alleviating effects notwithstanding, social expenditures have been cut within the last few years, against the political background of meeting the economic criteria of economic and monetary union (EMU), and as a means to reduce budget deficit. Despite the efforts of the government to improve allocation, there is some concern that the income poverty gap may have increased in recent years. This hypothesis has to be assessed as soon as more recent waves of ECHP data become available.

The latest reductions of social expenditures might also indicate a gradual withdrawal of the state from some of its traditional responsibilities, and indeed imply a shift towards more private responsibility. In this context, it is interesting to note that ECHP findings suggest a weak informal network for Austria. The population on average has less frequent contacts with neighbours, friends or relatives compared with many of the other countries in the study. Moreover, low income goes with even higher social isolation rates, above all with regard to men. Indeed, anecdotal evidence suggests that poor women, especially in their role as mothers, are more likely to look actively for help in the informal sector, for example by turning to non-profit organizations, than men or fathers. Given the withdrawal of the state, and the demographic and sociocultural changes (such as the dissolution of many families), policy should seek to strengthen and support informal networks.

INCOME POVERTY AND MULTIDIMENSIONAL DEPRIVATION OF YOUNG ADULTS AND RETIRED ADULTS IN AUSTRIA

Preliminary dynamic analysis provided ample evidence of both transitory and persistent income poverty, deprivation and isolation. The ways into and out of these disadvantages are determined by multiple factors, such as individual characteristics and behaviour, and the economic and policy framework. In general, different policies and policy instruments are aimed at different sub-groups of the population. Analysing risk groups separately will thus allow us to draw some inferences on the effectiveness of policies in preventing or alleviating income poverty and deprivation. In what follows, two life course risk groups, young adults and retired adults, will be analysed in this respect. First, some background information on, and policies for, these groups will be presented. Then findings of the cross-sectional and dynamic analysis with regard to income poverty and multidimensional deprivation will be provided, and the policy implications discussed.

Socioeconomic Characteristics of and Policies for Young and Retired Adults in Austria

The risk group of the retired comprised more than a fifth of the total Austrian population. Owing to their longer life expectancy and lower state retirement age,[6] the majority (60 per cent) were women. Roughly a third of the retired – especially elderly widowed women – lived alone, another third with their partner only. Retired people were on average more likely to be satisfied with their main activity, and their amount of leisure time, and with their financial and housing situation than the average Austrian adult. The main source of household income for most retired people was their pension.[7] Within the Austrian compulsory social insurance system, there are several types of retirement pension, the entitlement and level of which depend on previous occupations, the length of insured employment and previous employment income (Badelt and Heitzmann, 1998). People with no or only insufficient employment history and income – predominantly women – are either not entitled to retirement pension or subject to the receipt of a means-tested compensatory supplement (in 2001 amounting to €613 for a single person), that is, a 'minimum pension' for the insured. These characteristics of the Austrian insurance scheme explain the comparatively low pension levels of women, which on average amount to only 60 per cent of the male pension (Hauptverband der Österreichischen Sozialversicherungsträger, 2001). Consequently, retired women are likely to depend on family support, a potential survivor's pension or the means-tested social assistance.[8] This suggests that they are particularly likely to be vulnerable to income poverty and deprivation.

The risk group of young adults made up about a fifth of the total Austrian population. They were likely to experience multiple transitions, such as from full-time education to employment, from living with parents to living alone or with a partner, and from financial dependency to independence. All these transitions account for the heterogeneity of this population group. About a fifth of the young adults were in (unpaid) training or education, and while the vast majority were gainfully employed, they were more likely than the average adult to have experienced unemployment. Almost two-thirds were singles and about a third were married or cohabiting. In comparison to other adults, the young were less likely to live alone and more likely to live with their parents (Heitzmann, 2000). All these socioeconomic characteristics change with age. However, young females were less likely to be in paid employment, more likely to be married or cohabiting and achieving lower levels of education than their male counterparts – characteristics of life styles that account for an enhanced vulnerability of young women with regard to income poverty and multidimensional deprivation. In terms of public support, families with a young adult family member might be entitled to family allowance (up to €171 per month, see also below), which is paid up to a maximum age of 26 years for dependent children (that is, children in education or on apprenticeship). Young adults might be entitled to social insurance or assistance benefits (for example, unemployment benefit or parental leave allowance). However, as insurance benefits depend on the length of previous employment and the level of employment income, they are bound to be low, and limited in duration. This suggests that young adults might indeed be vulnerable when affected by, for example, unemployment.

Empirical Evidence of Income Poverty and Multidimensional Deprivation of Young Adults and the Retired in Austria

In 1996, 8 per cent of all young adults and 15 per cent of the retired were poor, which compares to the population average of 11 per cent (see Table 3.3). The income poverty rates depend on the poverty threshold and equivalence scales chosen. Lower poverty thresholds lead to a substantial reduction of the poverty rate of the elderly (Heitzmann, 2000), which implies that the incomes of many elderly are low, and just around the income poverty threshold.

Women accounted for two-thirds of all poor young adults and almost three-quarters of all poor retired. The gender poverty ratios amounted to 2.0 (young adults) and 1.7 (retired adults). Conversely, the gender poverty ratio for working-age adults, who were defined as neither young nor retired, was equal to 1.1. This indicates that being young or old and female increased the probability of being poor quite dramatically. Apart from gender, many other factors account for the extent and likelihood of young and retired adults to be poor, such as the activity status, the household type or the level of education (for a detailed analysis, see Heitzmann, 2000).

As has been mentioned earlier, income poverty adversely affects other dimensions of well-being, a finding that is confirmed in the ECHP for both young and retired adults. Low income increased their probability of experiencing multidimensional deprivation by two to three times. Consequently, women were more likely to be deprived than men, with gender deprivation ratios amounting to between 1.1 and 1.7 (retired adults) and 0.8 to 1.7 (young adults), respectively.[9] Low income also adversely affected social participation rates of these population groups. Interestingly, both poor male young and retired adults were less likely to have frequent social contacts than their female counterparts.

Dynamic data analysis confirms that more young and retired adults are affected by income poverty and multidimensional deprivation than cross-sectional data suggest (see Table 3.4). However, their low incomes were largely transitory – with an important exception: income poverty of retired adults. Overall, some 11 per cent of retired people experienced persistent poverty in 1995 and 1996. Moreover, more than three-quarters of all retired who were income poor in 1995 remained poor in 1996. These rates are considerably higher than the Austrian average (6 per cent and 64 per cent, respectively). As the pension is the main income source for the vast majority of the retired, their income level is unlikely to change.[10]

Table 3.3   Income poverty and multidimensional deprivation of young and retired adults in Austria, ECHP, 1996

Young adults	All			Poor			Non-poor		
	Total (%)	Female (%)	Male (%)	Total (%)	Female (%)	Male (%)	Total (%)	Female (%)	Male (%)
Income poverty	8	11	6	NA	NA	NA	NA	NA	NA
Amenities deprivation	10	12	8	21	[19]	[25]	9	11	7
Durables deprivation	11	14	8	33	38	[22]	9	11	7
Necessities deprivation	11	11	11	21	[23]	[16]	10	9	10
Talking to neighbours[1]	33	31	35	38	36	[41]	33	31	34
Meeting friends/ relatives[2]	15	15	15	[22]	[20]	[22]	14	14	14

Retired adults	All			Poor			Non-poor		
	Total (%)	Female (%)	Male (%)	Total (%)	Female (%)	Male (%)	Total (%)	Female (%)	Male (%)
Income poverty	15	18	11	NA	NA	NA	NA	NA	NA
Amenities deprivation	13	15	10	28	30	[22]	11	12	9
Durables deprivation	6	6	6	11	[11]	[10]	5	5	5
Necessities deprivation	15	19	10	39	44	[26]	11	13	8
Talking to neighbours[1]	16	16	17	26	[15]	[33]	16	16	19
Meeting friends/ relatives[2]	38	39	36	42	40	45	37	38	35

Notes:
[1] Adults only: 'talks to neighbours less than once a week'.
[2] Adults only: 'meets friends or relatives (not living with the person) at home or elsewhere, less than once a week'.
In all tables, * indicates a cell size of less than 10 unweighted observations; [ ] indicates a cell size of between 10 and 29 unweighted observations

The dynamics of social exclusion in Europe

Table 3.4   Dynamics of income poverty and multidimensional deprivation of young and retired adults in Austria, ECHP, 1995–6

Young adults	Income poverty	Amenities deprivation	Durables deprivation	Necessities deprivation	Talking to neighbours[1]	Meeting friends/ relatives[2]
	(%)	(%)	(%)	(%)	(%)	(%)
Transitions						
Persistence rate	49	72	48	58	63	38
Exit rate	51	28	52	42	37	62
Entrance rate	5	4	7	7	20	11
Avoidance rate	95	97	93	94	80	89
Turnover						
Remained poor/ deprived	4	7	5	4	19	6
Exited from poverty/ deprivation	4	3	6	3	17	11
Entered poverty/ deprivation	4	3	6	6	14	10
Never poor/ deprived	88	87	83	86	56	76
Base (un- weighted)	1475	1470	1469	1471	1474	1474
Retired adults						
Transitions						
Persistence rate	77	64	33	70	48	58
Exit rate	23	36	67	30	52	42
Entrance rate	6	4	5	10	10	24
Avoidance rate	94	96	95	90	90	76
Turnover						
Remained poor/ deprived	11	10	2	7	7	23
Exited poverty/ deprivation	3	6	3	3	8	17
Entered poverty/ deprivation	4	4	4	9	9	15
Never poor/ deprived	83	81	91	82	76	46
Base (un- weighted)	1664	1662	1653	1658	1659	1660

Notes:
[1] Adults only: 'talks to neighbours less than once a week'.
[2] Adults only: 'meets friends or relatives (not living with the person) at home or elsewhere, less than once a week'.

Nonetheless, some 7 per cent of retired people left or entered poverty. Multivariate analysis suggests that it is higher education that significantly reduces the odds of the retired moving into income poverty. Young adults were less likely to experience persistent income poverty (4 per cent) than the elderly, and indeed the population on average. Rather, many experienced movements into and out of income poverty, which were in part explained by the various transitions they undergo. For example, moving from full-time education to full-time employment increased the odds of young adults escaping income poverty by more than 16 times. Interestingly, multivariate analysis also provided statistically significant evidence that being young and female more than doubled the odds of entering income poverty (Heitzmann, 2000).

With regard to other dimensions of well-being, the retired in general, and women specifically, were more likely to experience persistent deprivation of amenities and necessities as opposed to the population on average. Also more than half lacked frequent contacts with their relatives or friends, even though more than three-quarters regularly talked to their neighbours. Young adults were less disadvantaged in terms of these deprivation factors. However, they were more likely to lack durables, and less likely to have frequent contacts with their neighbours than the population on average.

Policy Implications

ECHP findings for young and retired adults confirm the particular vulnerability of women to income poverty and deprivation. It has been possible to see that being young and female more than doubles the odds of becoming poor in Austria. Given the differences in the socioeconomic characteristics of young men and women, the traditional gender pattern, and thus gender inequality, still prevails. The positive correlation between low income and other dimensions of deprivation suggests that an improvement of the income situation of females will have positive repercussions on other aspects of their welfare, and indeed reduce gender inequality.

Employment income is the most important income source. Thus it is vital to encourage and support young females in terms of their entrance and re-entrance into the labour market. As has been mentioned earlier, strong incentives for women to leave employment, and weak incentives to re-enter, counteract this effort. Moreover, the status-preserving Austrian welfare state model translates low employment income into low or no insurance benefits. This helps to explain why almost three-quarters of all poor retired people were females: many did not qualify at all or only for low retirement pensions, despite recent policy efforts to take periods of unpaid caring into account. Against the background of an ageing society, and of increasing concerns with regard to the fiscal sustainability of the existing pension schemes, recent policy changes have resulted in restricted access to, and reduced levels of (early) retirement pension. One type of early retirement pension, the pension for people with reduced working capabilities, has been abolished altogether. Moreover, the government is inclined to adjust the different public pension systems in Austria, most notably by reducing the generous scheme of civil servants to the level of the less generous scheme of private employees (BMSG, 2001). Many of these reforms are bound to affect adversely the well-being of many elderly people. Moreover, the current government increasingly promotes private responsibility for old age (for example, by granting tax concessions for those who are privately insured), while a universal minimum state pension, which would primarily benefit elderly women, is still out of sight.

ECHP findings confirm the particular importance of higher secondary and tertiary education as a means to prevent income poverty in old age. However, it has also been possible to see that education significantly reduces the odds of young adults escaping from income poverty. Education is thus mainly an investment for future well-being, while it tends to decrease the welfare of those currently in education. Consequently, policy should seek to support young adults, and indeed women, to help them remain in education. Recently, however, the Austrian government introduced a university fee, which amounts to €727 per year. It still needs to be seen how this fee will affect the decision-making process of young adults. There is some concern that young females, who for some years now have formed the majority of university students, might be more likely than young men to renounce tertiary education because of this fee.

INCOME POVERTY AND MULTIDIMENSIONAL DEPRIVATION OF WORKING-AGE SICK OR DISABLED ADULTS AND LONE MOTHERS IN AUSTRIA

While every (living) person undergoes the life course risks described above, additional idiosyncratic risks only afflict parts of the population. However, they shape the extent and characteristics of income poverty and multi-dimensional deprivation within each group. Among these risks are sickness or disability and lone parenthood, which are discussed below. While both are individual risks, they affect large parts of the population: in Austria about a third of all families with children are headed by a lone parent, and about a quarter of the population has a physical disability (Badelt and Österle, 2001). However, the small ECHP sample sizes of working-age sick or disabled adults and lone parents[11] have severely constrained the possible analyses. A large group turnover – evidence of sickness and disability, and possibly explained by the very definition of this risk group, which is based on a subjective evaluation of well-being – hampered the dynamic analysis even further. Despite these data limitations, however, it has been possible to reveal a general pattern in terms of income poverty and deprivation of these groups. Before these findings are presented, some background information on their socioeconomic characteristics, and on the policies aimed at them, is provided. Then policy implications will be discussed.

Socioeconomic Characteristics of and Policies for Working-age Sick or Disabled Adults and Lone Mothers in Austria

Working-age sick or disabled adults were most likely to live with their partner, and be married. The relative majority was in (early) retirement, while employment rates were smaller and unemployment rates higher as compared with the non-sick (Heitzmann, 2000). Most of the working-age sick or disabled were men, while the vast majority of all lone parents are women.[12] The lone mothers were on average younger and more likely to be in paid employment than partnered mothers. Consequently, the latter more often reported themselves to be primarily occupied with caring for home and family, whilst lone parents rather said that employment was their main activity. The relative majority of lone mothers were divorced, about a third had never been married, and about one in eight were widowed. Most notably, lone mothers tended to have obtained a lower level of education than the population on average.

Families with dependent children in Austria are assisted by a comparatively generous family policy. It includes, for mothers who have been gainfully employed, fully paid maternity leave eight weeks before and after the projected delivery date, parental leave allowance (€412 per month in 2001) up to a maximum of two years,[13] which might be topped up by an additional €182 for lone parent and low-income families. A special assistant payment is paid for another 12 months if low-income families are unable to find child care facilities. In this context, it is important to note that these facilities are still scarce, although the government has recently put a lot of effort (and money) into reducing this gap. Moreover, as has been mentioned earlier, inflexible opening hours of existing kindergartens or child care crèches hamper the possibilities of parents (and indeed mothers) to reconcile work and family obligations. Families are entitled to a universal family allowance for each dependent child (up to a maximum age of 26 years), which amounts to between €105 and €171 per month, depending on the age and the number of children in the family. These cash benefits, together with tax concessions, and additional benefits from federal provinces, are evidence of the generous Austrian family policy. The current coalition government, moreover, is inclined to expand this policy, for example by changing the insurance-based parental leave allowance to a universal benefit for all mothers, regardless of previous insured employment.

Also sick or disabled adults are assisted by a broad mix of policy instruments (Badelt and Heitzmann, 1998). Most importantly, some 99 per cent of the Austrian population are covered by health insurance. People in need of care are entitled to a generous care allowance (amounting to between €145 and €1532 per month). Some 324000 Austrians receive this universal cash benefit, which was introduced in 1993. However, only about a sixth of the beneficiaries are below the age of 60. Working-age sick or disabled adults might be entitled to early retirement pension, the access to which has recently been restricted, as has been mentioned earlier. In addition to cash benefits, various in-kind benefits assist the sick or disabled mainly in terms of rehabilitation. Moreover, sheltered workshops, sheltered housing and – increasingly – supported employment are provided to improve integration and enhance the opportunities of working-age sick or disabled. This is also achieved through quota regulations that oblige companies with 25 or more employees to employ registered disabled people (Badelt and Österle, 2001).

Empirical Evidence of Income Poverty and Multidimensional Deprivation of Working-age Sick and Disabled Adults and Lone Mothers in Austria

Not least because of the generous benefits aimed at working-age sick or disabled people, the ECHP data showed that they were less likely to be poor than the population on average (see Table 3.5 and Table 3.1).[14] However, they were more likely to lack amenities, durables and necessities than the population in general and the non-sick or disabled – regardless of whether they were income poor or not. They were also among the least likely to have frequent contacts with neighbours, relatives or friends. There is some indication that income poverty of the sick or disabled was more persistent than that of the non-sick or disabled, a finding which was partly confirmed for deprivation of necessities (see Table 3.6). The working-age sick or disabled were also the most likely to be persistently socially isolated, compared with all other life course and risk groups analysed here. Small sample sizes, however, reduce the significance of these results.

While public benefits assist sick and disabled adults in preventing income poverty, the Austrian family policy is not so successful. Members of families with dependent children were more likely to be poor than the average population (see Table 3.5). As soon as all children are independent, however, the incidence of income poverty decreases. This general pattern,

Table 3.5   *Income poverty and multidimensional deprivation of working-age sick and non-sick adults and members of lone and partnered mother families with at least one dependent child in Austria, ECHP, 1996*

Indicators	Sick (%)	Non-sick (%)	Lone mothers (%)	Partnered mothers (%)
Income poverty	9	9	24	9
Amenities deprivation	[12]	9	8	8
Durables deprivation	[12]	9	20	8
Necessities deprivation	20	9	19	9
Talking to neighbours[1]	29	23	24	14
Meeting friends/relatives[2]	41	27	23	30

Notes:
[1] Adults only: 'talks to neighbours less than once a week'.
[2] Adults only: 'meets friends or relatives (not living with the person) at home or elsewhere, less than once a week'.

that dependent children lower the standard of living, also characterizes other dimensions of well-being: access to amenities, durables and necessities. While dependent children thus increased the income poverty and deprivation risk, lone parenthood led to an even more substantial deterioration in income and living standards. For example, the income poverty rate of members of lone-mother families with at least one dependent child was much higher (24 per cent) than that of partnered mother families (9 per cent). Not very surprisingly, therefore, lone parents were the most likely to be dissatisfied with their financial means and life. This did not translate into social retreat, however. While lone mothers were less likely to talk regularly to their neighbours, they were more likely to have frequent contacts with relatives and friends than the Austrian population in general.

Dynamic data analysis confirmed the disadvantaged position of lone-mother families with at least one dependent child, and added an additional concern: they were more likely to remain in income poverty (12 per cent) than two-parent families (5 per cent: see Table 3.7) which was also confirmed by the higher persistence rate of the former (68 per cent compared with 58 per cent). Interestingly, members of lone mother families were not worse off than two-parent families in terms of amenities. They were, however, more likely to renounce durables or necessities (see Table 3.5). Deprivation was predominantly transitory, though. For example, only 5 per cent of all lone mother family members experienced persistent deprivation of durables, while 23 per cent had to renounce durables in one of the

Table 3.6   Dynamics of income poverty and multidimensional deprivation of working-age sick or disabled and non-sick adults in Austria, ECHP, 1995–6

	Income poverty		Amenities deprivation		Durables deprivation		Necessities deprivation		Talking to neighbours[1]		Meeting friends/relatives[2]	
	S (%)	NS (%)	S (%)	NS (%)	S (%)	NS (%)	S (%)	NS (%)	S (%)	NS (%)	S (%)	NS (%)
Transitions												
Persistence rate	*	60	*	70	*	47	*	57	*	57	[66]	53
Exit rate	*	40	*	30	*	53	*	43	*	43	[34]	47
Entrance rate	*	4	*	3	*	5	[13]	6	*	13	[26]	19
Avoidance rate	*	96	*	97	*	95	87	94	*	87	75	81
Turnover												
Remained poor/deprived	*	4	*	7	*	4	*	3	[26]	12	[26]	15
Exited poverty/deprivation	*	3	*	3	*	5	*	3	*	9	[13]	13
Entered poverty/deprivation	*	4	*	2	*	5	[10]	6	*	11	[15]	14
Never poor/deprived	87	89	85	88	81	87	76	88	60	69	46	59
Base (unweighted)	85	4878	83	4855	84	4851	84	4865	85	4875	85	4879

Notes:
[1] Adults only: 'talks to neighbours less than once a week'.
[2] Adults only: 'meets friends or relatives (not living with the person) at home or elsewhere, less than once a week'.
S = working-age sick or disabled adults; NS = working-age non-sick adults; * indicates a cell size of less than 10 unweighted observations and [ ] indicates a cell size of between 10 and 29 unweighted observations.

Table 3.7   Dynamics of income poverty and multidimensional deprivation of lone mother and partnered mother families with at least one dependent child in Austria, ECHP, 1995–6

	Income poverty		Amenities deprivation		Durables deprivation		Necessities deprivation		Talking to neighbours[1]		Meeting friends/ relatives[2]	
	LM (%)	PM (%)	LM (%)	PM (%)	LM (%)	PM (%)	LM (%)	PM (%)	LM (%)	PM (%)	LM (%)	PM (%)
Transitions												
Persistence rate	[68]	58	*	65	[39]	47	[47]	54	[62]	47	[44]	54
Exit rate	[32]	42	*	35	[61]	53	[53]	46	[38]	53	[56]	46
Entrance rate	14	4	*	3	17	4	15	7	*	10	*	20
Avoidance rate	86	96	*	97	83	96	85	93	*	90	*	80
Turnover												
Remained poor/deprived	12	5	[7]	6	[5]	5	[6]	3	[17]	6	[12]	17
Exited poverty/deprivation	[6]	3	*	3	[8]	5	[6]	3	[11]	7	[15]	15
Entered poverty/deprivation	12	4	*	2	15	3	13	6	*	8	*	13
Never poor/deprived	71	88	89	89	72	87	75	88	65	79	62	55
Base (unweighted)	251	3320	251	3291	251	3293	251	3304	90	790	89	790

Notes:
[1] Only adults

LM = members of lone mother households with at least one dependent child; PM = members of partnered mother households with at least one dependent child; * indicates a cell size of less than 10 unweighted observations and [ ] indicates a cell size of between 10 and 29 unweighted observations.

years analysed. The dynamic is also evidenced by a low persistence rate: only 39 per cent of those deprived in 1995 remained deprived in 1996 (see Table 3.7). Lone parenthood thus seems to be characterized by profound variations in life style – a dynamic that is reduced as soon as all of the children become independent. With regard to social isolation, lone parents rank worse than partnered mothers in terms of persistent isolation in talking to neighbours. They were, however, more likely to meet friends or relatives frequently (see Table 3.7).

Policy Implications

Sickness or disability and lone parenthood are idiosyncratic risks even though they affect large parts of the population. The very definition of these risk groups (see Chapter 1) resulted in small sample sizes which restricted the analysis severely. Nonetheless, some general patterns can be revealed. Working-age sick or disabled adults were less likely to be affected by income poverty,[15] but they were more likely to be deprived and isolated than the non-sick or disabled. This suggests that public transfers successfully assist sick or disabled adults in preventing income poverty. Owing to their additional needs, however, expenditures tend to be higher than in an average household (Badelt *et al.*, 1997). This might explain their lower than average standard of living, as measured by the supply of durables and necessities. In this context, it is vital to note that the universal care allowance, a benefit granted to many sick or disabled adults in need of care, only aims at covering a *part* of the total costs of care, while the family or informal sector is expected to cover the rest. Thus the government insists on a shared responsibility regarding sickness and disability. It has, however, recently allocated one billion ATS (€73 million) to improve labour market integration of disabled people. At the same time, the receipt of early retirement pension has been restricted, and the pension for reduced working capabilities abolished. The effects of these policy changes are twofold. On the one hand, the so-called 'disability billion' ought to increase labour market chances of the sick or disabled (and thus their household income). On the other hand, those unable to participate in the labour market might end up receiving low unemployment benefits rather than the higher early retirement benefits. The net effect of these policy changes in terms of income poverty and deprivation of the sick or disabled has to be assessed, once more recent waves of the ECHP become available.

Empirical evidence suggests that the Austrian family policy only covers part of the additional expenditures caused by raising children.[16] It is far away from preventing income poverty of families with dependent children. Again it is the traditional gender pattern, enforced by the corporatist welfare state model, that accounts for the specific vulnerability of families. Most mothers tend to take on full-time care as long as their children are small, which reduces household income. This loss of income, and the additional expenditures of raising children, are apparently only partially covered by the benefits aimed at families.

The current government, however, is inclined to reform one of the main transfer payments to families, namely parental leave allowance. It intends to extend the entitlement to this benefit to all mothers, regardless of their employment history. While this will improve the income situation of many females who did not qualify up to now for this transfer payment (for example, students), there is some concern that this universal benefit will reinforce the role of women as mothers rather than encourage women to enter or remain in paid employment. Currently, parental leave allowance is a type of unemployment benefit and thus – arguably – is aimed at women as workers rather than mothers. According to the existing stipulations, moreover, mothers or fathers entitled to parental leave allowance lose this transfer payment if their employment income exceeds a certain minimum level. The coalition government is inclined to relax this constraint, which will enable parents to generate higher employment income – if they manage to reconcile paid employment and caring obligations.

As it has been possible to see, the absence of the (male) breadwinner worsens the economic circumstances of lone mother families profoundly.[17] Although lone mothers are more likely to be employed than partnered mothers, employment income tends to be low. Their, on average, lower educational levels and obstacles to the reconciliation of work and family obligations lead them into low-paid, atypical and unsecured jobs. Not least due to their permanent struggle to combine employment and care-taking, accompanied by low employment incomes, many lone mothers feel very dissatisfied with their lives. As regards policy, this implies the need to provide better support for lone mothers to enable them to reconcile employment and care work, for example by providing enough and adequate child care facilities, and by promoting further education and professional training.

SUMMARY AND CONCLUSIONS

The availability of the ECHP allows us for the very first time to conduct dynamic analysis of income poverty and multidimensional deprivation for Austria. However, analysis is limited both by the existence of two waves only and by the small (for the purpose of dynamic analysis of various risk groups) number of sample observations.[18] A large group turnover, as has been evidenced for the working-age sick or disabled, is bound to restrict in-depth dynamic analysis of sub-groups, such as on gender. Despite these data limitations, however, it has been possible to gain new insights. Findings for Austria confirm that it is important to differentiate between persistent and transitory income poverty and deprivation. While larger proportions of the population are affected by income poverty and deprivation compared with the levels found in cross-sectional data, a large part of that was transitory. The in-depth analysis of selected risk groups does however suggest that different population groups are affected differently in this regard. For example, retired adults, lone mothers with at least one dependent child and working-age sick or disabled adults were more likely to be persistently poor, compared with young adults or the Austrian average. Within all of the population groups analysed here, women were more likely to be persistently poor than men, and thus deserve particular consideration in terms of policy.

ECHP findings provide evidence of a positive correlation between income poverty and other dimensions of welfare, most notably deprivation of necessities. For example, income poverty increased the probability of the population, and indeed young and retired adults, being deprived of amenities, durables and necessities by two to three times. This confirms the significance of income as a means of enhancing welfare. As women are much more likely to be income poor than men, policy should help women to earn higher wages, and more generally to improve their employment opportunities, for example by providing more child care facilities, as has been discussed above. This would not only decrease their relatively worse position in terms of income poverty and deprivation, it would also decrease their dependency upon their partner, family and, indeed, public social assistance. As mentioned earlier, there is some concern that current government policy reinforces the traditional gender roles.

Even though ECHP data suggested a positive correlation between low income and social isolation, this was less pronounced than with regard to other dimensions of welfare. Moreover, existing evidence suggests that low income affects the social participation of men and women differently. Men seem to be more likely than women to retreat from social life when their income is low. This different behaviour might partly be explained by the very responsibilities the corporatist Austrian welfare state attributes to gender. The male breadwinner is responsible for generating income, while the primary role of the female care-taker comprises the provision of services, continuity and stability beyond the market (and the state). The prevalence of income poverty might thus be interpreted as a failure of the male breadwinner, who retreats – often out of shame for this failure – from social life. Moreover, for many men their social contacts are often identical to their professional contacts. Thus, by losing their jobs, which often causes income poverty, men often also lose many of their social contacts.

In general, policy makers would be well advised to assess the compatibility of old and new policy instruments with regard to their effects on income poverty, multidimensional deprivation and gender inequality. The requirement of the European Commission for all member states to prepare National Action Programmes against social exclusion might indeed help to ensure that policies and policy reforms will be considered in this respect.

NOTES

1. Historically, poverty was *the* dominant social problem after World War II and in the 1950s. In the following two decades, Austria's economy performed well, as evidenced by impressive growth rates and low unemployment. Poverty seemed to be eradicated, affecting fringe groups only. In the late 1970s, parts of the middle-class population increasingly became affected by poverty. This 'new poverty' caused tremendous political turmoil, and encouraged many smaller-scale studies (for example, Schneidewind, 1985; Hawlik, 1981). After that agitation poverty disappeared again from the political (and research) agenda. Only after the country prepared to join the European Union, a pressure derived to keep pace with existing evidence at EU level.
2. With the exception of social isolation, analyses of poverty and deprivation are based on examinations of households rather than individuals, suggesting an under-representation of women who are assumed to share equally income and other material factors within the household (Millar and Glendinning, 1989; Reinl, 1997; Heitzmann, 2001), an assumption that has been disproved by several smaller-scale studies (for example, Middleton *et al.*, 1997).
3. See Chapter 1 for definitions of risk groups and other key variables and concepts.
4. That is, €637.33 (= ATS 8400) per month; for a definition, see Chapter 1; for a discussion of the relevance of this poverty line for Austria, see Heitzmann (2000).
5. A recent study found that only 3 per cent of the Austrian population had been persistently poor between 1994 and 1997 (Förster, 2001).
6. As mentioned previously, state retirement age is 60 years for women and 65 years for men. However, average entrance age is lower (in 1999: 56.7 years for women and 58.4 years for men) thanks to generous possibilities of early retirement.
7. Also the care allowance might be a potential income source for the retired in need of care; this benefit, for the sick or disabled adults, is discussed below.
8. Private insurance is not very prevalent in Austria. However, it is bound to increase.
9. Female poor young adults were less likely to be affected by deprivation of amenities than men.
10. Moreover, household income had to improve by at least five percentage points to account for movements out of poverty; that is, a higher proportion than the rise of the pension levels on average.
11. There is only information for 85 persistently sick or disabled adults, 89 lone mothers with at least one dependent child, and 31 lone mothers with non-dependent children available. To enable the analysis, the risk group of lone mothers has been enlarged to comprise all family members.
12. Therefore the following findings are based on analysis of lone mother families only.
13. If only one parent takes parental leave, the maximum duration is 18 months. Despite this monetary incentive for fathers to take on parental leave, only 1.5 per cent of those on parental leave are men.

14. While there is some evidence of an enhanced poverty risk for female sick or disabled, the small sample sizes do not allow for an in-depth analysis of gender.
15. There is some evidence that the sick or disabled are more likely to be persistently poor than the non-sick.
16. However, various in-kind benefits improve the situation for families with children by lowering expenditures (for example, schoolbooks and transfer to schools are free).
17. Cross-sectional data analysis has shown the importance of private transfers (partly alimony payments) as an important income source that helps prevent poverty.
18. There is only information for 8555 individuals available who participated both in 1995 and in 1996.

4. The dynamics of social exclusion in Germany: solving the east–west dilemma?

Wolfgang Voges and Olaf Jürgens

Traditionally, poverty research has been concerned with the economic and social causes of poverty. Labour market variables such as low pay, unemployment and under-employment, as well as familial conditions, such as single parenthood or divorce, are usually investigated as conditions that determine poverty. 'Individual' causes of poverty mainly refer to the lack of poor people's capabilities regarding participation in the labour market or regarding the setting up and successful management of family or household constellations. From this point of view, public policies assume the function of combating poverty, either in a structural way by intervening in the labour market and in family relations to moderate processes of exclusion and marginalization, or by direct measures designed to improve the individual capabilities and inclinations of poor people to become self-sufficient.

However, if the structure of society has changed – as in the former socialist countries including the former East Germany – the welfare state will not only combat or alleviate poverty arising from socioeconomic factors but may also produce poverty itself as an effect of the transition process. This type of poverty can be perceived as being caused by politically institutional mechanisms and these causes are, of course, not quite the same as the socioeconomic ones. Poverty brought about by socioeconomic factors can be seen as a kind of individual poverty, whereas poverty induced by the welfare state and its reconstruction can be perceived as societal poverty. In some cases the state also induces individual poverty, for example when welfare services are minimized owing to cuts in social spending and thus result in unemployment and poverty. The term 'societal poverty' thus denotes a situation of deprived people who suffer as a consequence of relying on institutional mechanisms intended to safeguard against poverty or to maintain income, but which fail to do so. It could be assumed that, after political unification and the transformation of political–institutional mechanisms, societal poverty would increase in the former East Germany.

A transformation of social policy for firms and a general policy of subsidiarity as the main anti-poverty strategy in the former socialist East German welfare state were replaced by social policies mainly based on local government strategies and individually focused policy with income maintenance benefits in the former West German welfare state. Such changes may have led to a shortfall in income for former East Germans. In this chapter we seek to explore poverty and deprivation in Germany, drawing out comparisons between the western and eastern parts of the country. The first main section of the chapter reviews some of the existing evidence on poverty rates and risks, focusing in particular on the 1990s but also setting this evidence within the pre-unification context. The second main section then turns to the analysis of the European Community Household Panel data, and again makes comparison between the west and the east in respect of poverty and deprivation across our four main risk groups.

INCOME POVERTY IN GERMANY: PRE- AND POST-REUNIFICATION

The changes in poverty rates over time are closely connected to economic development. In former West Germany, the first half of the 1960s was characterized by a successful economic upswing (the so-called 'West German economic miracle') and by full employment (unemployment rate 0.7–0.8 per cent). Furthermore, the important pension reform of 1957 greatly improved the situation of old people. It was a period later seen as a phase of seemingly perpetual prosperity (Lutz, 1984), where prosperity had stripped poverty of its traditional character as a social phenomenon that could be experienced directly. It is therefore not surprising that income poverty decreased on all measures from the early 1960s until the onset of the first oil crisis in 1973. But, halfway through the 1970s, this trend towards declining poverty was completely reversed, being strongly affected by the unemployment rate, which increased steadily from 1974 onwards. On a poverty line of 40 per cent of average income, the poverty rate more than doubled between 1973 and 1993, on a 50 per cent line it doubled, and on a 60 per cent line it increased by a quarter. The major changes were below this 60 per cent poverty line. The social security system was obviously most helpful above that line, while not as helpful for people in the lower wage categories. It also has to be remembered that foreign residents, who largely occupy lower wage groups and who live at an average risk of becoming unemployed, were not included in the data before 1993. The degree of growing income poverty since the middle of the 1970s is therefore probably rather underestimated.

The monetary union with the GDR (German Democratic Republic, the former East Germany) in 1990 and shortly thereafter the change of system and reunification of the two states into an economic and social union was a serious hiatus with long-term and far-reaching economic and social results (Hauser and Hübinger, 1993; Hauser *et al.*, 1996). Even if the effects of a changing system, of reunification, and of global economic development cannot, strictly speaking, be separated from each other, there are many indications to suggest that an important part of the increased unemployment rate has resulted from this change. In the western part of the country, the unemployment rate increased from 7.9 per cent to 10.5 per cent between 1990 and 1998, while in the eastern part the unemployment rate increased from 4.9 per cent (second half of 1990) to 19.5 per cent in 1998 (Statistisches Bundesamt, 2000, p. 98; Buhr *et al.*, 1998, Table 1).

Table 4.1 shows estimates of poverty in post-unification Germany in 1993 and 1998, based on three relative poverty lines, using data from two national surveys, and showing the western and eastern parts of the country separately. Obviously, the higher the poverty line the greater the proportion in poverty. Thus, in Germany as a whole, the rates of poverty in 1993 varied from 3.5 per cent of the population below 40 per cent of the median, to 5.2 per cent below 50 per cent of the median, to 11.7 per cent below 60 per cent

Table 4.1   Relative income poverty in Germany, 1993 and 1998

	Proportion of population below poverty line								
	Western			Eastern			Germany		
	40%	50%	60%	40%	50%	60%	40%	50%	60%
EVS									
1993	3.9	6.1	12.5	(0.7)	(1.7)	5.8	3.5	5.2	11.7
1998	4.3	6.6	13.1	(1.1)	2.8	7.9	3.8	5.7	12.4
GSOEP									
1993	—	9.5	17.0	—	3.7	8.5	—	8.1	15.8
1998	—	9.5	16.0	—	5.8	10.0	—	8.5	14.5

Note: The alternative poverty lines are based on the median of the equivalised household income. Numbers in parentheses indicate very low case numbers. Net equivalence income: head of household 1.0, further members of the household from the age of 15 0.7, children 0.5. For the EVS (Income and Consumption Survey) results are based on incomes of the year (including rental values of owned property) and relate to households with German heads. Calculations with the use of GSOEP (German Socio-Economic Panel) for 1993–1998 are based on monthly incomes and relate to households with German heads.

Source: Hauser and Becker (2001); special calculations of Irene Becker on the basis of the EVS database; Krause *et al.* (2001, Table 3–9.3, p.52).

of the median. In 1998, the equivalent proportions were 3.8 per cent, 5.7 per cent and 12.4 per cent, respectively.

In the former East Germany the rise in unemployment has been lower (by about one-third) than the total decrease of employment, because a great variety of sociopolitical measures have been set up temporarily to tackle underemployment (Sachverständigenrat zur Begutachtung der gesamtwirtschaftlichen Entwicklung, 1996, Table 2; Hauser *et al.*, 1996, ch. 2.4). However, increased unemployment has had a major influence on the further increase in income poverty in both parts of Germany, as shown in Table 4.1.

In the former West Germany an increased proportion in poverty on all three poverty lines is apparent between 1993 and 1998. This might partly be a consequence of methodological differences in the database, and of the inclusion of foreign residents. The highest increase of the proportion in poverty was on the 60 per cent poverty line, probably because the social security system has been changed and weakened through various reforms, especially with regard to safeguarding unemployed people. Generally speaking, the distribution of the net equivalence income among the lower wage groups is similar to the situation at the beginning of the 1960s.

In the former East Germany a strong increase on all poverty lines is noticeable, despite the immediate change to the existing West German social security system and the introduction of special provisions for the new East German Bundesländer (states). This tendency still remains, even if the data from 1990 are excluded, because of the subventions on basic foodstuffs which still existed and which constituted an advantage for poorer members of society.[1] In the former East Germany, the proportion in poverty between 1993 and 1998, raised to a higher extent than in the former West Germany on all three poverty lines.

In fact, the new Bundesländer were confronted by a deep socioeconomic crisis during reunification, leading to huge changes in nearly every aspect of everyday life and also affecting the chances of impoverishment (Hanesch *et al.*, 1994). The result was an increasing risk of poverty and exclusion for whole sections of the population (Lutz and Zeng, 1998). But with regard to the differences in financial and material deprivation between the eastern and western parts of the country, Böhnke and Delhey (1999) demonstrated that, on the basis of the German Welfare Survey of 1998 via means of a proportional deprivation index, although the extent of deprivation is still higher in the east, material and financial deprivation is due to the same risk factors: the unemployed, lone parents and persons without adequate qualifications are identified as the classic risk groups in both east and west.

Therefore the next question is whether the proportion in poverty among different population groups has moved above or below average and, subsequently, whether there are differentiated policy outcomes and effects in relation to poverty and the groups of people affected by it. Poverty risks affect not only classic risk groups, but also, to an increasing extent, members of the middle class (Adamy and Steffen, 1998). Eckardt (1997) revealed that even the average family (with two or more children) is as threatened by poverty as are lone mothers, children, young people and the retired. Using the 50 per cent poverty line, research (Becker, 1997; Hauser, 1997) has revealed the following.

1. If we make the distinction between the gender of the persons con-
    cerned, it becomes obvious that in the last two decades the proportion
    of men in poverty has increased more than the proportion of women
    in poverty. The latter was higher from the start but now the proportion
    of men in poverty is almost as high as that of women in both parts of
    the country. We can therefore no longer speak of poverty as a problem
    that mainly concerns women (*feminization of poverty*), contrary to the
    situation in the United States.
2. However, in both the west and the east, the members of lone-parent
    families headed by a woman belong to the group of the population very
    likely to be affected by poverty. In 1962/63, their poverty rate in West
    Germany was about twice as high as for the total population; by 1995
    the rate had tripled (31 per cent). In the former East Germany their
    poverty rate in 1990 was much higher than the already very low total
    rate of 3.5 per cent, whereas its increase by 1995 was slightly lower than
    average (27.2 per cent).
3. The proportion in poverty amongst people living in households with at
    least one unemployed member can only be established from 1983
    onwards in the west. At that point they already numbered a third of the
    total proportion; the ratio remained the same in the following years.
    The percentage in poverty in the east changed from probably almost
    nothing in the year 1990 to more than double the overall rate (20 per
    cent).
4. In both parts of the country the number of children under the age of
    16 who belong to those affected by income poverty has steadily
    increased since 1990 (in 1995 this was 38 per cent in the eastern part of
    the country and 28 per cent in the western part). In the west this ten-
    dency was already visible at the beginning of the 1980s. We can there-
    fore speak of an *infantilization of poverty* (see, in general, Otto 1997;
    Weick, 1999).
5. In the west the proportion of old people (over 65) in poverty was twice
    as high as the overall poverty rate at the beginning of the 1960s. Since
    then this rate has constantly decreased and at the end of the 1980s it

even fell below the overall rate. In 1990, the proportion in the east had reached the same level as that in the west (9 per cent). Thanks to special provisions for pensioners, there is hardly any old-age poverty in the western part of the country.

6. Poverty among foreign residents has also increased in the west. At the beginning of the 1980s, the proportion of foreigners in poverty was about twice as high as that of the German population (Seifert, 1994). Especially the higher risks in the labour market for foreign employees has helped increase their numbers in poverty (Habich and Krause, 1997).

In general, with regard to the unemployed, lone parents and retired people, Ehlers (1997) explored multidimensional poverty and deprivation using an ordinal data concept. This showed that in the last half of the 1980s the extent of poverty for these three risk groups decreased, while in the first half of the 1990s, after unification, it either levelled off or increased. But if we look at all households affected by poverty and deprivation, the differences between the poor and the rest of the population are not so great that we could speak of social exclusion of whole parts of the population, although some of them might be deeply affected by poverty (Andreß, 1999).

The Development of 'Societal' Poverty

At the beginning of the 1960s, the reform of the former West German public welfare system through the Federal Social Assistance Act (SAA) initiated a discussion of the function of minimum income support. The reason for this was the assumption that non-monetary assistance towards specific living conditions, the lowest level of support offered by the welfare state, would become less important over time because of the expected rise in income through higher wages and the dynamic pension system. As a result, this sort of assistance would then become the main part of social assistance in general. Whether these expectations turned into reality will be shown in the following overview.[2]

At first sight it is clear that these expectations did not materialize – in fact, the development shows quite the opposite. In former West Germany, the proportion of recipients of social assistance was 1.3 per cent in 1963 and increased only by a small amount during the following decade. There was, however, a big increase in the second half of the 1970s, while yet another increase led to a level twice as high in 1988. In 1993,[3] the proportion in receipt of social assistance benefits (including refugees and asylum seekers) had reached 5.1 per cent. The gradual increase of the social assistance proportion mainly followed the worsening economic situation and the reduced possibilities of gainful employment, which were mirrored by the gradual increase in the unemployment rate.

In the former East Germany only a few thousand people lived on minimum income support and there was practically no unemployment in 1989. After the change to the West German welfare system, and even with increasing unemployment in the new German Bundesländer (the states in the former East Germany), the social assistance ratio did increase (by 3.2 per cent in 1993), but has not yet reached the levels in the western part of the country.

As mentioned above, the changes in social assistance receipt are also affected by the development of the social assistance threshold. Only when this threshold is regularly brought into line with the average rise in income can the increasing rate of social assistance recipients be interpreted as an increase in the level of 'combated' poverty. In general, the social assistance standard did increase in proportion to the net wage per employee from 1963 to 1993. However, the increase in the average net equivalence income could be considered as a more relevant reference, because the net wage per employee increase was held back by an increasing number of part-time jobs. Moreover, the average level of affluence has become increasingly determined by households with two wage earners. If we take the average net equivalence household income, the level of social assistance lags behind, even if not by much (about 10 per cent after rent and heating bills). A similar picture is found from data from official statistics on the net equivalence income of social assistance recipients as compared to the average total economic net equivalence income: between 1972 and 1993, this percentage decreased from 53 per cent to 48 per cent (Hauser, 1995). These results suggest that, since the beginning of the 1980s, the proportion in receipt of social assistance, and with it combated poverty, would have increased more if the social assistance limit had been brought into line with changes in average incomes.

When comparing the development of combated poverty with the development of relative poverty, differences appear during the decade from 1962/63 to 1973. While relative income poverty decreased until the mid-1970s, the proportion in receipt of social assistance slowly increased. This may be due to the fact that knowledge of the improved social assistance only spread among the population slowly in comparison with their knowledge of the former welfare system. From the mid-1970s until the end of the 1980s, there was a parallel increase in the social assistance rate and relative income poverty on the 40 per cent and 50 per cent poverty lines, while there was hardly any change on the 60 per cent poverty line. This divergence means that the risk of poverty is still concentrated below the 60 per cent poverty line among wage earners with a very low income. It was only after the reunification of the two German states that a parallel development started taking shape in the west between relative poverty on all three poverty lines and the social assistance rate. Even if we exclude combated poverty resulting from the large increase in numbers of asylum seekers, the parallel remains. Because of the obvious increase in income poverty on the 60 per cent poverty line, a greater risk of poverty for lower groups of wage earners with medium income can be expected (Hauser and Hübinger, 1993; Kronauer, 1998). In the former East Germany, a similar development can be traced.

Concerning combated as well as relative poverty, we can ask whether particular groups are more likely than the average to be in receipt of social assistance. Such differences would indicate group-related specific risks of poverty and their change over the course of time. As a result we might obtain indications of new poverty problems and the need for group-specific measures in the fight against poverty. The main features of structural change among social assistance recipients are the following.

1. When we look at combated poverty in the former East Germany, it becomes evident that the poverty rates for women and men between 1963 (men 0.9 per cent; women 1.7 per cent) and 1992 (men 4.6 per cent; women 4.0 per cent) have gradually been brought into line with those in the former West Germany. No gender-specific differences concerning the risk of poverty have been traceable in the past few years.
2. The number of lone-parent households who have to live on social assistance is rising, especially where these households are headed by a woman.
3. The most important structural change noticeable when considering age-specific rates of social assistance receipt in the former West Germany is that, while the proportion of children under seven in receipt of social assistance was approximately the same as the proportion of people over 70 years in receipt (about 2.0 per cent according to figures at the end of the year), an enormous discrepancy has developed since then. The percentage of young children under seven in families receiving social assistance is now at 7.3 per cent, the percentage of old people at 1 per cent (Neuhäuser, 1995, p. 796). The aforementioned problem of infantilization of poverty again becomes obvious and is likely to have heavy psychosocial consequences for the affected children (Mansel and Brinkhoff, 1998).
4. Another important structural change can be seen when looking at receipt of social assistance amongst foreigners, both resident and those who have only recently immigrated to Germany. While the rate of social assistance granted to foreign residents was below that of the German population until 1980 in the former West Germany, it was five times higher than the rate for German residents in 1993 (Voges and

Weber 1998). It would be a mistake to explain this increase simply with reference to the increase in the number of foreign residents, because the German rate also doubled over the same period of time. However, if we look at the German Micro census database on foreign male residents, their risk of being dependent on social assistance benefit in 1995 was nine times that of German men. German women are more likely than German men to be social assistance recipients, and so the risk for foreign female residents is only three times higher than for German women (Voges *et al.*, 1999).

The Dynamics of Poverty

The fact that there has been a certain poverty rate from the early 1960s does not mean that the same people are affected during the whole period and that a lower class of society is constantly affected by poverty. Some people may escape poverty while others find themselves in that situation, thus replacing them. Hence three questions arise: (1) which people live at a higher risk of becoming impoverished and of falling below the poverty line; (2) which people live at a higher risk of short- or long-term or even long-lasting poverty, and how long does such an individual situation of impoverishment last; (3) which people can escape from that situation on a temporary or long-term basis? Such questions can only be answered on the basis of statistics and reports on the same people over a long period of time. The dynamics of individual relative poverty over any period of time can be identified by using the data from GSOEP.[4] Questions about the dynamics of combated poverty (social assistance dynamics) in the western part of the country can be answered on the basis of data from the Longitudinal Social Assistance Study (LSA) for Bremen,[5] and for the eastern part there is an analogous survey called the Halle Longitudinal Study on Social Assistance (HLS) for Halle.[6]

Data from the GSOEP, 1984 to 1995, show that 4 per cent of the population lived in income poverty (50 per cent poverty line) for five years or more. In such cases we are talking about long-lasting poverty. The data also show that, on the one hand, three-quarters of the population in the former West Germany have never been affected by the 50 per cent poverty line and, on the other hand, that the remaining quarter did fall below this poverty line at least once over the same period (Habich and Krause, 1997). Sopp (1994) critically examined the thesis of a two-thirds/one-third society, which implies that a deprived or poor segment of the population exists on a long-term basis. When he looked at processes of social mobility and the extent to which people remain in the same area, he used GSOEP as well.

A second perspective on poverty is based on an income line that separates those in the lower 10 per cent (or 20 per cent) of the population from the upper 90 per cent (80 per cent). In both the west and the east some people belong to these lower income groups every year. The percentage of people who do not belong to the lower tenth or fifth at any time is higher in the former West Germany. The risk of falling below this poverty line at least once is higher in the east than in the west. However, the risk of remaining in a situation of impoverishment is higher in the west than in the east. The percentage of people who belong to the poor segment of the population is at any time in the west in relation to the lower tenth more than five times as high, and in relation to the lower fifth more than twice as high, as in the east. Moreover, as a consequence of the existence of low-wage jobs, even a full-time employment does not protect people from falling below the (relative) poverty line (Strengmann-Kuhn, 1997).

The results show that many lower-income groups are at risk of impoverishment. However, among wage earners of lower-income groups there is a great dynamic regarding poverty. Thus the people affected by poverty stand a comparatively good chance of escaping from this situation in the following years. It cannot be said to what extent social assistance benefits help people escape from impoverishment. Long-term or long-lasting social assistance receipt involves the risk not only of remaining in poverty, but also of social exclusion from relevant peer groups of the population, of forming a sub-class, and, owing to segregation, of spatial concentration in closed poverty areas.

THE EUROPEAN HOUSEHOLD PANEL SURVEY: DYNAMICS AND THE EAST–WEST DILEMMA

In contrast to the studies in pre-unification West Germany which, until the 1980s, were mainly centred on income poverty, the few unofficial studies in pre-unification East Germany emphasized the meaning of different life situations and thus referred to the concept of relative or, rather, multiple deprivation in which the monetary impact was excluded. This implied an understanding of poverty as a direct and perceptible phenomenon that can be directly 'measured', for example by the level of provision of consumer goods, services or accommodation. Whereas, in the previous section, the poverty research discussed focused on income poverty, in this section we focus on different kinds of material deprivation and their connection to income poverty.

To examine the extent of deprivation, we used the German version of the European Community Household Panel (ECHP), which allowed us to distinguish between the western and eastern parts of the country. We calculated three different indicators for deprivation with regard to housing conditions. Each indicator consisted of different items, weighted by the proportion of the population that has each at its disposal. The absence of items widely distributed within the population was therefore weighted to a stronger extent than the absence of items not so common within the population. The three indicators were household amenities (consisting of whether a household has its own kitchen, a bath, a toilet, hot running water and so on), household durables (whether, for example, a TV set, phone or car is available) and household necessities (whether the accommodation is adequately warm, whether worn-out furniture or clothes can be replaced and so on). See Chapter 1 for a full description of these measures. We have to bear in mind that there are large differences in household amenities between the former East and West. Therefore we used the German version of the ECHP[7] and matched the variable with the regional information to the Eurostat public use file.

If we look at the household amenities (Table 4.2), it turns out that comparatively few households were deprived in this category in the west, compared to the other two types of deprivation, and the extent of deprivation did not increase between waves two and three. Most households in Germany possess amenities such as a separate kitchen and inside flushing toilet. In the east there was a comparatively high extent of deprivation in this respect, but it was declining across the waves. The proportion without durables was higher in the east, and it rose between the successive waves, but to a lower extent than in the west. The proportion without necessities is highest for Germany as a whole (although we used a lower deprivation line), but in the former East Germany deprivation of necessities is lower than the other types of deprivation, and it fell between waves two and three, whereas it rose in the former West Germany.

Table 4.2   Deprivation rates, Germany, ECHP, 1995–6

	Percentage deprived of amenities			Percentage deprived of durables			Percentage deprived of necessities		
	West	East	All	West	East	All	West	East	All
Wave 2 (1995)	3	17	6	5	19	8	8	15	10
Wave 3 (1996)	3	13	5	11	20	13	9	12	10

Note: Amenities and durables deprivation line set at 80 per cent median proportional deprivation score; necessities deprivation line set at 60 per cent. The percentages may not add up to 100 per cent because of rounding. All ECHP tables based on weighted sample, see Chapter 1.

Table 4.3   Deprivation dynamics: all adults 16 plus, Germany, ECHP,
*   1995–6 (turnover)*

	Weighted percentage			Unweighted numbers		
	West	East	All	West	East	All
Amenities						
Remained in deprivation	2	10	4	126	172	298
Exited from deprivation	1	7	3	81	135	216
Entered deprivation	1	3	1	74	43	117
Never in deprivation	95	80	93	6292	1568	7860
Durables						
Remained in deprivation	2	6	3	138	102	240
Exited from deprivation	3	12	4	141	264	405
Entered deprivation	8	13	9	408	187	595
Never in deprivation	87	68	83	5775	1358	7133
Necessities						
Remained in deprivation	5	8	5	279	134	413
Exited from deprivation	4	7	4	236	129	365
Entered deprivation	5	4	5	269	81	350
Never in deprivation	87	81	86	5689	1539	7228

Note: Amenities and durables deprivation line set at 80 per cent median proportional deprivation score, necessities deprivation line set at 60 per cent. The percentages may not add up to 100 per cent due to rounding.

For the whole of Germany, there were very low entrance rates for all kinds of deprivation measured (Tables 4.3 and 4.4). This was partly due to the comparatively low levels of deprivation found at wave two. However, persistent deprivation rates for household amenities and household necessities were higher than the exit rates, whereas this was not the case for household durables. For the latter, we can observe a turnover for exiting that was in general higher than the persistency rates, and for the east was twice as high.

The higher exit rate for durables (Table 4.4) may be the outcome of the so-called 'generosity' of the German welfare system. This allows people below the social assistance threshold to use telephones without a flat rate charge and with a budget of a given amount of free calls; recycled furniture will be given to this section of the population by charity organizations, and so on. On the other hand, the highest entrance rate into deprivation was for deprivation of durables for both the eastern and western parts of the country. For this type of deprivation there was a very high dynamic with a high number of people exiting or entering, but with a higher proportion of

Table 4.4 *Deprivation dynamics: all adults 16 plus, Germany, ECHP, 1995–6 (rates)*

	Weighted percentage			Unweighted numbers		
	West	East	All	West	East	All
Amenities						
Persistence rate	61	59	60	126	172	298
Exit rate	40	41	40	81	135	216
Entrance rate	1	3	2	74	43	117
Avoidance rate	99	97	99	6292	1568	7860
Durables						
Persistence rate	49	35	42	138	102	240
Exit rate	51	66	58	141	264	405
Entrance rate	9	16	10	408	187	595
Avoidance rate	91	84	90	5775	1358	7133
Necessities						
Persistence rate	55	52	54	279	134	413
Exit rate	45	48	46	236	129	365
Entrance rate	5	5	5	269	81	350
Avoidance rate	95	95	95	5689	1539	7228

Note: Amenities and durables deprivation line set at 80 per cent median proportional deprivation score, necessities deprivation line set at 60 per cent. The percentages may not add up to 100 per cent because of rounding.

those exiting and with a comparatively low number of persons remaining deprived in both waves. To a more limited extent we can observe these dynamics also in the case of household necessities, where in the west more or less the same proportion exited, entered or remained in deprivation (Table 4.3). Only in the east did the proportion in deprivation remain higher than those exiting. For household amenities, the weighted percentages indicate that the number of those who exited was only slightly lower than the number of those who remained. The extent to which people entered this type of deprivation for the first time was very low. Again there was a worse picture in the east, where a high proportion remained deprived.

In the case of the durables and necessities, the extent of deprivation was rising slightly, mainly in the west. Only for household amenities did the extent of deprivation in the west remain more or less the same; in the east it was, again, declining. These findings do not seem to confirm that, in the west, overall rates of deprivation were decreasing faster than increasing between the waves, whereas in the east, although the overall extent of deprivation was still higher there, there was a decline in deprivation.

Income Poverty and Deprivation Dynamics for Risk Groups

By differentiating between different risk groups defined according to life course transitions (see Chapter 1) we can examine which kind of changes within individual life courses lead to a substantially higher risk of being affected by income poverty or deprivation. After German unification in 1990, nearly every aspect of everyday life was affected by the socio-economic changes, with increasing risks of income poverty and deprivation for entire sections of the population (as discussed at the beginning of this chapter). Therefore, we can expect the same kind of transition to lead to different risks of income poverty or deprivation, depending on whether the affected person is in the west or in the east. If we look at the different risk groups and divide them into east and west, we have to face the general problem of very low case numbers, especially in the east. We report the tables for the different risk groups only if most of the cells have numbers higher than 30.[8] Thus, on that level of the analysis, a comparison between east and west with regard to the different risk groups was omitted for certain kinds of deprivation, mainly in the case of lone parents and sick or disabled persons (Tables 4.5 and 4.6).[9]

Lone parents
Interpretation of these data is very difficult, because of the very low case numbers, especially in the east. Therefore the numbers are not reported. However, we could expect a relatively high income poverty entrance rate for lone mothers, an outcome of the inadequate child care situation, largely affecting the west, where there is a large deficit in child care. In the former East Germany, by contrast, there is still a very comfortable child care situation. We can thus assume that the entrance rates of lone parents in the former West Germany are affected by a lack of child care facilities, while in the former East Germany poverty is a consequence of limited labour market opportunities. If we look at deprivation, the case numbers are again too low for analysis.

Retired people
The case numbers in the west for exiting from or entering income poverty were again too low for detailed analysis; thus interpretation is very difficult. For the whole of Germany, the income poverty exit rates for retired people were comparatively low; this is a consequence of retired people having fewer opportunities for earning an income through paid employment. Low entrance rates, on the other hand, were more or less due to numerous programmes for income support, for example higher social assistance rates and pre-retirement support. We can observe in the west higher proportions of

Table 4.5 Income poverty dynamics for panel members: Germany, ECHP, 1995–6, young adults, retired, lone mothers (rates)

	Retired			Young adults			All adults 16+		
	West (%)	East (%)	Total (%)	West (%)	East (%)	Total (%)	West (%)	East (%)	Total (%)
Transitions									
Persistence rate	81	[100]	80	57	[55]	56	67	63	66
Exit rate	[19]	*	20	43	[45]	44	33	37	34
Entrance rate	3	*	2	7	[5]	6	4	2	3
Avoidance rate	97	100	98	93	95	94	96	98	97
Turnover									
Remained in									
income poverty	7	[6]	6	7	[7]	7	6	5	6
Exited poverty	[2]	*	2	6	[6]	6	3	3	3
Entered poverty	3	*	2	6	[5]	6	3	2	3
Never in poverty[1]	89	94	90	82	83	82	88	90	89
Base (unweighted)	1525	498	2023	1251	386	1637	6603	1923	8526

Notes:
[1] 'Never', in this and subsequent tables, refers to the observation period: thus, never poor/deprived over the two years covered.
In all tables, * indicates a cell size of less than 10 unweighted observations; [ ] indicates a cell size of between 10 and 29 unweighted observations. Poverty line set to 60 per cent of the median equivalent monthly net income; the percentages may not add up to 100 per cent because of rounding.

those who remained deprived or in income poverty compared to the east. This is also true for the different kinds of deprivation: the proportion exiting from deprivation was higher in the east.

Young adults
When considering young adults, the most important problem is youth unemployment and the lack of available apprenticeships. The situation is especially bad in the east, therefore we could expect a higher proportion of those deprived or below the income poverty line. But, on the other hand, we can observe higher chances on the labour market for young adults with 'everybody qualification'.[10] Therefore the income poverty and deprivation exit rates in general were comparatively high for young adults, and there were no differences between east and west. The entrance rates, on the other hand, were not higher than the exit rates. This was probably the result of the elaborate programmes the Social Democratic Party established together with the Green Party to support unemployed young people.

Table 4.6   Deprivation dynamics: Germany, ECHP, 1995–6

	Retired			Young adults	All adults 16+		
	West (%)	East (%)	Total (%)	Total (%)	West (%)	East (%)	Total (%)
Amenities							
Transitions							
Persistence rate	63	59	61	59	61	59	60
Exit rate	[37]	41	39	41	39	41	40
Entrance rate	[2]	[3]	2	[2]	1	3	2
Avoidance rate	98	97	98	98	99	97	98
Turnover							
Remained in deprivation	2	13	5	5	2	10	4
Exited deprivation	[1]	9	3	3	1	7	3
Entered deprivation	[2]	[2]	2	[1]	1	3	1
Never in deprivation	95	76	90	91	95	80	92
Base (unweighted)	1516	496	2012	1632	6573	1918	8491
Durables							
Transitions							
Persistence rate	[54]	[44]	44	44	49	35	42
Exit rate	[46]	56	56	56	51	65	58
Entrance rate	19	35	35	6	9	16	10
Avoidance rate	81	65	65	94	91	84	90
Turnover							
Remained in deprivation	[2]	[7]	7	5	2	6	3
Exited deprivation	[2]	9	9	6	3	12	4
Entered deprivation	18	29	29	6	8	13	9
Never in deprivation	78	55	55	84	87	68	83
Base (unweighted)	1500	495	1995	1598	6462	1911	8373
Necessities							
Transitions							
Persistence rate	59	55	58	49	55	52	54
Exit rate	41	45	42	51	45	48	46
Entrance rate	7	[4]	6	5	5	5	5
Avoidance rate	93	96	94	95	95	95	95
Turnover							
Remained in deprivation	5	9	6	5	5	8	5
Exited deprivation	4	7	4	5	4	7	4
Entered deprivation	6	[3]	5	5	5	4	5
Never in deprivation	86	81	85	86	87	81	86
Base (unweighted)	1502	487	1989	1590	6473	1883	8356

Note: Amenities and durables deprivation line set at 80 per cent median proportional deprivation score, necessities deprivation line set at 60 per cent. The percentages may not add up to 100 per cent because of rounding. In all tables, [ ] indicates a cell size of between 10 and 29 unweighted observations.

Until now we have used purely descriptive methods to look at distributions of, and within, risk groups. In order to construct a typology on the basis of these distributions it seems to be important to try to identify factors that can help predict whether a household that belongs to a risk group falls below the income poverty line. Identifying these predictors should not be confused with causal analysis of longitudinal data: if this had been the aim, we would have had to construct models on a completely different basis (that is, hazard rates). We start with explorative techniques, thus allowing us to identify (possibly) important factors, which can then be examined in more detail through further analysis.

Explorative Analysis of Income Poverty over Time

For this analysis we used the approach developed by Kass (1975, 1980) and known as CHAID (Chi-Square Automatic Interaction Detection). On the basis of χ^2 tests, this programme detects correlation between different characteristics of people. This method allows us to take characteristics as values that follow a categorical scale, therefore it is a good predictor of relationships between dependent and independent variables (in this case, characteristics and income poverty).

The basic idea is that a given population is divided into sub-groups with the help of independent variables. These sub-groups should be – with respect to the dependent variable – as homogeneous as possible and, consequently, are clearly differentiated from each another. For example, if it is possible, with the help of a variable, to split poor and non-poor people into sub-groups that clearly differ from each other, this variable is a significant predictor for being/not being poor. This approach is obviously not restricted to one explanatory variable. If there are several independent variables, they can be used successively to form 'better' sub-groups, that is sub-groups that, with respect to the phenomenon that is going to be explained, are successively more clearly differentiated. Consequently, this is referred to as 'the method of successive splits' rather than contrast group analysis: from a given number of independent variables, the ones that allow the optimal split of the original population, or the optimal split of an already formed sub-group, are successively applied. The sub-groups are split in this way until the groups become too small or the sampling error becomes too large. The advantage of this technique within the framework of our study is that, by splitting the population, sub-groups with clearly differentiated risks of becoming (or not becoming) poor can be identified.

We set out to explain the reasons for being poor in 1995, that is in the third wave of the ECHP. We distinguish between the three waves: the first in 1993 (t_1), the second in 1994 (t_2), and the final one in 1995 (t_3). Being poor means having incomes below the 60 per cent threshold of the median of the weighted monthly net household equivalence income. To identify the best explanatory predictors for this phenomenon, we use the characteristics of the population both at t_3 (that is, in 1995) and at the preceding time points, t_1 and t_2. As predictors, we used indicators for being poor in the preceding waves, an age variable (grouped), the different risk groups,[11] employment status (having a full-time job or not, a part-time job or not, and being unemployed or not), whether the person concerned was economically inactive, whether he or she belonged to the hidden reserve (inactive people of workable age with terminated unemployment benefits), marital status, childbirth, marriage, divorce and, finally, whether he or she lived in the east or the west. The household size is also taken into account, although the interpretation has to rely on strong plausibility assumptions.[12] Only cases which were observable in all the three waves were used. All missing cases were excluded.

The results clearly show that the most accurate predictor for being poor at t_3 was whether or not the person concerned was poor at t_2 (Figure 4.1). About six in 10 (60.2 per cent) of those who were poor at t_2 remained poor in t_3. On the other hand, very few (only 5.9 per cent) of those who were not poor at t_2 became poor at t_3. On the next level, for both sub-groups, whether they were poor in wave 1 is most important: from those who were poor in t_1 and poor in t_2, 67.3 per cent (514 people, the far right branch of the tree) remained poor also in t_3. On the other hand, from those who were poor neither in t_1 nor in t_2, only 5 per cent (328 people, the left branch of the tree) became poor in t_3. In this case, the history of the poverty track record was the most important factor in explaining income poverty in wave three. On the next level, for those not poor in wave one, being unemployed or not was the most decisive factor, as well as for those poor in t_2, but not in t_1. One level beyond, the importance of the labour market becomes even more obvious: being unemployed or not was, on that level, the most important factor in an individual's chances of being affected or not by income poverty in the third wave. But also one of the risk groups under examination, the retired, has a significant effect: those active in wave two had a higher risk of becoming poor than those who were retired, owing to comparatively generous pensions in Germany. Only on the fourth level of our model was there a significant effect of the household size: a decrease in household size from wave two to three led to a higher risk of being affected by income poverty in the last wave.

Moreover, those with less than a full-time job at wave two were more likely to be poor at wave three than those with full-time work (34.4 per cent and 19.2 per cent, respectively). There would also have been an effect from being in the east or in the west at this last level of the tree, but, owing to the low case numbers, this branch had to be skipped.

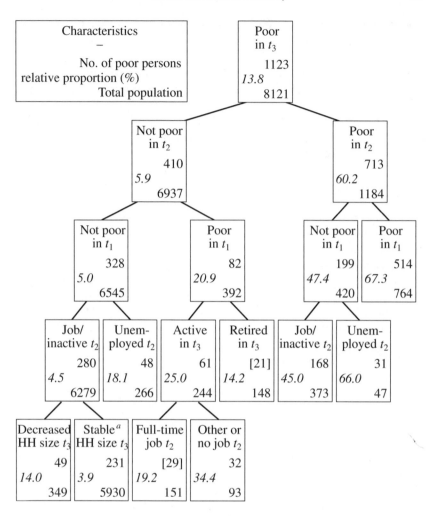

Note: Reading from top to bottom, the first value in each box is the number of persons who were poor in 1995 in the sub-group. The value in italics shows their relative proportion in the respective sub-group (per cent). The bottom value is the total number of people in this sub-group. Differences between sub-groups are significant at the 5% level; [a]*stable* could also mean an increase in household size.

Figure 4.1   Determinants for being poor at the end of a three-year observation period

Dynamics in a Multivariate Perspective: the Importance of the Life Course History

Logit models are often used for analysing cross-sectional data, but for the analysis of longitudinal panel data they are comparatively new. In panel data, the outcome is not observed only at one given point in time, but at several, successive points in time. The dependent variable here is being poor at wave three. We assume that unobserved heterogeneity terms are fixed effects that do not change across waves. The basic formula is:

$$Pr(Y_{it} = 1 | X_{i1}, \ldots, X_{iT}, c_i) = \frac{exp(\mathbf{X}_{it}\beta + c_i)}{1 + exp(\mathbf{X}_{it}\beta + c_i)}.$$

Y_{it} is the dependent variable for the ith individual in wave t ($i = 1,\ldots,8121$; $t = 1,2,3$) and can take on two different values: Y_{it} {0,1} with 1 = poor in wave 3 and 0 = not poor in wave 3; $\mathbf{X}_{it}$ is a row vector of observed covariates, for individual i in wave t; c_i is an individual-specific scalar introduced to account for unobserved heterogeneity across individuals. The c_i terms do not change across waves, but they may be correlated with the observed variables in an arbitrary manner.

The results of the conditional logit model, as shown in Table 4.7, show that transfer income out of the social security system strongly reduces the risk for (so-called) traditional target groups (traditional in the sense that they were traditional target groups within the German system of social protection). In the observed period the pension in Germany was related to net income obtained over the previous couple of years. This time lag generates income positions for pensioners that may mean they are relatively better off than employed workers in phases of economic downswing. Furthermore, people who stay on unemployment benefits (67 per cent of last net income) or sickness benefits (100 per cent of last net income) have better chances of overcoming a situation of income poverty. The social capital associated with a large number of household members also reduces the risk of remaining below the income poverty line. The birth of a child and a transition into the status of lone parent increases the risk of falling below the income poverty line.

The model shows also whether (and to what extent) there are significant differences between the east and the west. However, if we separate the population into those who stay within the observation period in one particular part of Germany, the results become much clearer. In the former East Germany the labour market offers work opportunities, especially for the young. This reduced their risk of remaining below the income poverty line. Retirees from the former West Germany have higher pensions than those from the former East Germany and so were less likely to fall below the

Table 4.7 Determinants for being poor in wave 3: conditional logit model, Germany, ECHP, 1995–6

Variable	Germany		West Germany		East Germany	
Age <30	−0.2495	(−0.8122)	0.3238	(0.8674)	−1.4470**	(−2.3287)
Age >65	−0.6212***	(−1.9837)	−1.0254*	(−2.5806)	0.2367	(0.4176)
Married	−0.4977	(−1.3287)	−0.7186	(−1.5548)	−0.2845	(−0.3967)
Divorced	0.5361	(1.0315)	1.8388**	(2.2355)	−0.8610	(−1.0810)
HHSize2–3	−0.7567*	(−3.6389)	−0.3346	(−1.3347)	−1.5107*	(−3.7186)
HHSize4–8	−1.0969*	(−4.6417)	−0.8461*	(−3.0684)	−1.6397*	(−3.3673)
Birth	0.6830**	(2.3583)	0.7130**	(2.2019)	0.7574	(1.0497)
Lone Parent	1.2314*	(3.2719)	1.4130**	(3.0625)	0.9874	(1.4360)
Unemployed	−0.4289**	(−1.9465)	−0.7291**	(−2.6543)	0.4312	(0.9453)
Hidden Reserve	0.2370	(1.3257)	0.3374***	(1.6857)	−0.3650	(−0.8008)
Retired	0.3896	(1.3678)	0.3835	(1.1595)	0.3285	(0.5264)
Sick	−0.0861*	(−2.7290)	−0.0643***	(−1.8389)	−0.2402*	(−2.6397)
East Germany	0.5829	(0.7163)				
Cases	8130		6279		1833	
Poor in Wave	1:14.2 2:14.6 3:13.8		1:13.6 2:14.1 3:13.3		1:16.2 2:16.4 3:15.7	

Notes:
*** = p<0.01, ** = p<0.05, * = p<0.10

income poverty line. But sickness benefits had a better protective function for those in the east. Unemployment benefits had no significant effect on income poverty status. This is an outcome of the specific salary situation in the east, where wages are generally as much as one fifth below those in the west. Unemployment benefits do not seem to have had the same cushioning effect in the east as in the west. In the west, we can find the income poverty-increasing effect of a transition to the status of a hidden labour market reserve. These are inactive people who are in the right age category to be in employment and who have terminated unemployment benefits. This phenomenon is often used to describe young people and women in the former West Germany. Owing to socialization, in the former East Germany, particularly the 'Right to Work' in the GDR constitution, transitions to the hidden labour market reserve occur more seldom. People there accept more varied job offers, even if this implies a discontinuous career for a specific profession. Divorce, the birth of a child and lone parenthood are characteristics that increased the risk of falling below the income poverty line in the west. The better child care situation in the east still means that there are much better chances for people with children to participate in the labour market there. The lack of child care facilities makes it difficult for people to accept job offers in the west and increases the risk of their falling below the income poverty line. The impact of social capital is much greater in the east than in the west. This phenomenon is sometimes described as being a consequence of higher family solidarity among families in the former East Germany.

CONCLUSION

With descriptive, explorative and multivariate methods we have examined the extent and the dynamics of income poverty and deprivation in Germany and compared, as far as possible, the eastern and western parts of the country. In the first stage of the analysis of the ECHP, as regards deprivation, the situation in the former East Germany was worse than that of the former West Germany. But across the three years of the data the extent of deprivation in durables and necessities in the new Bundesländer in the east was decreasing, whereas in the western part of the country it was increasing. Looking at the different risk groups, low sample sizes meant that we had to exclude sick or disabled people and, to some extent, also lone mothers, from much of the detailed analysis. For the latter, in the case of income poverty we can assume that the child care situation in the east is slightly better than in the west, but we cannot check empirically what kind of effects are produced. For young adults, the situation in the east was comparatively worse owing to high youth unemployment. Again, we cannot distinguish between east and west, but the reported numbers for the whole of Germany revealed only a small difference between young adults and all adults. For retired people, the situation was worse in the east than the west, although in general the extent of income poverty and deprivation was only slightly higher compared to that of all adults.

Using CHAID as an explorative mechanism (including all the risk groups, also lone mothers and sick or disabled people) to detect interaction between being poor in wave three and all the other possible explanatory factors showed that the history of a poverty career was the most important single factor. On the third and fourth levels, the importance of the labour market was revealed. Only on the third level do we find one of our risk groups, the retired, but they have a low risk of falling below the income poverty threshold because their pension benefits act as protection.

Finally, we used a hazard rate model to include the history of the process and the different panel waves. As explained, in general the traditional target groups are relatively better off, because the social security system reduces the risk of their falling below the income poverty threshold. But if we distinguish between east and west, it becomes clear that, for persons with children and the young adults, the situation is better in the east than in the west, as well as for large households with high social capital, whereas for retirees the propensity for being poor is lower in the west. For the sick or disabled the differences between east and west are small. All in all, their risk of falling below the income poverty line is comparatively slim.

NOTES

1. The data for the year 1990 refer to several months before the German monetary union (May to July 1990), when the change in the price systems had not yet been carried out.
2. Numbers and selected characteristics of the affected people (not counting homeless persons) can be found in federal statistics for welfare use. Because all recipients are counted per annum, these statistics can only be used for time series.
3. 1993 is the last year of the old form of statistics. From the following year onwards more detailed statistics were set up with more varied facts about recipients. Facts about political asylum seekers can be found in specialized statistics.
4. The GSOEP is a representative panel study of private households. It provides information on all household members: for example, occupational biographies, employment, earnings, health and satisfaction indicators. The Panel was started in 1984.
5. The LSA was initiated in September 1987 and has been continuously extended by sampling new recipients after that date. The data are derived from administrative files. The LSA compiles monthly data on the duration of social-assistance receipt, is able to distinguish first-time recipients, and tracks multiple spells of receipt during the entire panel period. The initial sample was 10 per cent of the records in the central welfare registry, which covers all newly registered and non-benefit cases of recipients in the city of Bremen. The first-time recipient cohorts of 1983 and 1989 and the single-mother

first-time recipient cohort of 1984 are analysed in the Special Collaborative Programme 186 and the Centre for Social Policy Research at the University of Bremen. Cf. Buhr and Voges (1998), Duncan and Voges (1995).

6. This research concept for the HLS in Halle is oriented towards the LSA in Bremen. The database contains information on the first cohorts for the years 1990–94 (Rentzsch and Buhr, 1996; Olk and Rentzsch 1997). The following comparison is based on the 1991 data (Olk and Rentzsch, 1998).

7. 100 per cent sample; for reasons of data protection, the data set is not accessible as a public use file.

8. Where there were few cells with numbers between 20 and 30, we indicated that by bracketing the corresponding percentages.

9. Owing to low case numbers (for the descriptive analysis), income poverty rates and deprivation indices are not reported for sick and disabled people. This is a disadvantage of the data base, because, although we do not know how long these adults have been in a continuous state of ill health, it is clear that a prolonged experience of a sickness or disability can have negative effects on household income.

10. 'Everybody qualification' ('Jedermann-Qualifikation') refers to qualifications and skills which can be activated immediately by everybody; they are not connected to a certain occupation or industry. Workers with these qualifications can easily be exchanged and transferred to other companies or industries (Voges, 2001, p. 360).

11. Young adults were excluded, because they are covered by the age variable.

12. These assumptions would refer mainly to the 'Within-Household Income Distribution' (Jenkins, 1991): especially in households affected by social problems, the internal income distribution can differ to a large extent from what can be observed in normal families.

5. The dynamics of poverty and multidimensional deprivation in Greece

Eleni Apospori

INTRODUCTION

Welfare provision in Greece is relatively new, especially when compared with many other European countries. It was founded in 1917 with the foundation of the Ministry of Social Assistance. However, its development came much later, in the early 1980s. Despite the stagnation of national productivity and GDP, and the extraordinary military spending during the early 1980s, expenditure on social protection was unprecedented. Social insurance was extended to cover both the rural and urban sectors. The lowest pensions were upgraded considerably. For example, the average old age pension increased from 48.5 per cent per capita of GDP to 78 per cent, the highest percentage in Europe. Social care services and means-tested public assistance pensions for elderly people were established. The first steps towards a non-contributory universal health scheme were also made in this period by establishing the Greek National Health Service (ESY). However, clientelistic policies continued to exist to some extent (Katrougalos, 1996; Venieris, 1997).

After 1985, the government introduced a stabilization programme for the economy. The great expansion of social policy in the early 1980s, combined with existing and long-standing fragmented social policy practices and with unfavourable demographic changes, had brought the system to the verge of collapse. Since the early 1990s, an effort at readjustment has started. Social policy expenditures have been reduced and benefits restricted. At the same time, support has been given to the most endangered insurance funds. Other readjustment measures included the gradual harmonization of social security contributions, stricter eligibility criteria for invalidity pensions, and greater transparency and objectivity in the processes of evaluating invalidity. Despite the efforts made, the system can still be characterized as inadequate, fragmented, inefficient and administratively overcentralized.

These problems, combined with the new forms of poverty emerging in Greek society and with the gradual weakening of the primary type of relationships which in Greece have for a long time been acting as a safety net for unprivileged social groups of the population (such as unemployed youth, lone parents, elderly and disabled people), have created a mixture of social conditions that bring an increasing number of people in those groups close to social exclusion.

Several studies have pointed out the problems of poverty and other forms of deprivation in the population in general as well as in particular social categories such as the young, sick or disabled, elderly and so forth (EKKE, 1996). Although valuable in their own right, these studies were using measurements taken at one point in time. Poverty and deprivation, like all social phenomena, are susceptible to social changes. These changes call for a dynamic rather than static approach to the study of the problems related to poverty and deprivation. The dynamic approach requires the collection and use of panel data. Panel data are a relatively new methodological tool used in Europe for the study of social phenomena. The present study is among the first attempts at the European level and the first at the national level to study the dynamics of income poverty and deprivation on several dimensions among the Greek population in general and various social categories in particular. For this purpose, the present study makes use of the second and third wave of the Greek version of ECHP data;[1] the second wave of data refers to 1995 and the third wave to 1996.

However, the use of panel data may not be considered as the panacea to the study of the social phenomena. The collection and analysis of panel/longitudinal data require very careful research design. One of the problems inherent to panel data collection difficulties is the attrition of the sample subjects between the waves of data. This difficulty may turn into a serious methodological problem for a study. Poor design of panel surveys may result in high sample attrition rates inhibiting the generalization of the results to the population under study, especially if the distribution of the lost subjects between the waves is not random.

For Greece, the ECHP attrition rate between the first wave (1994) and third wave (1996) for the adult panel members was 18.26 per cent, while for the entire sample, that is, including child panel members, it was 17.82 per cent. In comparison with other EU countries, this attrition rate is relatively low (Eurostat, 2000). This might be partially due to the fact that spatial mobility in Greece is not as common as in other EU countries, especially for families with children and, therefore, it is somehow easier to follow the sample subjects between the various waves of data collection.

This chapter is organized as follows. The next section gives a brief description of the dynamics of income poverty and multidimensional deprivation of the Greek population using the ECHP.[2] In the following four sections the analysis is shifted from the total population to each one of the particular four 'risk groups'. In general terms, the analysis of each group focuses on two aspects: first, the transition rates of income poverty and multidimensional deprivation within the group, and, second, where possible, the factors related to movement of the various group members in and out of poverty and multidimensional deprivation. Finally, the last section summarizes the main findings of the empirical analysis of the four 'risk groups'' living standards in comparison to the rest of the population.

DYNAMICS OF INCOME POVERTY AND MULTIDIMENSIONAL DEPRIVATION IN GREECE

About one-fifth of the population in Greece were in households living in income poverty in both waves of the ECHP (19.9 per cent in wave two and 20.7 per cent in wave three) (Table 5.1). As the evidence of the rest of this book shows, Greece, compared to the other four EU countries participating in the study, had higher income poverty rates than Austria, Germany and the United Kingdom and lower rates than Portugal. In addition, income poverty showed high stability over the two waves of the study. Likewise, the indices of material deprivation, apart from necessities, showed a relative stability over the time. The rate of those deprived of various household amenities decreased from 14.6 per cent at wave two to 11.2 per cent at wave three. The rate of those falling below the deprivation line for durables (such as television, telephone, or access to a car or van) was almost stable between the two waves of measurement, at just over 17 per cent. The most significant decrease among the three material deprivation indicators between wave two and wave three was found in the rate of those falling below the line of deprivation of necessities, which fell from 26.8 per cent in wave two to 15.9 per cent in wave three. Levels of social isolation (not talking to neighbours and not meeting friends) were much lower than the measures of material deprivation, and declined slightly between the two waves.

Overall, with regard to income poverty and various dimensions of deprivation, as the evidence of the rest of this book shows, Greece, in both waves, had the second highest proportion, after Portugal, of poor people and of people deprived of household amenities and durables. However, Greece had the highest rate of deprivation of necessities among the participating countries at wave two, while at wave three Greece had the third lowest rate after Austria and Germany. With regard to social isolation, Greece had the lowest rates of isolation from neighbours, friends and

*Table 5.1   Income poverty and multidimensional deprivation in Greece,
            ECHP, 1995– 6 (per cent)*

	Wave 2 (1995)	Wave 3 (1996)
Income poverty[1]	19.9	20.7
Deprivation of amenities	14.6	11.2
Deprivation of durables	17.9	17.6
Deprivation of necessities	26.8	15.9
Talking to neighbours[2]	6.1	5.2
Meeting friends/relatives[3]	11.2	10.1
Base (unweighted)	15308	14390

Notes:
[1] Poverty line set at 60 per cent of the median net equivalent household income per capita
using the 'modified OECD equivalence scales' (Hagenaars *et al.*, 1994) which, in
comparison to other sets of equivalence scales used in empirical studies, imply moderate
household economies of scale (Buhmann *et al.*, 1988).
[2] Adults only: 'talks to neighbours less than once a week'.
[3] Adults only: 'meets friends or relatives (not living with the person) at home or elsewhere,
less than once a week'.
All ECHP tables are based on weighted sample; see Chapter 1.

relatives. Finally, most of the indices showed a relatively high stability over time.

Table 5.2 reports more detailed estimates of the dynamics of income poverty[3] and multidimensional deprivation in the entire Greek sample. In particular (lower part of Table 5.2) about one-quarter (24 per cent) of the sample experienced poverty over the two waves, slightly higher than the proportion (19–20 per cent) who were poor at any one time. About 17 per cent remained poor in both waves. Overall, at wave three, about 4 per cent of the sample individuals left income poverty, while 3 per cent entered it. The transition rates showed that 20 per cent of those who were income poor at wave two had exited from income poverty at wave three; this was the lowest income poverty exit rate, followed by the UK (22 per cent). Overall, according to the findings of the present study, between 1995 and 1996, Greeks had a probability of one in four of experiencing poverty and, once in it, only one in five could move out. This means that a very large proportion of the Greek population (compared to other EU countries of the study) may be trapped in poverty for a significant period of time.

In respect of the deprivation measures, 18 per cent experienced deprivation of household amenities over the two waves and 8 per cent remained deprived at both waves (lower part of Table 5.2). Just under half (46 per cent) of the panel individuals who were deprived of amenities at wave two had exited from deprivation at wave three, while 4 per cent of the

Table 5.2   Income poverty and multidimensional deprivation dynamics: all adults (16 years and over), Greece, ECHP, 1995–6 (per cent)

	Income poverty	Amenities deprivation	Durables deprivation	Necessities deprivation	Talking to neighbours[1]	Meeting friends/relatives[2]
Transitions						
Persistence rate	80	54	62	40	31	35
Exit rate	20	46	38	60	69	65
Entrance rate	5	4	8	8	3	7
Avoidance rate	95	96	92	92	97	93
Turnover						
Remained in poverty/deprivation	17	8	12	11	2	4
Exited poverty/deprivation	4	7	7	17	4	7
Entered poverty/deprivation	3	3	6	6	3	6
Never in poverty/deprivation[3]	76	82	75	66	92	83
Base (unweighted)	11125	11125	11119	11119	11125	11125

Notes:
[1] Adults only: 'talks to neighbours less than once a week'.
[2] Adults only: 'meets friends or relatives (not living with the person) at home or elsewhere, less than once a week'.
[3] 'Never' in this and subsequent tables, refers to the observation period: that is, never poor/deprived over the two years covered.

non-deprived at wave two had entered deprivation at wave three (upper part of Table 5.2). The relative estimates for deprivation of household durables were very similar, showing high proportions of people in this state and the relative stability of this index between the two waves of measurement. Between wave two and wave three a very similar percentage of individuals in Greece left (7 per cent) and entered (6 per cent) this deprivation state while, of those deprived in 1995, two in three remained deprived in 1996. As the turnover for deprivation of necessities shows in the lower part of Table 5.2, one in three members of the households in the sample had experienced this dimension of deprivation over the two waves of the study. This figure placed Greece in the worst position among the five countries participating in the study. At the same time, six out of the 10 people living in households deprived of necessities at wave two could escape deprivation at wave three; this means that deprivation of necessities may be transitory for the majority of those who had experienced it. Furthermore, for every three people who exited from deprivation in 1996 only one entered it. There were few changes in the measures of social isolation over the two waves, except that many – about two-thirds – (of the small proportion) – who had been socially isolated at wave two had exited by wave three.

In conclusion, between 1995 and 1996, Greece in comparison to the other four EU countries participating in the study showed very high proportions of poor and materially deprived people. In addition, it showed very high levels of stability of poverty and deprivation. Poor and deprived people were more likely to remain in this state over time, while non-poor and non-deprived tended to avoid this state at rates of 92 to 98 per cent.

Next, our analysis focuses on four groups whose life course experiences have been related to higher risk of income poverty and multidimensional deprivation than the rest of the population according to studies based on cross-sectional data (Barnes *et al.*, 2002). The four groups of interest are those of sick or disabled, retired people, young adults and lone mothers.

SICK OR DISABLED PEOPLE

Of all male adults under state retirement age, 6 per cent said that they had been sick or disabled at some time over the two waves of the study, that is, 1995–6; for female adults, the proportion was slightly lower, at 4 per cent.

Income Poverty and Deprivation Dynamics among Sick or Disabled People

While 76 per cent of all adults had not experienced poverty over the two waves of the study, among the sick or disabled people the corresponding

Table 5.3   *Income poverty and non-monetary deprivation dynamics: sick or disabled people (adults under state retirement age), Greece, ECHP, 1995–6*

	Income poverty		Amenities deprivation		Durables deprivation		Necessities deprivation	
	S/D[1] (%)	AA[2] (%)	S/D[1] (%)	AA[2] (%)	S/D[1] (%)	AA[2] (%)	S/D[1] (%)	AA[2] (%)
Transitions								
Persistence rate	79	80	49	54	67	62	46	40
Exit rate	21	20	51	46	33	38	54	60
Entrance rate	10	5	6	4	8	8	11	8
Avoidance rate	90	95	94	96	92	92	89	92
Turnover								
Remained in poverty/ deprivation	22	17	9	8	14	12	21	11
Exited poverty/ deprivation	6	4	10	7	7	7	24	17
Entered poverty/ deprivation	7	3	5	3	7	6	6	6
Never in poverty/ deprivation	65	76	76	82	72	75	49	66
Base (unweighted)	384	11 125	384	11 125	384	11 119	384	11 119

Notes:
[1] In this and all the tables, S/D = sick or disabled.
[2] In this and all the tables, AA = all adults, 16 years and over.

rate was much lower; that is, 65 per cent of the sick or disabled people were not in income poverty in 1995 and 1996 (lower part of Table 5.3). Furthermore, 29 per cent of the sick or disabled either remained in or entered income poverty between 1995 and 1996, while 20 per cent of all adults either remained in or entered income poverty at the same period of time. Of the people who were not poor in 1995, those who had been sick or disabled at some point over the two waves entered income poverty between 1995 and 1996 at a rate (10 per cent) that was twice the rate of all adults (5 per cent). Overall, the dynamic comparative picture showed that in Greece sick or disabled people were at higher risk of falling into or remaining in income poverty than were the adult population as a whole (Table 5.3).

Cross-sectional studies have shown that certain demographic and social characteristics, such as gender, age, education and employment, may be related to poverty among various social categories and sick or disabled people in particular. However, the lack of panel data before the present study in Greece had precluded a dynamic consideration of this relationship. The present study looked at preceding factors (at wave two) such as gender, age, education and work transitions which might be related to movement of sick or disabled people into income poverty at wave three. Dynamic analysis showed that *being over 45 years* or *out of work for more than one year* or *having less than second-stage secondary education* were statistically significant factors contributing to the movement of sick or disabled people into poverty between wave two and wave three. However, for all adults, the only statistically significant factor related to their movement into poverty between waves two and three was *exit from work at wave two.* In respect of movement out of income poverty, none of the factors mentioned above contributed significantly to the movement of sick or disabled people, while for all adults *being younger: 16 to 29 years*, *having higher education* or *entering work* were found to be statistically significant factors related to exit from income poverty.

Over the two waves of the study, almost one in four sick or disabled people experienced deprivation of amenities, a very high proportion by any standard; among all adults, one in five experienced deprivation of amenities (lower part of Table 5.3). With regard to the dynamics of deprivation of amenities among the sick or disabled, the pattern was very similar to the pattern observed among all adults. In 1996, the great majority (94 per cent) of sick or disabled people who were not deprived in 1995, as well as the majority of all non-deprived adults (96 per cent), remained non-deprived. Of those who were deprived in 1995, almost half remained in deprivation in 1996. This pattern holds for both groups of sick or disabled people and for all adults. However, among sick or disabled people the proportion of those who remained in deprivation of amenities or who entered this deprivation status (14 per cent) was slightly higher than the proportion of all adults (11 per cent) (Table 5.3).

Sick or disabled were slightly more likely (28 per cent) than all the adults of the sample (25 per cent) to experience deprivation of durables, at some point over the two waves. Although their mobility pattern is very similar to the pattern of all adults – that is, almost the same percentages of the two groups left (7 per cent) and entered (7 and 6 per cent) deprivation – sick and disabled people, once in deprivation, had a slightly higher probability of remaining in it than the entire sample of adults.

Among all the indicators used in the present study, the necessities indicator showed clearly the relative deprivation of sick or disabled people compared to all adults. Although a very large proportion of all the adults (34 per cent) had been deprived at some point over the two waves of the study, an even higher proportion of sick or disabled had that experience;

specifically, more than half of them (51 per cent). Among the sick or disabled, 21 per cent remained deprived during the two waves of the study, while among all adults 11 per cent remained in this status. In addition, sick or disabled who were deprived of necessities in wave two had a lower exit rate (54 per cent) than all adults (60 per cent) in wave three (Table 5.3). Also the rate at which they entered this state was considerably higher (11 per cent) than the respective rate of all the adults in the study (8 per cent).

Social Isolation Dynamics among Sick or Disabled People

Some social groups are more vulnerable than the rest of the population to various kinds of social isolation or exclusion. The present study used two indicators of social isolation: rare or no contact with neighbours, and rare or no contact with friends or relatives. With regard to these two indicators of social isolation, higher proportions of sick or disabled people (16 and 23 per cent) than of all adults (9 and 17 per cent) had experienced isolation from neighbours and from friends or relatives at some point over the two waves of the study (Table 5.4). In addition, both of the indicators of

Table 5.4   Social isolation dynamics: sick or disabled people (adults under state retirement age), Greece, ECHP, 1995–6

	Talking to neighbours[1]		Meeting friends or relatives[2]	
	S/D (%)	AA (%)	S/D (%)	AA (%)
Transitions				
Persistence rate	[36]	31	[50]	35
Exit rate	[64]	69	[50]	65
Entrance rate	[6]	3	11	7
Avoidance rate	94	97	89	93
Turnover				
Remained in isolation	[4]	2	[7]	4
Exited isolation	[7]	4	[7]	7
Entered isolation	[5]	3	9	6
Never in isolation	84	92	77	83
Base (unweighted)	385	11 125	385	11 125

Notes:
[1] Adults only: 'talks to neighbours less than once a week'.
[2] Adults only: 'meets friends or relatives (not living with the person) at home or elsewhere, less than once a week'.
[ ] indicates a cell size of between 10 and 30 unweighted observations

isolation and in particular the indicator of isolation from friends and relatives showed that, among those isolated at wave two, the sick were more likely to remain isolated and more likely to enter the status of isolation at wave three than all adults (upper part of Table 5.4). In conclusion, sick or disabled people in Greece were at higher risk of social deprivation than all adults. However, compared to the other four countries participating in the study, Greeks in general and the group of sick or disabled in particular were better off in experiencing social isolation over the two-year period than the respective groups in the other countries.

Overall, the dynamic comparative picture showed that in Greece sick or disabled people were at higher risk of falling into or remaining in income poverty than the overall adult population. Older age, long-term unemployment and lower education were found to be risk factors contributing to their movement into poverty.

RETIRED PEOPLE

Almost six out of 10 adults over the age of 45 had experienced retirement at some point of time over the two waves of the study. As expected, more women (62 per cent) than men (56 per cent) of this age group had been retired over these two years. In addition very few (1 per cent) of those who were retired at wave two left this status at wave three. However, between the two waves about one in 10 of the adults over 45 years of age entered retirement. The proportion of those who entered retirement (4 per cent) at wave three was four times as high as the proportion of those who exited (1 per cent).

Income Poverty and Deprivation Dynamics among Retired People

Retired people were more likely than all the adults of the sample to experience poverty at some point over the two waves of study (Table 5.5). In particular, of the people who were retired in 1995 and remained retired in 1996, 37 per cent experienced income poverty at some time over these two years; of those who entered retirement in 1996, 35 per cent had a similar experience while, among all adults, 24 per cent did. In addition, while there was no difference in the income poverty exit rate among those who were in retirement (16 per cent) and those who entered retirement (15 per cent) between 1995 and 1996, there was a difference between the retired in general and all the adults of the sample; in particular, those who were not in retirement seem to have left income poverty at a higher rate (20 per cent) than the two groups of retired. Also, with regard to the income poverty entrance rate, it is clear that those who had never been retired had the lowest entry rate (5 per cent) compared to those who were retired in 1995 (8 per cent) and to those who became retired in 1996 (13 per cent). This means that the more recently retired population runs a higher risk of entering into a state of poverty than people who retired before 1996.

Table 5.5   *Income poverty dynamics: retired people (adults 45 years and over), Greece, ECHP, 1995–6*

	RR (%)	ER (%)	AA (%)
Transitions			
Persistence rate	84	85	80
Exit rate	16	15	20
Entrance rate	8	13	5
Avoidance rate	92	87	95
Turnover			
Remained in poverty	28	24	17
Exited poverty	5	[4]	4
Entered poverty	4	[7]	3
Never in poverty	63	65	76
Base (unweighted)	2888	287	11 125

Notes:
RR = remained in retirement between 1995 and 1996; ER = entered retirement in 1996; AA = all adults.
[ ] indicates a cell size of between 10 and 30 unweighted observations.

Looking at the various risk and protective factors, we found that, among the retired people, *those who had finished secondary education* were 10 times less likely to move into income poverty between 1995 and 1996 than those who had lower levels of education. A similar pattern was observed for the entire sample of adults; that is, among the entire sample of adults, those who had finished secondary education had four times less probability of moving into income poverty between 1995 and 1996 than those who had lower levels of education; however, the intensity of the effect of education was much lower for all adults than it was for retired people. At the same time, tertiary-level education also reduced the chances of all adults moving into income poverty, but it did not reduce the chances for the group of retired people. This may have been due to the fact that retired people were older people and that very few of those who belong to older age groups have had tertiary-level education in Greece.

Overall, the analysis supported the hypothesis that higher levels of education as compared to lower levels reduce the probability of becoming poor among retired people. A similar pattern was observed in Austria, Germany and the UK, but not in Portugal. In addition, retired individuals *living in households with other people* were four times less likely to move into income poverty than those living in households with partner and no children. A similar pattern of lower probability of moving into income poverty was observed for the entire sample of adults. A quite opposite pattern was observed in the UK, Portugal and Germany. Finally, in Greece, but in none of the other EU participating countries, when all the members of the household of the retired person were *in employment* the probability of moving into income poverty was lower compared to that of retired persons living in households where none of the members of working age were in employment. In none of the other countries was a similar pattern observed. Several factors could affect the probability of retired people moving out of income poverty. The data analysis showed that having had upper level of secondary education may be one of those factors. In particular, the retired people who had upper level secondary education were five times more likely to leave poverty than the retired people who had lower levels of education. In conclusion having had higher levels of education was found to be a protective factor that either keeps retired people out of income poverty or helps them to move out of it. In addition, the extended family was found to play a significant role in keeping retired people out of poverty or helping them to escape from it.

Both of the groups of retired people – those who remained in retirement in 1995 and 1996 and those who entered retirement in 1996 – shown in Table 5.6 were more likely to have some experience of deprivation of amenities (24 and 28 per cent) over the two waves of the study than all the adults of the sample (15 per cent). In regard to the turnover, in the three groups, the proportion of those who exited from deprivation was higher than the proportion of those who entered across all of the groups. However, among those who were not in retirement only 6 per cent remained in deprivation, while for the two groups of retired people this proportion was 9 and 12 per cent. In addition, considering the group of deprived in 1995, all the adults of the sample had a considerably higher exit rate from deprivation of amenities (49 per cent) than the two groups of retired (35 per cent and 44 per cent). But no differences in deprivation entrance rate were observed among the groups.

The estimates of the dynamics of deprivation of durables (Table 5.6) showed that those who were retired at both waves, that is, in 1995 and in 1996, were more likely to have some experience of deprivation over the two waves (30 per cent) followed by the group who retired in 1996 (28 per cent). Both groups were more likely than all adults (23 per cent) to have experi-

Table 5.6   Non-monetary deprivation dynamics: retired people (adults 45 years and over), Greece, ECHP, 1995–6

	Amenities deprivation			Durables deprivation			Necessities deprivation		
	RR (%)	ER (%)	AA (%)	RR (%)	ER (%)	AA (%)	RR (%)	ER (%)	AA (%)
Transitions									
Persistence rate	65	56	51	60	45	65	47	47	38
Exit rate	35	44	49	40	55	35	53	53	62
Entrance rate	5	5	3	10	[6]	6	13	13	8
Avoidance rate	95	95	97	90	94	94	87	87	92
Turnover									
Remained in deprivation	9	12	6	15	13	11	21	23	9
Exited deprivation	9	11	6	8	11	6	23	25	16
Entered deprivation	6	5	3	7	[4]	6	7	[8]	6
Never in deprivation	76	72	85	70	72	77	49	44	69
Base (unweighted)	2888	287	11125	2888	287	11125	2888	287	11125

Notes:
RR = remained in retirement; ER = entered retirement; AA = all adults.
[ ] indicates a cell size of between 10 and 30 unweighted observations.

enced deprivation of durables. Considering those deprived of durables in 1995, both groups of retired had lower exit rates (40 and 55 per cent) than all the adults of the sample (35 per cent).

Deprivation of necessities was another indicator that clearly showed the vulnerability of retired people. Regardless of how recent was the transition into retirement status, all retired people were much more likely to have experienced this form of deprivation at some point in time over the two waves (51 and 56 per cent) than all the adults of the sample (31 per cent). In addition, retired people who were deprived at wave two showed considerably higher rates of persistence in deprivation of necessities (47 per cent) compared to all adults (38 per cent). They also had considerably higher necessities deprivation entrance rates (13 per cent, compared with 8 per cent).

Of the four indicators used to measure the different dimensions of disadvantage among retired people, income poverty and deprivation of necessities were those that more clearly than the other two showed the disadvantage of retired people compared to all the adults of the sample. Further analysis showed that income poverty and deprivation of necessities were closely related among retired people (Table 5.7). In particular,

Table 5.7 *Income poverty and deprivation of necessities dynamics: retired people (adults 45 years and over), Greece, ECHP, 1995–6*

	Income poverty dynamics: transitions							
	Persistence rate		Exit rate		Entrance rate		Avoidance rate	
Deprivation of necessities	RP (%)	AA (%)	RP (%)	AA (%)	RP (%)	AA (%)	RP (%)	AA (%)
Transitions								
Persistence rate	65	57	34	37	81	69	30	28
Exit rate	35	43	66	63	[19]	31	70	72
Entrance rate	28	22	*	15	[24]	20	10	6
Avoidance rate	72	78	98	85	76	80	90	94
Turnover								
Remained in deprivation	42	31	[23]	21	41	23	10	6
Exited deprivation	23	24	45	36	[10]	11	22	15
Entered deprivation	10	10	*	[6]	[12]	13	7	4
Never in deprivation	25	35	31	36	37	53	61	74
Base (unweighted)	888	2201	†	419	†	350	1746	8149

Notes:
RP = retired people; AA = all adults.
† Numbers are not reported for reasons of confidentiality.
In all tables, * indicates a cell size of less than 10 unweighted observations; [ ] indicates a cell size of between 10 and 30 unweighted observations.

among the retired people, those who had experienced poverty at some time over the two waves – poor in 1995 and poor in 1996 – were more likely to have experienced deprivation of necessities, that is, remained in, left or entered deprivation (75, 69 and 63 per cent, respectively) than those who had not been poor (39 per cent) (lower panel of Table 5.7). In addition, the relationship between income poverty and deprivation of necessities was more prominent among retired than non-retired. Among those who had experienced poverty at some time between 1995 and 1996, retired people were more likely (75, 69 and 63 per cent) than all adults (65, 63 and 47 per cent, respectively) to have experienced deprivation of necessities as well. Focusing on the two most disadvantaged groups of retired people, that is, the persistently poor (1995 and 1996) and the new poor (1996), we observe that they were more likely (42 and 41 per cent) than the other retired people (23 and 10 per cent) to remain in a state of deprivation of necessities; likewise they were more likely than the persistently poor and new poor adults (31 and 23 per cent) to remain in this state of deprivation. In addition among the retired people who exited from poverty in 1996, 45 per cent exited from deprivation of necessities as well, a percentage substantially higher than the relevant figure in the rest of the three categories of retired (23, 10 and 22 per cent) and the respective category of all the adults (36 per cent).

Furthermore, the rates of the changes in income poverty and deprivation of necessities in 1995 and 1996 among the four groups of retired and the adults (upper panel of Table 5.7) give a picture very similar to the picture of the distribution of changes (lower part of Table 5.7). On the one hand, among the retired, those who were poor in 1996 – either because they remained poor or because they had just gained this status – showed a persistence in deprivation of necessities at much higher rates (65 and 81 per cent) than those who were not income poor the same year (34 and 30 per cent). Likewise, the respective persistence rates of all the adults who remained poor or had just entered income poverty were considerably lower (57 and 69) per cent. On the other hand, the retired who were not poor in 1996 – because they either exited from poverty in 1996 or had not been poor in 1995 and 1996 – avoided deprivation of necessities status in 1996 at considerably higher rates (98 and 90 per cent) than those who were poor in 1996, either because they remained poor during 1995 and 1996 or because they had just become poor in 1996 (72 and 76 per cent). Overall, the above findings did not disprove the hypothesis that deprivation is more likely to be present when income poverty is present, and that this relationship is more prominent among the retired people in particular than the adults in general.

Social Isolation Dynamics among Retired People

However, looking at the dynamics of social isolation (Table 5.8), the retired people in Greece seem not to have been different from the other adults in terms of having or not having relationships with neighbours, relatives and friends. Further analysis also showed that poor retired people were not different from non-poor retired people in this respect. The same was true for the non-retired adults, poor and non-poor. Compared to Germany, Austria, the UK and Portugal, retired people in Greece were better off in terms of social participation. Greece had the highest proportion of retired people who had never been in social isolation (96 and 93 per cent), according to the indicators used in this study, and the highest rates of retired people who exited from social isolation between 1995 and 1996 (68 and 64 per cent).

Overall, the dynamic picture of the Greek population showed that, over the time of the ECHP, a substantial proportion joined the already disproportionately large retired population. Furthermore, experiencing retirement was clearly related to experiencing income poverty. On the other hand, exiting from or never experiencing retirement was associated with favourable changes in access to household amenities and/or the possession or use of durable goods. The experience of retirement at some point over the two waves of the study was associated with unfavourable changes in access to necessities. Furthermore, changes in income poverty were associated with changes in deprivation of necessities. In conclusion, retired people in Greece constitute a high-risk group of income poverty and multi-dimensional disadvantage in general.

Table 5.8   Social isolation dynamics: retired people (adults 45 years and over), Greece, ECHP, 1995–6

	Talking to neighbours[1]		Meeting friends/relatives[2]	
	RP (%)	AA (%)	RP (%)	AA (%)
Transitions				
Persistence rate	32	31	36	35
Exit rate	68	69	64	65
Entrance rate	4	3	7	7
Avoidance rate	96	97	93	93
Turnover				
Remained in isolation	2	2	5	4
Exited isolation	3	4	9	7
Entered isolation	3	3	6	6
Never in isolation	92	92	79	83
Base (unweighted)	2888	11125	2888	11125

Notes:
[1] Adults only: 'talks to neighbours less than once a week'.
[2] Adults only: 'meets friends or relatives (not living with the person) at home or elsewhere, less than once a week'.
RP = retired people; AA = all adults.

YOUNG ADULTS

During the last decades Greek society has undergone rapid social change. At the macro social level, among other changes, it has become more urbanized and less homogeneous. At the micro social level the Greek family, one of the crucial socializing agents, has become less stable. In the 1990s, the Greek youth became more internationally oriented. The 'MacDonaldization' of society, the hedonistic outlook, the participation in sports that create pseudo-heroes and violent reactions before, during and after the game, and the search for time to waste are some of the prevailing elements for a considerable section of Greek youth. At the same time, official statistics show a tendency for increased involvement in delinquency and drug use among the young (Spinellis *et al.*, 1994). Overall, the changes mentioned above, along with unemployment, poverty and material deprivation, may place a considerable number of young adults on the verge of social exclusion and marginalization. The purpose of this section is to explore the dynamics of poverty, material deprivation and social isolation among the young and to estimate factors inhibiting or facilitating movement into or out of poverty.

Income Poverty and Multidimensional Deprivation Dynamics among Young Adults

One-fifth (21 per cent) of the sample of all Greek adults in wave two and wave three were young adults, that is, adults aged between 16 and 29 years. The proportion of young adults who showed persistency in income poverty – that is, they retained this status throughout 1995 and 1996 – was slightly lower (13 per cent) than the respective proportion of all adults (17 per cent) (lower panel of Table 5.9); the proportion of those who exited from (4 per cent) and entered poverty (3 per cent) was identical among young adults and all adults. Similarly, the transition rates (upper panel of Table 5.9) show that, among the poor in 1995, young adults had a higher exit rate in 1996 (23 per cent) than all adults (20 per cent); at the same time they entered the income poverty state at the same rate with all adults: 5 per cent (Table 5.9). Overall, young adults in Greece were at slightly lower risk of being poor or remaining in poverty than all adults, and at the same risk – with all adults – of becoming poor (Table 5.9).

Estimates of possible factors that may affect the probability of young adults moving into income poverty showed that the young adults who were *living with their parents* were 10 times less likely to become poor between 1995 and 1996 than young adults living with people who were not relatives. Among the other four countries participating in the study, only Portugal showed a similar pattern. For these two countries, living with parents seemed to be a protective factor against income poverty for young adults. Also *full-time work* reduced the probability of moving into income poverty for the young adults as well as for all adults. Similar patterns were observed in all the other countries. On the other hand, estimates of factors that may affect the probability of young adults moving out of income poverty showed that *being unemployed* decreases significantly the chances of

Table 5.9   *Income poverty and non-monetary deprivation dynamics: young*
          adults (16–29 years), Greece, ECHP, 1995–6

	Income poverty		Amenities deprivation		Durables deprivation		Necessities deprivation	
	YA (%)	AA (%)	YA (%)	AA (%)	YA (%)	AA (%)	YA (%)	AA (%)
Transitions								
Persistence rate	77	80	42	54	65	62	31	40
Exit rate	23	20	58	46	35	38	69	60
Entrance rate	5	5	4	4	10	8	6	8
Avoidance rate	95	95	96	96	90	92	94	92
Turnover								
Remained poor/ deprived	13	17	5	8	13	12	8	11
Exited poverty/ deprivation	4	4	7	7	7	7	17	17
Entered poverty/ deprivation	3	3	4	3	8	6	5	6
Never in poverty/ deprivation	79	76	84	82	72	75	70	66
Base (unweighted)	2 348	11 125	2 348	11 125	2 342	11 119	2 342	11 119

Note: YA = young adults; AA = all adults.

moving out of income poverty. This finding is in line with other empirical studies (see Tsakloglou and Papadopoulos, 2003) which give evidence that participation in the labour market can provide a safe barrier against all sorts of deprivation, and social exclusion in general.

With respect to the turnover of deprivation of amenities, the distribution of changes over the two waves among young adults and all the adults were similar; 5 per cent of young adults remained deprived from 1995 to 1996, and 16 per cent experienced deprivation at some point during these two years, compared to 8 and 18 per cent of all adults who had the respective experiences. However, young adults left the deprivation of amenities status between 1995 and 1996 at a higher rate (58 per cent) than did all adults (46 per cent) (upper panel of Table 5.9). Looking at the deprivation of durables, 28 per cent of young adults had experienced this over the two waves, compared to 25 per cent of all the adults; also, among those deprived in 1995, young adults were slightly more likely (65 per cent) than all the adults (62 per cent) to remain deprived in 1996. Among those not deprived in 1995, young adults were slightly more likely (10 per cent) than all the adults

(8 per cent) to enter deprivation in 1996. Young adults seemed to be slightly better off with regard to necessities: 70 per cent of them had not experienced deprivation in 1995 and 1996, compared to 66 per cent of all adults. Of those deprived in 1995, young adults were more likely (69 per cent) than all the adults (60 per cent) to exit from deprivation in 1996. Of those not deprived in 1995, 6 per cent of young adults, compared to 8 per cent of all adults, became deprived in 1996. These dynamic findings do not disprove the conclusions that cross-sectional studies have shown so far for the young adults in Greece, namely that they do not seem to run a considerably higher risk of poverty and multidimensional deprivation (see Tsakloglou and Papadopoulos, 2003) compared with all adults.

Although, overall, young adults seemed to be better off compared to all the adults, the question is whether among the poor, young adults are more deprived or more likely to become deprived than all adults and whether changes in poverty status among young adults are related to changes in deprivation. As shown in Table 5.10, among the persistently poor, 55 per cent of young adults, compared to 65 per cent of all adults, had experienced deprivation of necessities at some time during 1995 and 1996 (lower panel

Table 5.10   Income poverty and deprivation of necessities dynamics: young adults (16–29 years), Greece, ECHP, 1995–6

	Income poverty dynamics							
	Persistence rate		Exit rate		Entrance rate		Avoidance rate	
	YA (%)	AA (%)	YA (%)	AA (%)	YA (%)	AA (%)	YA (%)	AA (%)
Deprivation of necessities								
Transitions								
Persistence rate	46	57	[31]	37	48	69	25	28
Exit rate	54	43	69	63	52	31	75	72
Entrance rate	18	22	[22]	15	[20]	20	4	6
Avoidance rate	82	78	78	85	80	80	96	94
Turnover								
Remained in deprivation	21	31	[16]	21	16	23	5	6
Exited deprivation	24	24	35	36	*	11	16	15
Entered deprivation	10	10	[11]	[6]	16	13	3	4
Never in deprivation	45	35	38	36	57	53	76	74
Base (unweighted)	375	2201	98	419	—	350	1792	8149

Notes:
In all tables, * indicates a cell size of less than 10 unweighted observations; [ ] indicates a cell size of between 10 and 30 unweighted observations. YA = young adults; AA = all adults.

Table 5.10). Poor young adults were more likely (54 per cent) to exit from deprivation than all poor adults (43 per cent) and less likely to become deprived (18 per cent, compared to 22 per cent). Also, among the new poor (those who became poor in 1996), young adults seem to be better off compared to all adults. Among young adults, those who were not income poor in 1995 and 1996 or who exited income poverty in 1996 had higher exit rates from deprivation of necessities (75 per cent and 69 per cent, respectively) than those who either remained poor for these two years (54 per cent) or entered income poverty in 1996 (52 per cent) (upper panel of Table 5.10). However, the relationship between income poverty and deprivation was more clear among all adults where the deprivation exit rate for those who remained poor (43 per cent) or who entered income poverty (31 per cent) was much lower than the exit rate of those who exited from income poverty (63 per cent) or who were never in income poverty (72 per cent). Overall, young adults hit by income poverty had better chances than all adults in poverty status to avoid or exit from deprivation. Also avoidance of, or exit from, income poverty increased the chances of young people to avoid or exit from deprivation.

Social Isolation Dynamics among Young Adults

Young adults in Greece seem to have been slightly less social than the other adults, with regard to having or not having relationships with their neighbours (Table 5.11). However, they more often reported that they socialized with their friends and relatives than did other adults. Further analysis showed that income-poor young adults were not different from non-income-poor young adults. Both groups had a very low risk of social isolation. The same was also true for other adults, poor and non-poor.

Compared to other countries, young adults in Greece were better off in terms of social participation. Apart from the UK, Greece between 1995 and 1996 had the highest proportions of adults, young or not young, who had not been in social isolation and for the same period of time the highest exit rates (69 and 65 per cent) from this state of deprivation. In the UK, young adults were almost as likely as young people in Greece to report that they socialized with friends and relatives relatively frequently and at the same time to have high exit rates from the state of social isolation.

Overall, the dynamic analysis of the ECHP data for Greece did not find that young adults run a higher risk of unfavourable economic and social changes than the rest of the population. However, several studies have shown that particular sections of the population of young adults are at a higher risk of facing problems such as unemployment, violence and drug addiction than the rest of the population.

Table 5.11   Social isolation dynamics: young adults (16–29 years), Greece, ECHP, 1995–6

Social isolation	Talking to neighbours[1]		Meeting friends/relatives[2]	
	YA (%)	AA (%)	YA (%)	AA (%)
Transitions				
Persistence rate	35	31	25	35
Exit rate	65	69	75	65
Entrance rate	5	3	6	7
Avoidance rate	95	97	94	93
Turnover				
Remained in isolation	2	2	2	4
Exited isolation	4	4	5	7
Entered isolation	4	3	6	6
Never in isolation	89	92	87	83
Base (unweighted)	2348	11125	2348	11125

Notes:
[1] Adults only: 'talks to neighbours less than once a week'.
[2] Adults only: 'meets friends or relatives (not living with the person) at home or elsewhere, less than once a week'.
YA = young adults; AA = all adults.

LONE MOTHERS

Among all mothers, lone mothers in Greece are a very small group (6 per cent), and in particular lone mothers with at least one dependent child are just 2 per cent of all mothers. However, given the absence of second parent and potential breadwinner and the higher unemployment rates of women as compared to men in Greece (Apospori, 1998), lone mothers and their families are considered particularly vulnerable to poverty and to material and social deprivation.

For the purpose of this study, the group of lone mothers was split into two: lone mothers living with at least one dependent child, and lone mothers living with all non-dependent children. The operational definition of 'dependent children' is children under 16 years or in full-time education. In the following analysis, comparisons are made between lone mothers (and their families) and partnered mothers (and their families).

Between 1995 and 1996, the exit rate from the status of lone motherhood in Greece was much higher (14 per cent and 20 per cent) than the exit rate

Table 5.12   Income poverty dynamics: mothers, Greece, ECHP, 1995–6

	Lone mothers in 1995 and 1996		Partnered mothers in 1995 and 1996	
	With some dependent children	With all non-dependent children	With some dependent children	With all non-dependent children
Income poverty	(%)	(%)	(%)	(%)
Transitions				
Persistence rate	82	72	81	81
Exit rate	[18]	28	19	19
Entrance rate	[9]	[5]	3	2
Avoidance rate	91	95	97	98
Turnover				
Remained in poverty	24	16	10	13
Exited poverty	*	[6]	2	3
Entered poverty	*	[4]	3	2
Never in poverty	65	74	85	83
Base (unweighted)	151	315	5355	1710

Note: In all tables, * indicates a cell size of less than 10 unweighted observations; [ ]
indicates a cell size of between 10 and 30 unweighted observations.

from the status of partnered motherhood (6 per cent and 2 per cent). At the
same time, the entrance rate was in the opposite direction; that is, it was less
than 1 per cent for lone mothers (0.4 per cent and 0.3 per cent) and 2 to 3
per cent for partnered mothers. Overall, not only was the group of lone
mothers in Greece very small, but also the mobility in lone motherhood was
almost non-existent. Given the extremely low numbers of lone mothers
in the sample, the following results should be interpreted with extreme
caution.

Income Poverty and Multidimensional Deprivation Dynamics among Mothers

Among mothers, lone mothers with dependent children were more likely
than the rest to experience income poverty at some point during 1995 and
1996 (35 per cent), followed by lone mothers with non-dependent children
(26 per cent). (See Table 5.12.) Partnered mothers and their families seemed
to be the least vulnerable to income poverty (15 to 17 per cent). With regard
to income poverty dynamics, the entrance rate for individuals in house-

Table 5.13   *Deprivation of amenities dynamics: mothers, Greece, ECHP, 1995–6*

Deprivation of amenities	Lone mothers in 1995 and 1996		Partnered mothers in 1995 and 1996	
	With some dependent children	With all non-dependent children	With some dependent children	With all non-dependent children
	(%)	(%)	(%)	(%)
Transitions				
Persistence rate	67	55	47	47
Exit rate	33	45	53	53
Entrance rate	*	*	4	3
Avoidance rate	100	99	96	97
Turnover				
Remained in deprivation	10	[7]	5	6
Exited deprivation	*	[6]	6	7
Entered deprivation	*	*	3	3
Never in deprivation	85	86	86	85
Base (unweighted)	—	—	5355	1710

Note: In all tables, * indicates a cell size of less than 10 unweighted observations; [ ] indicates a cell size of between 10 and 30 unweighted observations.

holds consisting of lone mothers with at least one dependent child was about two to four times higher (9 per cent) than the rate for individuals in households consisting of the other three groups of mothers (2 to 5 per cent). The income poverty exit rate for lone mothers with dependent children was the lowest of all the groups (18 per cent); members of households with lone mothers with non-dependent children were more likely to exit from income poverty (28 per cent) than members of other lone-mother households. Overall, higher proportions of members of households with lone mothers were more likely to move into and remain in income poverty between waves two and three than members of other types of households.

Overall, it was found to be more difficult for lone mothers to escape the deprivation of amenities status than it was for partnered mothers. In particular, the exit rate from deprivation of amenities was higher among members of households with mothers who remained partnered between wave two and wave three (53 per cent) than the members of lone-mother households (33 and 45 per cent) (Table 5.13). Because of the small number of observations among lone-mothers, no more particular comparisons can be made.

Table 5.14   Deprivation of durables dynamics: mothers, Greece, ECHP, 1995–6

	Lone mothers in 1995 and 1996		Partnered mothers in 1995 and 1996	
	With some dependent children	With all non-dependent children	With some dependent children	With all non-dependent children
Deprivation of durables	(%)	(%)	(%)	(%)
Transitions				
Persistence rate	78	65	64	61
Exit rate	22	35	36	39
Entrance rate	[15]	11	5	8
Avoidance rate	85	89	95	92
Turnover				
Remained in deprivation	32	18	8	10
Exited deprivation	[9]	10	4	6
Entered deprivation	[9]	[8]	5	7
Never in deprivation	50	64	83	77
Base (unweighted)	—	—	5355	1710

Note: In all tables, * indicates a cell size of less than 10 unweighted observations; [ ] indicates a cell size of between 10 and 30 unweighted observations.

Households with lone mothers with dependent children were more likely to experience deprivation of durables at some point during the two years of the research (50 per cent), followed by the households with lone mothers with non-dependent children (36 per cent); households of partnered mothers were much less likely to have a similar experience (17 to 23 per cent). Furthermore, the exit rate from deprivation of durables was lower among members of households with lone mothers with at least one dependent child between waves two and three (22 per cent) than for other types of households and for the entire population, and at the same time their entrance rate was higher (15 per cent) (Table 5.14). Also this group had the highest proportion of individuals that remained in deprivation of durables (32 per cent) between the two waves, followed by the group of members of households with lone mothers with no dependent children (18 per cent).

Deprivation of necessities was another indicator of the disadvantaged position of members of households with lone mothers. About half of those households had experienced this type of deprivation at some point during the two years of the study, while about one-quarter to one-fifth of the

*Table 5.15   Deprivation of necessities dynamics: mothers, Greece, ECHP,
1995–6*

Deprivation of necessities	Lone mothers in 1995 and 1996		Partnered mothers in 1995 and 1996	
	With some dependent children (%)	With all non-dependent children (%)	With some dependent children (%)	With all non-dependent children (%)
Transitions				
Persistence rate	36	49	30	31
Exit rate	64	51	70	69
Entrance rate	*	12	4	9
Avoidance rate	99	88	96	91
Turnover				
Remained in deprivation	[17]	20	5	9
Exited deprivation	[29]	21	11	20
Entered deprivation	*	[7]	3	7
Never in deprivation	54	52	81	64
Base (unweighted)	—	—	5355	1710

Note: In all tables, * indicates a cell size of less than 10 unweighted observations; [ ]
indicates a cell size of between 10 and 30 unweighted observations.

households with partnered mothers had a similar experience. Furthermore,
members of households with lone mothers exited from the deprivation of
necessities status at lower rates than members of households with partnered mothers and the entire population. Overall, higher proportions of
lone mothers and their household members remained in deprivation of
necessities (17 per cent and 20 per cent) than the other two groups and all
individuals.

The present study showed that lone mothers were as likely to have social
contacts with their neighbours as were other mothers and all adults. With
regard to frequency of meeting friends and relatives, they showed a slightly
lower level than the other two groups. Greek lone mothers had the lowest
proportion of socially isolated people in comparison with lone mothers in
Austria, Germany and Portugal. Lone mothers in the UK showed similar
patterns of social isolation/participation to those of Greek lone mothers.

The population of lone mothers in Greece is very small and its turnover
is almost non-existent. For this reason the results drawn from the dynamic
analysis of the Greek Household Panel data must be interpreted with

extreme caution. However, the small numbers of lone mothers should not inhibit researchers from looking at the real problems of this section of the population. Greek lone mothers, and especially those with dependent children, run higher risks of unfavourable economic and social changes than partnered mothers.

CONCLUSIONS AND POLICY IMPLICATIONS

The results from the dynamic/longitudinal analysis of poverty and social exclusion in Greece were compatible with the results from our cross-sectional analysis of the second wave of the ECHP (Barnes *et al.*, 2002). Two of the four risk groups – sick or disabled people and the retired – were at high risk of income poverty and social exclusion in Greece. Similar but not as strong evidence was found for lone mothers, and particularly lone mothers with dependent children. Conversely, little, if any, evidence was found that those undergoing transition to young adulthood were at high risk of income poverty and social exclusion.

Sick or disabled people were at substantially higher risk of falling into or remaining in income poverty and all forms of material and social deprivation than the adult population as a whole. However this risk was lower in Greece than it was in the three northern countries in the study. Older age, long-term unemployment and lower education were found to be risk factors contributing to their movement into poverty. However, the reverse factors, that is younger age, higher education and employment, were not found to contribute to their exit from poverty as they did with non-sick adults. In terms of social policy, this means that the supportive mechanism for sick and disabled people should go beyond securing jobs and education for them in order to help them move from a state of poverty.

Retired people in Greece, along with retired people in Portugal, were found to be at much higher risk than were retired people in the UK, Austria and Germany. Experiencing retirement was found to be associated primarily with negative changes in income. Those who were or became retired ran a substantially higher risk than all adults of becoming and of remaining income poor. In addition, changes in income poverty were closely related to changes in deprivation of necessities. The extended family, especially when most of its members were in employment, seemed to play a supportive role in keeping retired people from poverty and deprivation. At the social policy level, this means that measures should be taken to improve, first, retired people's income and, next, their overall welfare status. Securing employment of members of extended families with retired people living in them seemed to help towards this end.

Young adults in general were not found to run a higher risk of unfavourable economic and social changes than the rest of the adult population. However, specific pockets of young adults are at a higher risk of facing problems such as unemployment, violence and drug addiction than the rest of the population. In accordance with the estimates of the ECHP data, social policy should focus on education, employment and support of families with young adults as they seem to be factors protecting young people from risks such as income poverty, social exclusion, marginalization and deviance.

Despite their small number, lone mothers in Greece, and especially those with dependent children, were found to run considerably higher risks of unfavourable economic and social changes than partnered mothers. However, the risks were not as high as they were in Portugal, the UK and Germany. This implies that social policy should focus on lone mothers' employment opportunities, along with the provision of child care facilities and the financial facilitation of the education of the children in lone-mother families.

NOTES

1. For details of the methodology used for the collection of information in the ECHP, see Eurostat (1996); for the quality of the collected information see Eurostat (1999).
2. See Chapter 1 for definitions of the risk groups, income and deprivation measures, and changes in these over time.
3. As noted earlier, the definition of income used for the poverty analysis is net equivalent household income per capita. It should be stated that this definition of resources consists only of monetary income components and no incomes in-kind of any type (from private sources or in the form of public goods) are included. This is not uncontroversial, since evidence from Smeeding *et al.* (1993) suggests that the inclusion of non-cash public transfers in the fields of health, education and housing in the concept of resources results in a decline in measured inequality and poverty. Furthermore, Rodrigues (1999), for the case of Portugal, and Tsakloglou and Papadopoulos (2002), for the case of Greece, report that the omission of private incomes in-kind increases substantially the recorded levels of inequality and poverty in both countries. In any case, a large number of EU publications on empirical poverty analysis utilize distributions of disposable monetary income (see ISSAS, 1990; O'Higgins and Jenkins, 1990; Hagenaars *et al.*, 1994).

6. The dynamics of income poverty and social exclusion in Portugal

Alfredo Bruto da Costa, Ana Cardoso, Isabel Baptista and Pedro Perista

INTRODUCTION

Poverty has been a persistent phenomenon in Portuguese society, presenting strong structural characteristics. Although unemployment is relatively low, the Portuguese poverty rate is the highest in the EU, in part because the poverty rate among employed people is much higher than the EU average. This highlights the fact that in Portugal exclusion from the labour market must not be seen as the major factor in explaining poverty. Other factors are vital in order to understand this phenomenon.

The first factor relates to a strong persistence of the informal economy that reduces unemployment but contributes to an increased vulnerability to poverty both during the active life of the individuals and also in their transition into retirement. A second factor is the precariousness of employment. The labour market is characterized by a diminishing number of permanent contracts and the simultaneous rise in short-term contracts; by an increase of the number of workers whose working hours are much above or below the normal number of working hours; and by the existence of a very wide range of salaries. Thirdly, there is a high degree of inequality in income distribution: in 1995, 20 per cent of the poorest households received only 6 per cent of the total income, whereas 20 per cent of the richest households received around 44 per cent (Barreiros, 2000).

Apart from these labour market characteristics, poverty in Portugal is also related to the relative weakness of the welfare state and above all to the low level of benefits it provides, as well as to the existence of gaps in the social security system. This system for a long time left totally unprotected entire groups of the population who, for various reasons, were not entitled to any social benefit. The Portuguese social security system – in its present formulation of universal entitlement of rights – dates back to the 1974 revolution, although the Social Security Basic Law was published only in 1984. In spite of its comparative newness, the social security system has already been faced with a crisis of financing. It has also been characterized by various forms of discretionary behaviour in the granting of social assistance benefits, and some sections of the population still remain out of the range of most benefits, because of restrictive eligibility criteria. These, among other reasons, raise the issue of how universal the system actually is in practice. However, since the late 1990s, with the implementation of the Guaranteed Minimum Income scheme, which is the only benefit granted as a right within social assistance, it has become possible to start to reduce the discretionary character of the system and to implement it on a more universal basis.

However, in a society where high income poverty rates only represent one feature of social exclusion, it is possible to identify an important number of individuals and groups who are still in a situation where they do not achieve fulfilment of their citizens' rights. These rights include not only work and social security, but also access to housing and education, and these are two areas where Portugal has also experienced extensive problems.

In respect of housing, problems include the existence of 'shanty towns' – very precarious housing settlements – in the large cities of Lisbon and Oporto (which in 1993 were housing around 155000 people),[1] the existence of overcrowding, the persistence of bad housing conditions (lack of running water, lack of electricity, and so on) and the degradation of houses in the historical centres of cities and in rural areas. Faced with the lack of state intervention on the land and housing markets, houses reach excessively high prices for low- or medium-income families and, in particular, for younger households.

In respect of education, there has been a significant increase in schooling since the 1974 revolution. Expectations of social mobility through education have risen and there has been a widening of the state's educational provisions, accompanied by the principles of free and universal basic education. However, although there has been a significant growth of the school population (an increase of 96 per cent between the 1960s and the 1990s), and also an increase in the levels of education of the population, both of these still remain, comparatively, very low. At the same time, school failure and dropout remain high, especially among children from the most disadvantaged social layers.

This chapter starts with an overview of the ECHP data in respect of the four risk groups and their experience of poverty and deprivation. The second section examines the dynamics of income poverty and social exclusion, looking at each of the four risk groups in turn. The final section reflects on the implications of this analysis for Portuguese research and policy.

FACING INCOME POVERTY AND DEPRIVATION IN PORTUGAL: EXPERIENCING DIFFERENT TRANSITIONS, FACING SIMILAR DIFFICULTIES

Turning to the ECHP data, the analysis performed on the four risk groups (as defined in Chapter 1) found substantial differences among the risks faced by the individuals involved in these different life course events, but at the same time highlighted the persistence of structural problems in Portugal.

Whilst high vulnerability to income poverty and deprivation was clearly apparent in the case of the retired and the sick or disabled groups, the same did not apply to transition into young adulthood, since, contrary to the other groups, the youth income poverty rate was lower than the average for the total population. The situation of lone parents also confirmed their vulnerability to income poverty and deprivation, but at the same time it showed a clear national specificity in respect of older lone mothers with non-dependent children, who accounted for the largest group of lone-parent households in Portugal.

Age was one of the factors that increased the risk of suffering income poverty or deprivation. Being a lone parent and being over state retirement age increased the risk of becoming income poor and the risk of experiencing high levels of deprivation. The sick or disabled individuals in income poverty were more likely to be older than other poor adults. The retired population presented the highest income poverty and deprivation rates both among the groups under study in Portugal and in general among the countries involved in this study.

Low educational levels and inactivity were also identified as negative assets for those involved in these risk groups. Portugal is the country where young people had the lowest levels of education and a weaker presence in the labour market. Income poverty rates rose with low levels of education for sick or disabled people and less educated lone mothers are more likely to be income poor than lone mothers in general. Inactivity also seemed to reinforce vulnerability to income poverty among the different groups, whereas participation in the labour market to some extent protects individuals – and often families – against monetary poverty.

The low levels of state benefits are no doubt responsible for the income poverty situation in which many of the Portuguese retired population live. Furthermore, these results have shown that, no matter what life course transition is being studied, those households mainly dependent on pensions or on other social transfers have repeatedly been identified as being more likely to be living in income poverty and in deprivation than those depending on wages or salaries. Resorting to family support is one of the strategies used by individuals in the different risk groups in order to reduce or help cope with income poverty and deprivation risks.

Cohabitation is one of the most obvious strategies identified among the risk groups, as can be seen by the extremely low percentage of individuals living alone and by the high percentage of lone parents living with their non-dependent children, or even the high percentages of people living with 'others', which very often refers to housing arrangements also including relatives (see Table 6.1, below).

Looking at the transition into adulthood, Portugal is a country where young adults leave their parents' home at a later stage and for whom marriage does not necessarily mean leaving the parental home. Portugal (and Greece) had higher percentages of couples living with dependent children and also with non-dependent children. Lone mothers living with their adult (non-dependent children) represented the largest group of lone mothers in Portugal, contrary to the situation in the other countries, where this type of lone parenthood is almost non-existent. Sick or disabled people in Portugal were the most likely, compared with the other countries, to be living in a household consisting of a couple with at least one dependent child, but they were the least likely to be living alone. Living as a couple with no children was the most common situation among the retired people, followed by living in 'other' household types. The latter include extended

Table 6.1   Household arrangements among the risk groups, Portugal, ECHP, 1995

	All (%)	Young adults (%)	Lone parents (%)	Retired (%)	Sick and disabled (%)
Alone	13	1	0	15	4
Not alone	87	99	100	85	96
With partner, no children	21	3	n.a.	43	15
With partner and children	46	10	n.a.	15	53
Lone parent with at least one dep. child	3	0	38[1]	0	2
Lone parent with all non-dep. children	5	0	62[2]	6	9
With parents	n.a.	68	n.a.	n.a.	n.a.
Other	12	18	n.a.	21	17
Total	100	100	100	100	100

Notes:
[1] Representing 6 per cent of all households with children.
[2] Representing 10 per cent of all households with children.
All ECHP tables are based on weighted sample; see Chapter 1.

family households, which very often consist of retired persons living with their adult children and respective families.

In all these risk groups there was thus a strong presence of family networks that can be explained not only from a cultural perspective, but also as a strategy to cope with difficulties at different stages in the individual's life. For young people, staying with their parents may help them face the difficulties they encounter in their transition to adulthood, not only concerning their entrance into the labour market but also concerning their access to housing. These difficulties may also be underlying the presence of such a large number of lone mothers living with their adult children. Housing difficulties and low incomes may also help explain the high percentage of retired people who live with their adult children, difficulties which may be better overcome when the household income depends mainly on wages, rather than on pensions.

INCOME POVERTY AND SOCIAL EXCLUSION: LIFE COURSE TRANSITIONS AND EVENTS

The analysis of the dynamics of income poverty in Portugal showed an increase in the poverty rate from 21 per cent to 24 per cent between 1995 and 1996.[2] This was contrary to the evolution for deprivation rates of amenities and necessities that registered a decrease over the same period, as shown in Table 6.2. The data also show (Table 6.3) that there was a close similarity between movements into and out of poverty over the two years, although for those already in poverty in 1995 the rate of remaining poor was almost three in every four poor individuals.[3]

A closer look into deprivation dynamics (see Table 6.4) from 1995 and 1996 showed that the different deprivation indicators – amenities, durables and necessities – were associated with different patterns of change over

Table 6.2   Deprivation rates, Portugal, ECHP, 1995–6

Percentage below deprivation line	Wave 2 (1995) (%)	Wave 3 (1996) (%)
Amenities	15.3	13.3
Durables	30.5	32.3
Necessities	18.5	15.6

Note: Amenities and necessities: deprivation lines set at 60 per cent median proportional deprivation score; durables: deprivation line set at 80 per cent median proportional deprivation score.

Table 6.3   Poverty dynamics, equivalized monthly household income, individuals, Portugal, ECHP, 1995–6

Income poverty	(%)
Transitions	
Persistence rate	72
Exit rate	28
Entrance rate	10
Avoidance	90
Turnover	
Remained in poverty	15
Exited poverty	6
Entered poverty	8
Never in poverty[1]	71
Total	100

Note:
[1] 'Never', in this and subsequent tables, refers to the observation period: that is, never poor/deprived over the two years covered.

Table 6.4   Deprivation dynamics, individuals, Portugal, ECHP, 1995–6

	Amenities (%)	Durables (%)	Necessities (%)
Transitions			
Deprivation persistence rate	78	74	61
Deprivation exit rate	22	26	39
Deprivation entrance rate	2	14	5
Deprivation avoidance	98	86	95
Turnover			
Remained in deprivation	12	22	11
Exited deprivation	3	8	7
Entered deprivation	2	10	4
Never in deprivation	83	60	77
Total	100	100	100

time, mostly associated with the nature of the indicator itself. Thus the lowest percentages of entrances and exits from deprivation were found for the amenities indicator. This is consistent with the fact that this indicator is composed of items such as having or not having a bathroom or a separate kitchen, which are basic items with a considerable inherent stability.

Bearing these characteristics in mind, there was nevertheless a 'high' percentage of people (2 per cent) who did not manage to avoid entering this type of deprivation. On the other hand, the highest percentages of deprivation were found in an indicator that consists of more volatile items, that is, the durables indicator. This was the one with the highest percentage of people having experienced deprivation, such that four in every 10 individuals had already experienced durables deprivation in at least one of the years corresponding to waves two and three of the ECHP.

Having briefly presented some of the findings for the dynamics of deprivation for the whole population, we now examine the four risk groups in more detail.

Young Adults and the Risk of Income Poverty: the Role of Education and Work

In spite of the lack of longitudinal data, various studies have shown an 'intergenerational reproduction' of income poverty in Portugal, which means that there is a strong propensity of poor children to remain poor throughout their life cycle. For example, a study carried out in the major degraded urban areas showed that 79 per cent of those who considered their respective parents as poor also considered themselves as poor (Silva *et al.*, 1989).

This 'reproduction of poverty' is generated by successive processes of discrimination that have been called the 'vicious circle of poverty'. As a result of the awareness of such a circle, and of the relative incapacity of some institutions (in particular the schools) to break it, children and young people have become, in recent years, the main target group for local projects against poverty. On the other hand, the growth of youth unemployment and of drug addiction and youth delinquency are some of the aspects that attach a 'youth face' to social exclusion in Portugal.

However, the youth[4] income poverty rate in the ECHP was lower than the average for the total population: 17 per cent and 24 per cent, respectively. Turning to the dynamic analysis, Table 6.5 shows that the percentage of young people 'never in poverty' (78 per cent) was higher than that of all adults (71 per cent).[5] Furthermore, income poverty was less persistent among the young than among adults: 73 per cent of the adults that were in income poverty in wave two were also poor in wave three; among young people the figure was 68 per cent.

In other words, young people are more likely to exit from income poverty than the adults (32 per cent of young people who were poor in wave two were not poor in wave three, compared with 27 per cent of other adults). This 'dynamism' of youth income poverty is certainly linked to the multiple nature of the transitions experienced by young people at this stage of their

Table 6.5   Poverty dynamics: young adults, Portugal, ECHP, 1995–6

	Young adults (%)	All adults (16+) (%)
Transitions		
Persistence rate	68	73
Exit rate	32	27
Entrance rate	10	5
Avoidance rate	90	95
Turnover		
Remained in poverty	9	15
Exited poverty	4	6
Entered poverty	9	8
Never in poverty	78	71
Total	100	100

lives. Perhaps the most important of these is the transition from school to work, which means moving from a dependent economic situation to an independent one.

For a better understanding of this transition in the actual context of the Portuguese society it is important to note one of the most relevant changes during the last three decades, the general increase in the educational level of the Portuguese population. The extension of compulsory education,[6] the enlargement of the network of public schools and the improvement of the general standard of living of the population are all factors that have led to an upgrading of the educational standards of the population and have increased the aspiration to higher qualifications in the younger generations. According to the ECHP data, 8 per cent of the age group between 25 and 29 had the 'third stage' of education, while among all adults the corresponding percentage was 5 per cent. Nevertheless, Portugal is a country where educational levels among young people are still comparatively low in a cross-national perspective.

Low educational levels are a cause of poverty as well as a consequence of a life course in poverty. The school system in Portugal has not yet succeeded in being effective in the correction of social inequalities and in promoting children and youngsters from the most disadvantaged families. The ECHP data confirmed the selective character of the school by showing that poor young people had lower educational levels than the non-poor young people. Indeed, referring to data from wave three, 81.5 per cent of the former group had less than the 'second stage' of education, compared with 69 per cent of the latter.

Table 6.6   *Poverty dynamics and education levels: young adults, Portugal,*
             ECHP, 1995–6

	Educational level		
	Third stage	Second stage	Less than second stage
	(%)	(%)	(%)
Remained in poverty	4.7	6	11.2
Exited poverty	1.6	2.2	5.1
Entered poverty	6.3	6	9.9
Never in poverty	87.5	85.7	73.7
Total	100	100	100

The dynamic analysis of the ECHP data provided enough evidence (see Table 6.6 above) to state that young people with a lower educational level were more likely to move into and remain in income poverty. Nevertheless, educational levels were not the only explanation for moving into, and out of, income poverty. In fact, those who moved out from income poverty were slightly less educated (85 per cent had less than second stage) than those who fell into income poverty or who remained poor (82 per cent had the same level of education), which seems to suggest the existence of other strategies to help young people exit from income poverty. Furthermore, although higher educational levels reduced the probability of being poor, they did not provide complete protection against the risk of income poverty, since 6.3 per cent of those who had completed the third stage of education were in income poverty. This could be one of the reasons why poor people sometimes underestimate the importance of education as a means of improving their life.

Given the limited number of the ECHP waves, it is not possible to know whether these movements into and out of income poverty are consistent or are just due to casual factors. Nevertheless, there seem to be two types of situations that may correspond to two different strategies among the young:

- poor young people who give up school with low educational levels, in order to get a job as soon as possible and, thus, escape from income poverty. According to the ECHP data, the young people who moved out of income poverty were younger than the average and were also those who had a higher probability of already being working;
- the non-poor youth (older than the average), who extend their school

life with the aim of getting not only a better job but also the type of
work that corresponds to their expectations, even at the cost of
unemployment and financial stress.

Access to employment is, certainly, in this case, the factor with the strongest influence on situations of income poverty and social exclusion.
Employment is a source of income but it is also an important means of
social inclusion, by providing the establishment of daily life routines, the
acquisition of a social status and the settlement of wider social networks.
However, the more visible consequences of the participation in the labour
market that we could find in the ECHP data concerned the protection
against income poverty. Indeed, 61.9 per cent of those young people who
were never in income poverty were employed. It should be recalled that it
was also in this group that we found higher levels of education. On the
other hand, the group that moved out of income poverty had the highest
percentage of entrance in the labour market (25 per cent). Here, employment and the income associated with it helps to explain their moving out
of income poverty. Contrary to this, those who moved into income poverty
had a higher percentage of individuals who stopped working (12.8 per
cent).

Similarly to the above point about education, it seems that the dichot-
omy of being in/out of the labour market is not the only explanation for
the exits and entrances in income poverty for young people, or for the risk
of remaining in this situation. The characteristics of the labour market also
have a significant influence, as may be seen in the following:

- the proportion of working young individuals who remained in
  income poverty was 58.8 per cent. This reflected their precarious jobs
  and particularly low wages. The average annual wage among those
  who were in income poverty during the two waves was 554 910 PTE
  (€2767.9) and 756 054 PTE (€3771.2) for those who were never in
  income poverty;
- it was among those who remained in income poverty and those who
  entered income poverty that we could find higher percentages of self-
  employment. This raises the question of the extent to which the
  resort to self-employment may be a disguised form of unemployment;
- according to the results of a logistic regression, young part-time
  workers were more vulnerable to income poverty.

Moreover, the percentage of those who stayed out of the labour market
in both waves was slightly higher among those who were never in income

poverty (42.4 per cent) than among those who remained in income poverty (40.8 per cent), which seems contradictory to what was said previously. We should, however, remember, once again the importance of the family in increasing the feasibility of young people's projects, namely through education: those who never experienced income poverty are the group with the highest percentage of students.

On the other hand, as stressed by Sérgio Grácio (n.d.), 'unemployment has a cost in ambitions; ambitions have a cost in unemployment'. This means that young adults with lower professional ambitions (who tend to match the less educated and the poorest) will find a job more easily because they are less demanding with regard to the type of job. Others, who have a higher objective, partially created by longer schooling, may have more difficulty, especially when the level of education attained is not sufficient to make them highly sought after.

The difficulties that young people face in their transition to adulthood concern not only their entrance into the labour market but also their access to housing. In this particular domain, family support emerges as one of the most important resources of young people. These difficulties were most apparent among those who remained in income poverty between the two waves of the ECHP. These young people were very likely to remain in their parents' home (75 per cent). On the other hand, those who exited from income poverty were also very likely to leave the home of their original family (20 per cent). One must also note that it was among those who exited from income poverty that there was the highest percentage of young people (22.9 per cent) already married or who married between the two waves. This could mean that some young people wait until certain economic conditions are in place (most of them being already in the labour market) in order to leave the parental home and set up their own family (sometimes the two phases are not simultaneous). Or, perhaps, for some, marriage is a strategy to improve living conditions.

It is also important to stress the (apparent) resemblance between those young people who remained in and those who were never in income poverty. In both cases there was a predominance of single individuals (86.1 per cent and 77.6 per cent, respectively) and a strong presence in the parental home (75 per cent in both cases). For those who remained out of income poverty, is it possible that the family played an important role in enhancing the feasibility of their personal projects, namely in helping them achieve higher levels of education? In fact, the percentage of young students was much higher (41.9 per cent) among those who never were in income poverty than in the other groups.[7] For those who remained in income poverty, their presence in the parental house was, no doubt, linked to their financial difficulties, given the lower wages among these young poor workers.

Lone Parenthood: Coping with Gender, Age and Family Responsibilities

In a context of poor social protection, the situation of lone parents in Portugal has repeatedly been mentioned by several authors as being particularly vulnerable to poverty and social exclusion (Ferreira, 1993; Perista *et al.*, 1993; Almeida *et al.*, 1992; Silva *et al.*, 1991). More recently, the first results from the Guaranteed Minimum Income scheme (introduced in 1997) also highlighted the poor economic situation of lone parents (IDS,1999).

In the ECHP data also, the incidence of income poverty among lone mothers was found to be higher than among couples and among adults in general. Among the lone mothers risk group, in 1995, the highest income poverty rate (34 per cent) was found among lone mothers with dependent children, compared with couples, adults in general and other lone mothers. Moreover, compared with other countries, the relative situation of lone mothers with non-dependent children was worse in Portugal, though it was better than that of lone mothers with dependent children at a national level. However, the fact that lone mothers with dependent children presented high levels of labour market participation helped to prevent – to a certain extent – even higher rates of income poverty.

A closer look at the characteristics of these lone parents with non-dependent children from a poverty point of view confirms the higher vulnerability of older, widowed, less educated, inactive and sick lone parents to income poverty (ECHP, second wave data). The stronger presence of this 'traditional' type of lone parenthood in countries like Portugal has been linked mainly to three different factors: 'the death of one of the spouses, single persons with children born out of wedlock and the absence/emigration of the spouse' (Wall, 1997). This type of lone parenthood has a significant weight in Portugal, representing a kind of situation repeatedly identified as one of the most vulnerable as far as poverty and social exclusion are concerned. This vulnerability derives, not only from the lone parenthood itself, but also from the overlapping of this situation with old age (health frailties, low pensions, isolation and so on) and with being a woman.

The dynamic analysis of the poverty and deprivation transitions experienced by lone mothers who remained lone parents between 1995 and 1996 showed a close similarity in the movements into and out of income poverty between lone-parent households and households in general. However, the probability of entering income poverty during that period was higher for lone-parent households than for households in general (9.4 per cent versus 6.3 per cent, respectively).

Table 6.7 shows that lone mothers with dependent children had a higher

Table 6.7   Poverty dynamics: lone mothers, aged below state retirement age, Portugal, ECHP, 1995–6

	Lone mothers		All individuals (including children)
Income poverty	Some dep. (%)	All non-dep. (%)	(%)
Transitions			
Persistence rate	74	78	72
Exit rate	[26]	[22]	28
Entrance rate	[7]	14	10
Avoidance rate	93	86	90
Turnover			
Remained in poverty	24	22	15
Exited poverty	[8]	[6]	6
Entered poverty	[5]	10	8
Never in poverty	62	62	71
Total	100	100	100

Note: [ ] indicates a cell size of between 10 and 29 unweighted observations.

probability of remaining poor between waves two and three than did lone mothers with non-dependent children. However, the latter had twice the risk of becoming poor within the same period. At the same time those with only dependent children had a higher rate of exit from income poverty. These movements, together with the behaviour of the sub-groups of lone mothers who were poor in 1995 and of those who were not poor in 1995, confirmed the fact that poor lone mothers with non-dependent children were a group at particularly high risk from a dynamic perspective, since they fell more often into income poverty and seemed to have fewer chances of getting out (as shown by the poverty persistence and avoidance rates in Table 6.7). This situation seems to be linked to the characteristics of lone mothers with non-dependent children, mentioned above.

Having older children living in the household could be expected to represent a way out of income poverty, since these young adults could potentially contribute additional sources of income. However, this did not seem to happen in the Portuguese context, although it did seem to do so in other European countries (in the cases of Germany and the UK). This apparent paradox should be understood in the context of the above points about families (not only lone parents or lone mothers) who in Portugal more often include non-dependent children. Furthermore, it should be noted that these non-dependent children are often young people over 16 years of age who are not in full-time education. This kind of cohabitation is very often linked to difficulties experienced by these young adults in relation both to the labour market insertion and to housing. The only choice available is, very often, to go on living with parents, who, in many cases, themselves face difficult living conditions. The result of these cumulative risks could easily translate into more persistent income poverty with less opportunity to escape.

The data on deprivation dynamics highlighted some other interesting points. Apart from the differences between the data concerning the three types of non-monetary deprivation (amenities, durables and necessities) there were certain trends that deserve to be highlighted:

- higher deprivation figures were found among lone mothers with non-dependent children than among lone mothers with dependent children for amenities deprivation (20 per cent and 11 per cent, respectively remained in deprivation from one wave to the other), but also a higher mobility for the former towards an exit from the deprivation situation;
- the particular situation of partnered mothers who had non-dependent children and whose levels of deprivation were very high should be noted. In some cases these were even higher than those of lone mothers with dependent children.

The fact that lone mothers with non-dependent children had a higher probability of remaining in deprivation, particularly at the level of amenities and durables, may imply the existence of long-term income poverty (probably more likely to be found among the older age groups among these women below the state retirement age). Such long-term poverty may have not allowed them to overcome housing difficulties or to gain access to durable goods. On the other hand, lone mothers with dependent children seem to have greater difficulties in overcoming deprivation in all the three areas considered (amenities, durables and necessities). One plausible explanation for this fact could be that, among the families with younger children, there are fewer resources available for expenses other than those connected with the children. For lone mothers with non-dependent children, this need to concentrate resources on the children does not exist and therefore priorities can be established in a different way, namely regarding better housing conditions or other needs.

The relationship between the dynamics of income poverty and deprivation in the case of lone mothers with non-dependent children presents some ambiguities: poor lone mothers with non-dependent children had the highest persistence rate from wave two to wave three and fewer possibilities of escape from income poverty. However, lone mothers with non-dependent children had more likelihood of exiting from deprivation.

Overcoming deprivation does not necessarily mean exit from income poverty; that is, it does not necessarily make people self-sufficient with regard to resources. Poor lone mothers with non-dependent children may have been able to overcome deprivation during this period, through having access to certain amenities or items for particular reasons, such as through family support. But this does not necessarily imply the availability of resources on a continual basis. Overcoming income poverty has other and more permanent implications.

Into Retirement, into Income Poverty: Trajectories, Choices and Constraints

Transition into retirement has been strongly associated with income poverty and social exclusion in Portugal.[8] The ECHP data showed an extremely high incidence of income poverty among the retired – the highest among the countries in this study. This was a result of several factors: precarious housing conditions as indicated by the lack of minimum basic housing standards and by high deprivation levels; the need to resort to paid work after retirement age; the extremely low value of retirement pensions and their relative lack of effectiveness in preventing income poverty among those who had no other income; and extremely low educational levels. These all contributed to the multidimensional nature of income poverty and to high rates of deprivation among retired people in Portugal.

The dynamic analysis of the ECHP data for waves two and three not only confirmed the extremely vulnerable situation of this risk group in the context of the Portuguese society, but it also shed some light on particular features of the transition into retirement among retired individuals. The first striking aspect concerns the fact that adults above the age of 45 years who entered this risk group had almost twice the probability of entering income poverty between the two waves than did all adults (15 per cent versus 8 per cent). Entering retirement meant a risk of moving into income poverty. Interestingly enough, for those individuals who left retirement status from one wave to the other – which means that they started working – that transition did not prevent them entering income poverty, with fewer than 10 per cent managing to exit from poverty.

Resorting to paid work after retirement age appears to be a strategy to cope with financial difficulties for those who depend on the pension as their main income. The low percentage of those who managed to escape from income poverty through this potential 'exit door' raises several questions, related to the type of work they do and the level of income it provides, and to the relationship between the individual income and the household income of this sub-group within the retired population. A closer look at this specific sub-group of the retired population who resorted to work after retirement revealed some signs of vulnerability which seem to confirm the fact that this is not at all a successful strategy for escaping from income poverty, although it can alleviate deprivation. The fact that this sub-group of 'retirement leavers' had mostly engaged in working activities traditionally connected to the informal sector (self-employment), along with their older ages and low educational levels, may help to explain why working, in these cases, did not seem to solve the income poverty situation of these retired people. However, this paid work did have some impact in respect of a slight increase in the household incomes and it may also have had other impacts related to self-perceived social status, feelings of social utility, higher self-esteem and so on, that cannot be evaluated in strict monetary terms.

Another interesting result from the dynamic analysis performed on waves two and three (see Table 6.8) was the fact that those who remained retired across the two years had the highest probability of remaining poor (28 per cent), although they seem to have had better chances of exiting from that situation than did adults in general, or even than those who exited from this risk group. On the other hand, the dynamics of the poor population revealed a very high income poverty persistence rate both among those who remained retired across the two waves (74 per cent) and among the adult population in general (75 per cent). However, entering the life course group appeared to be a risky transition for the non-poor (20 per cent of those who retired between the second and third waves entered income poverty), as well as for the poor (80 per cent of those who became retired were already poor and remained poor).

Those who continued to be retired from one wave to the other and who were not poor presented the highest probability of avoiding income poverty (92 per cent), even when compared with adults in general. It seems possible that having been able to overcome such a 'risky' transition and its impact 'untouched' by the spells of income poverty was an important 'passport' to a brighter and safer future.

Further analysis of this specific group of the retired revealed some of the reasons that may underlie their ability to resist income poverty spells. Compared with the total population that remained retired across the two waves, those who within this group did not experience income poverty in either wave seem to have resources that may be functioning as 'buffers' or 'passports'. They were more likely to have higher educational levels; they were less likely to be living alone and to have never been married; the household

Table 6.8   Poverty dynamics: retired people, adults over 45 years, Portugal, ECHP, 1995–6

Income Poverty	Remained in life course group (%)	Exited life course group (%)	Entered life course group (%)	Never in life course group (%)	All adults (16+) (%)
Transitions					
Persistence rate	74	*	80	78	75
Exit rate	26	*	[20]	22	25
Entrance rate	8	*	20	12	11
Avoidance rate	92	*	80	88	89
Turnover					
Remained in poverty	28	[24]	19	12	20
Exited poverty	10	*	[5]	3	7
Entered poverty	5	*	15	10	8
Never in poverty	57	61	62	75	66
Total	100	100	100	100	100

Note: In all tables, * indicates a cell size of less than 10 unweighted observations; [ ] indicates a cell size of between 10 and 29 unweighted observations.

income was more likely to be depending mainly on wages and salaries; and they were less likely to have been sick or disabled across the two waves. Education, family networks, health and salaries and wages as the main source of income seemed to play a positive role in the lives of these individuals and in their path of 'success', not only at this late stage of their trajectory but in the sense that they have probably been vital in the building up and the shaping of that trajectory throughout their lives, enabling them to better face hazardous events, including the risky transition into retirement.

From the dynamic analysis, some of the most striking results concerned the apparently paradoxical relationship between income poverty and deprivation dynamics. Deprivation of necessities is the area in which the nature of this relationship was clearest. One should remember that the very nature of the items involved in this category (replacing worn-out furniture, eating meat, chicken, buying new clothes and so on) is of a very changeable nature, more so than the other two deprivation indicators.

It is therefore not surprising that more than two in every three individuals already deprived in 1995 moved out of retirement between the two waves and at the same time also managed to exit from deprivation of necessities. If beginning to work – leaving retirement – as a strategy to overcome

Table 6.9   Poverty and deprivation of necessities dynamics for the retired, Portugal, ECHP, 1995–6

	Remained in poverty (%)	Exited poverty (%)	Entered poverty (%)	Never in poverty (%)
Remained in risk group				
Remained in deprivation	35	28	18	10
Exited deprivation	12	20	6	8
Entered deprivation	8	9	15	5
Never in deprivation	44	44	61	77
Total	100	100	100	100

income poverty was not generally successful, the same did not apply to solving deprivation problems.

On the other hand, the complexity of these dynamic processes and their interaction can also be illustrated by three different, although interconnected, movements into and out of income poverty and deprivation of necessities (see Table 6.9):

• retired individuals who entered income poverty in wave three had the highest probability of having never[9] been in deprivation, excluding those who had never been in poverty;
• retired individuals who exited from income poverty in wave three had the highest probability of overcoming deprivation;
• retired individuals who experienced income poverty in both years had the highest chances of remaining deprived.

Retired individuals who remained retired from one year to the other and who entered income poverty in the second year have probably been able to avoid deprivation at several levels, since they had the financial resources to do it. However, entering income poverty and having to cope with lack of resources may also trigger immediate responses and lead people to cut back on some of those items that belong to the category of necessities. Hence, perhaps, the fact that 15 per cent of the retired entered both income poverty and deprivation. On the other hand, those who managed to exit from income poverty, by solving the problem of lack of resources, may have the opportunity to acquire some of those necessities and thus overcome deprivation. However, it should not be forgotten that having been poor sometimes has long-lasting effects and can delay the possibility of overcoming deprivation: the fact that more than one in every four retired individuals who overcame income poverty continues in deprivation may illustrate the complexity of income poverty, not only in its causes, but also in the effects it has on the lives, choices and strategies of individuals and families. Finally, for those retired people who remained in income poverty, there seemed to have been few chances of overcoming deprivation, since they lacked the necessary financial resources.

Precariousness along the life cycle is, no doubt, one of the key aspects linked to the transition into retirement. Stepping into retirement very often means an aggravated continuity in the process of precarious living conditions that characterized people's lives during their active years; for others, it may mean a sudden drop in their financial (and emotional among other) resources and thus be one of the gateways to income poverty and social isolation.

The Sick or Disabled: Facing Income Poverty and Deprivation with Undermined Resources

The sick or disabled group is a highly dynamic one, particularly as far as the exit rates from wave two to wave three are concerned. About a third of the sick or disabled in wave two were no longer in this situation in wave three. This was particularly true for men, who seemed to exit more easily from this life course group than women. It was also a situation that seemed to affect a large number of people. Indeed, about one in every 10 individuals experienced ill health and/or disability in at least one of the two years considered.

With regard to income poverty, those who exited from the life course group showed the highest frequencies of entrance into income poverty, which apparently points to a situation in which the sick or disabled were protected against income poverty by an efficient safety net. However, in the Portuguese welfare state context, this is an unlikely hypothesis. Further analysis seems to increase the doubts. In fact, none of the 'exiting group' individuals were receiving social assistance in wave two and 80 per cent were not receiving sickness or invalidity benefits. Other attempts at an explanation also seem to fail. The analysis of the transitions by main activity, household composition, main income source and so on reveals stability and not changes which could explain this. Therefore the most reasonable explanation seems to be that this is a situation which, in the short term, does not give rise to changes that may be reflected in the monetary and non-monetary indicators. On the contrary, ill-health and/or disability seem to weaken the individual's resources in the medium/long term. Therefore changes derived from an entrance or an exit from this group might be identified in further waves of the ECHP.

Considering the non-monetary indicators, those who had been part of the sick or disabled group in at least one of the waves were much more likely than those never sick or disabled to have already experienced deprivation in amenities, durables or necessities. However, because the amenities indicator included items of a very basic nature, there were relatively few individuals deprived on this measure and the dynamics of deprivation were also low. Unlike durables and, especially, necessities, amenities are not easily acquired or lost. Therefore there were few individuals in the 'exited deprivation' and the 'entered deprivation' groups.

The necessities indicator seems to be the one that was most rapidly affected by changes in the individuals' lives, namely in income. Furthermore, all the items in that indicator may imply more subjective answers than, for instance, those in the durables indicator. Thus an increase in the disposable income can affect the necessities indicator, in subjective if not also in objective terms. This seems to be supported by the fact that it is among those who exit from the life course group that one finds the highest percentage of individuals exiting from deprivation.

Having briefly analysed the general dynamics of income poverty and deprivation concerning the sick or disabled in the Portuguese context, the following paragraphs will focus on some of the characteristics which may influence the movement into monetary income poverty of those experiencing an entrance into ill-health/disability.

A closer look at those who were not poor in wave two and who were also not sick or disabled in that wave but who entered this situation in wave three, makes it possible to identify some 'buffers' which seem to have protected individuals from this negative occurrence, preventing them from entering income poverty. With regard to personal characteristics, while gender did not seem to be meaningful (women were slightly less vulnerable to moving into income poverty when becoming sick), age seemed to be more relevant. In fact, those aged between 30 and 44 years were more likely to avoid entering income poverty, and registered almost half the probability of undergoing that change than those aged between 45 and the retirement age,[10] and almost one-third of the probability of young adults (16 to 29 years). Young adults are, generally speaking, less vulnerable to income poverty than adults above 29 years old (see above, on the transition to adulthood). However, it seems that the entrance into ill health/disability may alter this situation. One may easily imagine the additional difficulty that this transition may bring to young adults, 'caught' in a transitional stage of their lives, where autonomy is in many cases still in the process of being achieved.

Marriage or cohabitation also seemed to protect individuals, making them far less vulnerable to entering income poverty than widows (nearly five times less) and singles (rather more than five times). This is consistent with the characteristics identified earlier, regarding the situation of Portuguese widows (see above, regarding transitions to retirement and to lone parenthood). It is also consistent with a higher demand for support (for care but also a demand for financial support) among those becoming sick or disabled. In the absence of this support, the probability of entering income poverty would surely be higher.

The educational level of the individual may also represent an important buffer, as seems to be suggested by the fact that those who had less than the second stage of secondary education had more than one and a half times the probability of moving into income poverty when facing an entry into ill-health/disability than those who had at least that level of education. An interesting finding was that, in apparent contradiction to what is known about Portuguese retired people and their vulnerability to income poverty, among those who became sick or disabled between 1995 and 1996, the lower probability of entering income poverty was found precisely among those who were retired in wave three and among those whose main source of household income was a pension. These findings are, as noted above, an apparent contradiction because we seem to be analysing a very specific group of the retired, a group composed of those whose retirement did not mean an entrance into income poverty, people who probably had a stable contributory career, the opposite to the experience of most of the retired, and a characteristic which seems to buffer them from income poverty.

Those whose main activity was housework had the highest probability of moving into income poverty when becoming sick, being more than five times more vulnerable than those in paid employment and almost 20 times more so than those in retirement. This fact highlights the frailties commonly associated with this situation, which has implications in various domains.

Being dependent upon benefits, or upon self-employment or farming, increases by 1.5 and 1.7 times, respectively, the probability of moving into income poverty, when compared with those whose main source of income was 'wages and salaries'. This is not surprising considering the weak protection given by benefits (see above on retirement) and knowing that self-employment and farming often corresponds to precarious work that is not covered by the social security system.

Entitlement to sickness/invalidity benefits seems to have had a minimal effect on the probability of entering income poverty,[11] which reflects the above-mentioned weakness of the Portuguese welfare state. On the other hand, coverage by a private medical insurance (either directly or by a family member) reduces almost to zero the probability of moving into income poverty, permitting individuals to face the additional health costs that may come along with the transition into ill-health/disability. However, it should be stressed that the individuals covered by this type of insurance were already in a better financial situation. In wave two, these individuals had a mean of 75.4 in terms of income percentiles, while those not covered had a mean of 60.1.

The analysis of the health condition at wave two of those who became sick in wave three revealed that these individuals already had a higher level of resort to health care, as well as a more negative appreciation of their health, compared with those in the group who did not become sick or disabled. In addition, those who made a transition into ill-health/disability in wave three had higher chances of being poor and also deprived in wave two than those who had not become sick or disabled. The probabilities vary between around 1.6 (necessities) and 2.4 (income poverty) times higher. Thus health and income poverty seem to be strongly related. As much as health seems to be an important asset for buffering individuals from income poverty and deprivation, the conditions in which the individuals live also seem to play an important role in their probability of entering ill health/disability. As with so many other problems, health is not just a simple variable that influences an economic transition. It must be understood taking account of the complexity of social reality, in which these factors are often both the cause and the effect.

ECHP DATA ANALYSIS: NEW INSIGHTS FOR PORTUGUESE RESEARCH AND POLICY MAKING ON INCOME POVERTY AND SOCIAL EXCLUSION

Finally, we summarize and discuss the policy implications arising from the main results and consider the potentialities and the new insights for Portuguese research in this area. As far as policy implications are concerned, the dynamic analysis of the four risk groups has highlighted the persistence of structural problems in Portuguese society, which affect the lives, choices and strategies of individuals and families. Housing, education and the labour market are the areas in which these problems have gained more visibility along the different stages of the analysis.

The lack of affordable housing (either owned or rented) which affects the Portuguese population in general has particularly serious consequences for the younger generations, particularly those whose frail economic situation does not allow them to cope with the housing market's rising costs. Staying with their parents is very often the only choice available and the only help their parents can give them. On the other hand, recent measures implemented in housing policy (such as housing subsidies for young people) have mainly benefited those youngsters with more stable situations because the eligibility criteria exclude a large proportion of young people, namely the most deprived.

Very high deprivation levels registered in the amenities indicator reveal another major problem in this field: the precarious housing conditions which are still affecting many households, mainly older people and people living either in rural areas or in deprived neighbourhoods in the large cities. Major rehousing programmes in the latest years (more recent than the available panel waves) have reduced deprivation levels in these urban neighbourhoods. However, older people living in the city centres in very degraded rented houses have not in most cases benefited from regeneration programmes (which are mainly addressed to owners).

In this analysis education has also been systematically related to higher levels of vulnerability to income poverty. In fact, until now the educational system has not been able to transform the exclusive character (reproducing the existing social inequalities) of school into an inclusive one. Thus there is still a high proportion of young people who leave school without having completed their compulsory education.

Labour market insertion has been found to be one of the mechanisms that protects people from income poverty spells. However, it has also been stressed that having a job may not be enough as far as protection from income poverty is concerned (illustrated by the case of those retired individuals who start working and do not succeed in solving their income poverty problem). Precarious working conditions (low wages, lack of social protection, short-term contracts) very often accompany the individual's labour market trajectory, and contribute to his or her vulnerability towards income poverty and social exclusion. Self-employment has also emerged as a kind of unemployment disguise, rather than a real alternative to a previous job, often implying very precarious living conditions.

Access to health services and to other social facilities (such as kindergartens and day centres for the elderly) has also been pinpointed as another area to be taken into close consideration in order to improve the lives of families in general, and in particular the lives of the most deprived.

Finally, as far as policy implications are concerned, special attention should certainly be given to the family in its role of main carer. It is within the family that many solutions are still being found – for the children, for the young adults starting a new family, or for the elderly. In Portugal, the traditional supportive role of families (and particularly women) towards their members has been used both as an excuse and as a compensation for the, also traditional, low state support given to families. It is now time that the state recognized and supported this vital role played by the families.

In respect of future research, the availability, for the first time in

Portugal, of panel data is a major asset for research on income poverty and social exclusion. The possibility of following trajectories on such a large scale and of comparing them across the EU is vital for a better understanding of the mechanisms that push people into and out of income poverty and deprivation. At the same time, access to panel data widens methodological perspectives and offers opportunities for more complementarity between extensive and intensive methods. If exploring the causes of income poverty can be better achieved by using this new tool, studying its effects on the lives of individuals and families could now lead to a renewed interest in this topic from the research community.

Some limitations of the ECHP must, however, be highlighted. The fact that regional disparities may not be explored through panel data in Portugal seriously diminishes the ECHP potential at a national level for the study of income poverty. There is also the problem of the difficulty of studying specific groups of the population from a dynamic perspective given the declining numbers of individuals as the analysis probes more deeply into specific aspects and/or population sub-groups. This difficulty could be solved either by a wider panel or by resort to combined methodologies. Finally, the gap between the waves' reference years and the ECHP availability for research purposes needs to be shortened or else it will compromise the real pertinence and impact of the results achieved.

Having access to the ECHP at a national level could certainly enhance the evaluation (the lack of which is still a major drawback in Portugal) of current or future programmes and measures in different areas, since it allows a better understanding of the way mechanisms of exclusion and inclusion work. On the other hand, the recent introduction of important programmes in Portugal such as the Guaranteed Minimum Income scheme, necessarily raises the question of the need to introduce specific questions in the ECHP in order to grasp the impact of such programmes on the lives of individuals and families.

NOTES

1. In Portugal the urbanization process which occurred mainly after the 1950s in some seaside areas, namely Lisbon and Oporto, was the result of the migration of rural populations from the interior of the country, when people fled from bad living conditions on the fields towards the city, where they hoped for a better life. Urbanization is thus characterized by the settlement of a low-income population who, faced with the total absence of urban policies of housing and other urban infrastructures, tried to meet their housing needs by resorting to constructing their own in the context of an illegal market of housing production.
2. These figures should be treated with caution since there have been some problems with the reliability of the income data which led the Portuguese Statistical Institute to put forward correction procedures.

3. The poverty persistence rate and the poverty exit rate refer to only those individuals who were already poor in 1995, whereas the poverty entrance rate and the poverty avoidance rate refer to those who were not poor in 1995.
4. According to the ECHP, the age group of 16–29 years represents 25 per cent of the Portuguese population. Accordingly, Portugal has one of the highest percentages of young people in the context of the countries represented in this study.
5. Considered as those individuals from 16 years onwards.
6. The 'Lei de Bases do Sistema Educativo' created in 1986 establishes a compulsory schooling of nine years.
7. The next highest percentage is 25 per cent, among those who move into poverty.
8. Since the very first studies on poverty in Portugal (Bruto da Costa *et al.*, 1985) several authors have referred to the particular vulnerability of older people – who exclusively depend on their pensions – to poverty and social exclusion. These studies stress the extremely low values of state pensions which either worsen an already vulnerable situation of individuals and families whose professional life had been characterized by precariousness or, on the other hand, introduce poverty into the lives of older people whose new social status is thus translated into a significant deterioration of their living conditions.
9. Never, in the context of this analysis, must be read as 'in neither of the waves'.
10. In 1996 (wave three), 65 for men and 63 for women.
11. There is a difference between being dependent upon benefits, which means that this is the household's main source of income, which increases the probability of moving into poverty, and being entitled – on a personal basis – to benefits. These are so low that receiving them makes little difference to the probability of entering income poverty.

7. The dynamics of poverty and deprivation in the UK

Laura Adelman and Andreas Cebulla

INTRODUCTION

Welfare in the United Kingdom is based on the premise of minimum state provision. The public sector-provided social safety net serves as a last resort, whilst the state's role is seen as being to enable citizens to retain and improve personal welfare through work (Bennett and Walker, 1998). Social security is generally low-value and financed largely through national taxation. This approach sets the welfare regime of the UK apart from corporate welfare systems, such as in Austria and Germany, which combine active labour market policies with comparatively high social security protection (Standing, 2000). It is also unlike the system of 'Latin Rim' countries (Leibfried, 1992), such as Greece and Portugal, as it provides universal coverage, although this universality is achieved at the expense of residual, low benefit levels.

Welfare spending in the UK has remained fairly stable during the last three decades, amounting to between 21 per cent and 25 per cent of Gross Domestic Product (Hills, 1998). However, the demand for welfare services and social security increased, often cyclically, as a result of demographic and economic changes, such as population ageing, growth in lone parenthood and unemployment, and the opening of entitlement to newly eligible social groups (Walker and Howard, 2000). In the light of rising caseloads, in particular amongst groups such as lone parents, policy makers became concerned about potentially rising costs, but also about the threat of 'welfare dependency'. In response, key social security provisions in the country were curtailed. Some of the service and benefit reductions had a direct impact upon risk groups. Entitlements to Income Support and Housing Benefit amongst young adults under the age of 25 were either removed altogether or substantially reduced. One-parent benefit and a premium in Income Support, both payable to lone parents, were abolished. Sick or disabled people were subjected to more stringent ability-to-work tests, while the abolition of the earnings link to pensions eventually led to a steady erosion of the value of the state pension. All groups, with the exception of the retired, have also been targets for welfare-to-work programmes (see Trickey and Walker, 2000).

Between 1979 and 1998/9, the rate of income poverty (measured as below 50 per cent of mean household income) rose from 8 per cent to 24 per cent of families (DSS, 1999). The 'Breadline Britain' survey, undertaken in 1985, 1990 and again in 1999, furthermore revealed an increase in deprivation of 'socially-perceived necessities', such as food and clothes, and social interaction with friends and family (Gordon *et al.*, 2000). While the 1985 survey estimated that 14 per cent of households were living in deprivation, by 1999 this had increased to 24 per cent.

Although valuable in their own right, until the 1990s, poverty and deprivation indicators were typically point-in-time measurements. They did not, and could not, track people's experiences over time in order to explore changes in poverty and deprivation as they affected the same group or groups of people. Panel studies have made longitudinal measurements feasible. In the UK, the British Household Panel Survey (BHPS) was established in 1991, running annual surveys tracking the same individuals and therefore allowing detailed analysis of changes over time in the UK in the 1990s. The introduction of the European Community Household Panel (ECHP) also in 1991 allows researchers today to investigate social and economic developments across European Community countries and thus to compare income poverty and deprivation risks across borders.

This chapter examines the extent of income poverty and deprivation amongst risk groups in the UK between 1995 and 1996, presenting, in turn, evidence for young adults, lone mothers, sick or disabled people and the retired. The aim is also to describe movements into and out of poverty and deprivation, and the characteristics of people in these groups most likely to change their poverty or deprivation status from one year to the other. The impact of poverty on the social relations of risk groups is also explored. The findings highlighted the frequent independent effect of life-cycle and risk transitions on the risk of poverty and deprivation.

In comparison to the other countries in this study, the dynamic analysis revealed high levels of deprivation of consumer durables and of household and personal necessities, that is, consumer or private goods. Housing deprivation and deprivation of housing amenities, deprivation mainly concerning public goods, were comparatively low. In fact, low rates of housing and housing amenity deprivation in the UK prevented their detailed analyses owing to small numbers.

The risk groups accounted for variable proportions of the total household or individual population in the UK. Young adults and retired people were by far the largest groups, each accounting for 32 per cent of UK households in 1995, and 21 per cent and 26 per cent of the country's adult population (Table 7.1). Lone mothers, with at least one child under the age of 16 or in full-time education, constituted 6 per cent of households and 3 per cent of the adult population. Sick or disabled people also made up a small risk group, totalling 6 per cent of British households and 5 per cent of the adult population.

Table 7.1 Size of risk groups, UK, ECHP, 1995

Risk group	% of households	% of adult population
Young adults	32	21
Lone mothers	6	3
Sick or disabled people	6	5
Retired people	32	26

Note: All ECHP tables are based on weighted sample, see Chapter 1.

YOUNG ADULTS

The transition from youth to adulthood involves a series of fundamental changes in the lifestyles of young people. Young adults leave the parental home and learn to live independently. As compulsory education comes to an end, young people choose between entering the labour market, continuing in further and higher education, or inactivity. Early labour market experiences are typically unstable, subject to frequent changes in employment, a high risk of unemployment and fluctuating earnings (Endean, 1999). Instability in early working life, in particular extended periods of unemployment, adversely affect young people's employment prospects in later life (Gregg, 1999).

Income Poverty

Between 1995 and 1996, 14 per cent of young adults were in income poverty in both years (Table 7.2). Whilst 6 per cent of young people became poor from one year to the next, a further 6 per cent ceased to be poor. These poverty rates for young adults differed little from the poverty rates for the all-adult population.

However, these figures masked the greater frequency of movement into and out of income poverty amongst young people. On the one hand, proportionately more young adults (8 per cent) than all adults (6 per cent) not poor in 1995 were likely to have become poor in the following year. On the

Table 7.2   Income poverty dynamics: young adults, UK, ECHP, 1995–6

Income poverty	Young adults (%)	All adults (16+) (%)
Transitions		
Persistence rate	72	77
Exit rate	28	23
Entrance rate	8	6
Avoidance rate	92	94
Turnover		
Remained in poverty	14	15
Exited poverty	6	4
Entered poverty	6	5
Never in poverty[1]	74	76
Base (unweighted)	1 113	6 645

Notes:
[1] 'Never', in this and subsequent tables, refers to the observation period; that is, never poor/deprived over the two years covered.
Young adults: 0 missing values; all adults: two missing values.

other hand, young adults were also proportionately more likely to have left a state of income poverty between 1995 and 1996: 28 per cent did, compared to 23 per cent of all adults.

The risk of becoming poor from one year to the other was significantly higher amongst young adults who were unemployed, economically inactive or participating in education or training than amongst young adults in full-time employment. Young adults living alone, with or without children, were also at an increased risk of poverty compared to young people who, during the two years, continued living with their parents. However, the judicious choice of a partner, and the absence of children in a partnered household, also reduced the risk of income poverty. In essence, young adults' risk of becoming poor was most effectively reduced by their living in employed households, particularly if the young adults themselves were also in work.

Educational achievement also reduced the risk of entering poverty, at least up to the level of second-stage secondary education. Third-level education did not reduce the risk for young adults, although it did for all adults. The economic benefits of third-level education in terms of reducing poverty risks might thus not come to fruition until later in adult life. In fact, educational achievement played no role in determining young adults' chances of *leaving* a state of significant poverty from one year to the other. Employment status of the young adult and their household, however, were influential factors. Unemployment and economic inactivity reduced a young adult's chance of escaping poverty, whilst sharing a household with others who were in work made it more likely that he or she was able to move out of poverty from one year to the next.

Deprivation

Like income poverty rates, the rates of deprivation for young adults and the all-adult population were rather similar (Table 7.3). Focusing on necessities, 12 per cent of young adults and 11 per cent of all adults were deprived in both 1995 and 1996. As in the case of income poverty dynamics, young adults again experienced higher rates of exit from deprivation than all adults if they were already deprived in 1995 (39 per cent, compared to 36 per cent). Likewise, they were more likely to become deprived from one year to the next (8 per cent of young adults, compared to 6 per cent of all adults). Achieving second-stage secondary level education significantly reduced the risk of young adults encountering deprivation, although higher, third-level education did not.

Table 7.3   Deprivation (necessities) dynamics: young adults, UK, ECHP, 1995–6

Deprivation dynamics	Young adults (%)	All adults (16+) (%)
Transitions		
Persistence rate	61	64
Exit rate	39	36
Entrance rate	8	6
Avoidance rate	92	94
Turnover		
Remained in deprivation	12	11
Exited deprivation	7	6
Entered deprivation	6	5
Never in deprivation	75	78
Base (unweighted)	1 045	6 645

Note: Young adults, 68 missing values; all adults, two missing values.

In fact, there was a close correspondence between the risk of becoming deprived and the risk of becoming poor amongst young adults, in that the risk of *being* in poverty markedly increased the risk of *moving into* deprivation. While 33 per cent of *poor* young adults experienced material deprivation from one year to the next, only 26 per cent of all poor adults did (data not shown in table). Likewise, 29 per cent of young adults who became poor from 1995 to 1996 also experienced deprivation, compared to a national average for all adults who moved into poverty from 1995 to 1996 of 23 per cent.

However, for young adults not affected by poverty in either year, deprivation was less permanent than for all adults. A total of 64 per cent of non-poor young adults escaped deprivation from one year to the next, compared to 54 per cent of all non-poor adults. Only 3 per cent of both young and all adults not poor in 1995 became deprived of necessities by 1996.

Many young people also experienced deprivation of durables (data not shown), although the rates of deprivation were lower than in the case of deprivation of necessities. Of young adults, 17 per cent were deprived of durables in 1995 or 1996 (or in both years), which compared with 10 per cent of all adults. There was little difference in the rates at which young adults and adults in general were able to escape durable deprivation. Some 56 per cent of young adults overcame a state of deprivation of durables between 1995 and 1996, as did 54 per cent of all adults. However, young adults were twice as likely to become deprived between 1995 and 1996, albeit that only a small minority was affected: 4 per cent of young adults not deprived of durables in 1995 experienced deprivation in 1996, compared to 2 per cent of the entire adult population.

Income Poverty and Deprivation in International Comparison

Young people suffered a particularly high risk of deprivation if they were poor. In fact, this risk was considerably higher in the UK than in the other countries, despite the fact that poverty rates amongst young people were lowest in the UK (Barnes *et al.*, 2002). Young people, whose income kept them below the poverty line, were more than three times (3.2) as likely also to experience deprivation of private goods, that is, durables and necessities, as young adults whose income was above the poverty line (Figure 7.1). The odds of being poor and deprived over not being poor or deprived in the UK were by far the highest amongst the five countries in this comparison. The gap was particularly wide between the UK and the two examples of corporate welfare states, Austria and Germany. In these two countries, poor young people were only 1.3 times as likely to experience deprivation of consumer durables than young people who were not poor. Likewise, in Austria, they were 1.3 times as likely to experience deprivation of household necessities, whereas in Germany they were twice as likely to do so. The odds of poor young people also being deprived of consumer durables or household and personal necessities were somewhat higher in Greece and

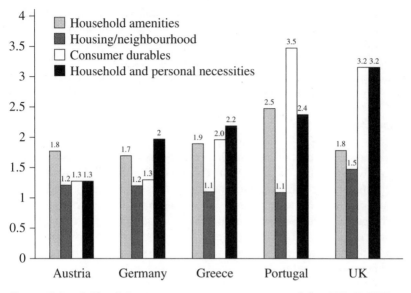

Figure 7.1   Odds of deprivation among poor young adults, UK, ECHP, 1995–6

Portugal, but still lower than in the UK, except for consumer durables in Portugal (3.5).

Poor young people in the UK also experienced a higher added risk of housing and neighbourhood deprivation than poor young people else-where, but the gap in the odds between the UK and the other countries was much reduced. In the case of deprivation of housing amenities, the additional risk of deprivation amongst poor young people in the UK (1.8) was the second lowest, together with Austria. The risk was lower only in Germany (1.7), but higher in Greece (1.9) and Portugal (2.5).

LONE PARENTS

The high poverty rate of lone parents in the UK has been widely documented (Millar, 1989; Bradshaw and Millar, 1991). However, lone parents suffer not only from an increased risk of poverty, but also from longer periods of poverty. Between 1991 and 1994, for instance, 42 per cent of lone parents were in the bottom three deciles of the income distribution in all four years, compared to the population average of just 13 per cent (DSS, 2000a).

This section analyses the experiences of income poverty and deprivation encountered by *individuals in lone mother households* and compares them to the experiences of *individuals in partnered mother households*. For ease, these individuals are simply described as 'lone mothers' and 'partnered mothers'. Owing to small sample sizes, only those who remained in lone mother and partnered mother households with dependent children in 1995 and 1996 were included in the analysis.

Income Poverty

As many as 63 per cent of lone mothers experienced income poverty in both 1995 and 1996 (Table 7.4, turnover). This was more than five times the rate of persistent poverty amongst partnered mothers (12 per cent). Over 70 per cent of lone mothers were poor in 1995 or 1996, compared to 16 per cent and 17 per cent, respectively, of partnered mothers; 9 per cent of lone mothers left a state of income poverty from 1995 to 1996, compared to 5 per cent of partnered mothers, while 7 per cent became poor from one year to the next, compared to 4 per cent of partnered mothers.

Table 7.4   Income poverty dynamics: mothers with dependent children, UK, ECHP, 1995–6

Income poverty	Lone mothers (%)	Partnered mothers (%)
Transitions		
Persistence rate	88	73
Exit rate	12	27
Entrance rate	23	5
Avoidance rate	77	95
Turnover		
Remained in poverty	63	12
Exited poverty	9	5
Entered poverty	7	4
Never in poverty	22	79
Base (unweighted)	449	3625

Note: Analysis includes mothers and other household members.

These figures for movements into and out of poverty, however, gave a mistaken impression of generally greater mobility amongst lone mothers than partnered mothers. In fact, rates of transition showed that lone mothers were *less* likely to exit from poverty, but more likely to enter it. Lone mothers who had not been in poverty in 1995 were also four times more likely than partnered mothers to become poor between 1995 and 1996: 23 per cent of lone mothers not poor in 1995 experienced poverty a year later, compared to 5 per cent of partnered mothers. Moreover, just 12 per cent of lone parents, who had been poor in 1995, left this state of poverty in 1996. This compared to 27 per cent of partnered mothers.

This discrepancy in findings reflects different base lines. The larger proportion of lone mothers (72 per cent) who were already poor in 1995 compared to partnered mothers (17 per cent) increased the risk of income poverty exit (turnover), as a proportion of the total population, despite a lower poverty exit rate (transition). Likewise, the comparatively smaller pool of lone mothers who were not already poor in 1995 reduced the poverty entry *risk* (turnover) relative to that of partnered mothers, despite a much higher entry *rate* (transition).

The key factor reducing the risk of income poverty amongst mothers was employment. Maintaining employment during both 1995 and 1996 approximately halved the chances of lone and partnered mothers encountering poverty from one year to the next. Thus, whereas 23 per cent of all lone mothers who were not poor in 1995 had become poor in the following year, this was the case for 'only' 11 per cent of working lone mothers. Likewise, whereas 5 per cent of all partnered mothers moved into poverty between 1995 and 1996, only 3 per cent of working partnered mothers did.

Lone mothers who had been educated to below second-stage secondary level were at greatest risk of poverty. Low levels of education increased the risk of becoming poor amongst lone mothers from the average of 23 per cent to 35 per cent. Likewise, the risk increased for partnered mothers from 5 per cent to 10 per cent. Lone mothers, therefore, were still more than three times as likely to become poor than partnered mothers, even if both reported low levels of educational achievement. Lone mothers were less likely to move into poverty if they were divorced: 14 per cent of lone mothers that were divorced moved into poverty.

Deprivation

Lone mothers were severely and adversely affected by the lack of consumer durables, and household and personal necessities. Lone mothers were over five times more likely than partnered mothers to be continuously deprived of durables (16 per cent compared to 3 per cent) (Table 7.5). With 7 per cent of lone parents experiencing deprivation of durable goods in 1996, but not 1995, the risk of becoming deprived was also considerably higher for lone mothers than for partnered mothers (1 per cent). The latter finding was confirmed by the transition rates. They showed that, whilst 11 per cent of non-deprived lone mothers experienced deprivation of consumer durables from one year to the other, only 1 per cent of partnered mothers did. Yet again, the larger pool of already deprived lone mothers in the sample gave the incorrect impression of greater deprivation mobility amongst this group, when in fact just 52 per cent of deprived lone mothers overcame deprivation of durables between the years, compared to 61 per cent of partnered mothers.

Table 7.5   Deprivation of durables dynamics: mothers with dependent children, UK, ECHP, 1995–6

Deprivation of durables	Lone mothers (%)	Partnered mothers (%)
Transitions		
Persistence rate	48	39
Exit rate	52	61
Entrance rate	11	1
Avoidance rate	89	99
Turnover		
Remained in deprivation	16	3
Exited deprivation	18	4
Entered deprivation	7	1
Never in deprivation	59	92
Base (unweighted)	449	3625

Note: Analysis includes mothers and other household members.

Likewise, as a proportion of the total population, more lone mothers escaped deprivation from 1995 to 1996 (18 per cent) than partnered mothers (4 per cent).

A similar pattern emerged with respect to deprivation of household and personal necessities (Table 7.6). However, a much larger proportion of lone mothers were deprived of these items in one or both years than of consumer durables. In addition, considerably more lone mothers were deprived of necessities than partnered mothers. Over two-fifths (44 per cent) of lone mothers were deprived of necessities continuously over the two years, whilst 12 per cent became deprived and 11 per cent overcame deprivation. These figures compared to 8, 4 and 7 per cent of partnered mothers, respectively.

Once again, the transition rates gave a more refined picture. Not only did they reveal that lone mothers deprived in 1995 were in fact less likely to exit from necessity deprivation than partnered mothers already deprived in 1995 (20 per cent, compared with 45 per cent), they also showed that lone mothers not deprived in 1995 were less likely to avoid becoming deprived than partnered mothers (73 per cent of lone mothers, compared to 95 per cent of partnered mothers). Moreover, in comparison to deprivation of consumer durables, lone mothers were at a substantially greater risk of entering and of failing to evade deprivation of necessities.

Table 7.6   Deprivation of necessities dynamics: mothers with dependent children, UK, ECHP, 1995–6

Deprivation of necessities	Lone mothers (%)	Partnered mothers (%)
Transitions		
Persistence rate	80	55
Exit rate	20	45
Entrance rate	27	5
Avoidance rate	73	95
Turnover		
Remained in deprivation	44	8
Exited deprivation	11	7
Entered deprivation	12	4
Never in deprivation	33	81
Base (unweighted)	449	3625

Note: Analysis includes mothers and other household members.

SICK OR DISABLED PEOPLE

A recent report estimated that about eight million adults in private households in the UK had physical and/or medical impairments in 1996/97 (Craig and Greenslade, 1998), including four million adults of working age. Although not directly comparable, this figure suggested a marked increase on 1985, when about 6.2 million adults were sick or disabled (Berthoud *et al.*, 1993). Approximately one-third of sick or disabled people receive one of the two main state benefits payable to people unable to work owing to illness, Incapacity Benefit and Severe Disablement Allowance (DSS, 2000b).

According to the ECHP, in the UK approximately 8 per cent of the working-age population were sick or disabled at one point during 1995 and 1996, which is in line with the estimates reported by Craig and Greenslade (1998); 3 per cent were sick or disabled in both 1995 and 1996. Sick or disabled people tended to be older and often lived alone, and included a disproportionate number of men (Barnes *et al.*, 2002).

Poverty

Sick or disabled people suffered disproportionate risks in terms of both becoming and remaining in income poverty (Table 7.7). Over two-fifths of the sick or disabled population (44 per cent) experienced income poverty at some point in 1995 or 1996, including 28 per cent of sick or disabled people who were in poverty in both years. Compared to people without impairment (20 per cent in poverty) and the UK's adult population in general (24 per cent), sick or disabled people were about twice as likely to be poor. Moreover, sick or disabled people were more than twice as likely to experience persistent income poverty (28 per cent), that is, poverty in both 1995 and 1996, than people without health problems (12 per cent).

Table 7.7   Income poverty dynamics: sick or disabled people, UK, ECHP,
1995–6

Income poverty	In the life course group at some time (%)	Never in the life course group (%)	All adults 16+ (%)
Transitions			
Persistence rate	82	75	77
Exit rate	[18]	25	23
Entrance rate	[15]	5	6
Avoidance rate	85	95	94
Turnover			
Remained in poverty	28	12	15
Exited poverty	[6]	4	4
Entered poverty	[10]	4	5
Never in poverty	56	81	76
Base (unweighted)	332	3872	6645

Notes: [ ] indicates a cell size of between 10 and 29 unweighted observations.

Transition rates also highlighted the greater risk of becoming poor amongst sick or disabled people. While 15 per cent of non-poor sick or disabled people became poor from 1995 to 1996, only 5 per cent of people without health problems did so. Conversely, sick or disabled people who were already in poverty in 1995 were less likely to have overcome poverty by the following year: 18 per cent of sick or disabled people left a state of income poverty between 1995 and 1996, compared to 25 per cent of people in good health and 23 per cent of the total adult population.

Deprivation

In addition to their disproportionate income poverty risks, sick or disabled people in the UK also experienced an increased risk of deprivation. As for the other risk groups, the added risk was particularly striking with respect to deprivation of household durables and necessities.

As many as 22 per cent of sick or disabled adults suffered deprivation of durable household goods in at least one year. This compared to approximately 10 per cent of all adults and adults without health problems (Table 7.8). One in 10 of sick or disabled adults were deprived of essential durable goods in both years, compared to one in 25 of other adults.

Table 7.8 *Deprivation of durables dynamics: sick or disabled adults, adults under state retirement age, UK, ECHP, 1995–6*

Deprivation of durables	In the life course group at some time (%)	Never in the life course group (%)	All adults 16+ (%)
Transitions			
Persistence rate	56	47	46
Exit rate	[44]	53	54
Entrance rate	[5]	2	2
Avoidance rate	95	98	98
Turnover			
Remained in deprivation	10	4	4
Exited deprivation	[7]	4	4
Entered deprivation	[5]	2	2
Never in deprivation	78	91	90
Base (unweighted)	332	3 867	6 645

Notes: Percentages may not add up to 100 due to rounding. [ ] indicates a cell size of between 10 and 29 unweighted observations.

Sick or disabled people were also often unable to afford household and personal items. Over half (56 per cent) of sick or disabled adults were deprived of household and personal necessities in 1995 or 1996. This was nearly three times the level of adults without health problems, and two-and-a-half times the level of all adults. The high incidence of material disadvantage amongst sick or disabled people again resulted from their lesser ability or lower opportunity to leave a state of deprivation, paired with a greater risk of experiencing deprivation from one year to the next. This was most apparent with respect to necessities. The rate of exit from necessity deprivation (22 per cent) was considerably below that of adults without impairment (40 per cent) or the all-adult population (36 per cent) (Table 7.9). At the same time, rates of entrance into deprivation were markedly higher (19 per cent, compared to 5 per cent for other adults and 6 per cent for the adult average).

Table 7.9   Deprivation of necessities dynamics: sick or disabled adults, adults under state retirement age, UK, ECHP, 1995–6

Deprivation of necessities	In the life course group at some time (%)	Never in the life course group (%)	All adults 16+ (%)
Transitions			
Persistence rate	78	60	64
Exit rate	22	40	36
Entrance rate	[19]	5	6
Avoidance rate	91	95	94
Turnover			
Remained in deprivation	35	9	11
Exited deprivation	10	6	6
Entered deprivation	[11]	4	5
Never in deprivation	44	82	78
Base (unweighted)	332	3867	6645

Note: [ ] indicates a cell size of between 10 and 29 unweighted observations.

Social Isolation

Sick or disabled people not only experienced a greater than average risk of poverty or deprivation, their sickness or disability appeared also to affect their social networks. For instance, membership of clubs or (community) associations was less common amongst sick or disabled people than amongst people without health problems. During 1995 and 1996, just over one-quarter of the sick or disabled (26 per cent) were members of a club, compared to 36 per cent of able-bodied adults and 37 per cent of the all-adult population (Table 7.10). Half of all sick or disabled were never members of clubs during this time, compared to just over 40 per cent of able-bodied and all adults.

Arguably of greater social and political significance were differences in sick or disabled people's contact with friends, relatives and neighbours when compared to unimpaired people. Sick or disabled people were nearly one-and-a-half times as likely to be excluded from contact with friends or family in 1995 or 1996 (or in both years) (31 per cent) than able-bodied people, or indeed the all-adult population (both 23 per cent). Moreover, sick or disabled people's social relations with friends and relatives appeared adversely affected by impairment: 12 per cent of sick or disabled people were socially isolated from friends and family persistently, that is, in both 1995 and 1996, compared to just 7 per cent of other adults.

Table 7.10   Social isolation dynamics: sick or disabled people, adults under state retirement age, UK, ECHP, 1995–6

Social relations	In the life course group at some time (%)	Never in the life course group (%)	All adults 16+ (%)
Not a member of a club			
Remained in exclusion	50	42	43
Exited exclusion	13	11	10
Entered exclusion	[11]	11	10
Never in exclusion	26	36	37
Talks to neighbours[1]			
Remained in exclusion	[5]	9	8
Exited exclusion	[8]	7	7
Entered exclusion	[7]	7	7
Never in exclusion	80	77	79
Meets friends/relatives[2]			
Remained in exclusion	12	7	7
Exited exclusion	10	8	8
Entered exclusion	9	8	8
Never in exclusion	70	78	77
Base (unweighted)	332	3872	6645

Notes:
[1] Adults only: 'talks to neighbours less than once a week'.
[2] Adults only: 'meets friends or relatives (not living with the person) at home or elsewhere, less than once a week'.
Errors due to rounding; [ ] indicates a cell size of between 10 and 29 unweighted observations.

Sickness or disability however, appeared to have little impact on people's contact with neighbours: 80 per cent of sick or disabled people had regular contact with their neighbours, as did 77 per cent of unimpaired adults and 79 per cent of the total adult population. In other words, about 20 per cent of sick or disabled and 23 per cent of able-bodied people at some point experienced social isolation. Sick or disabled people

were therefore markedly more likely to be isolated from friends and relatives than from neighbours. Persistent social isolation from friends and
relatives was almost twice the level amongst sick or disabled people as
amongst able-bodied people, whereas the reverse was the case for social
isolation from neighbours.

RETIRED PEOPLE

Low income and poverty amongst pensioners have been UK policy makers'
concern for some time. The country's Basic State Retirement Pension
(BSRP) pays a flat-rate £67.50 per week to single persons and £40.80 per
week to wives and retired adult dependants (1999/2000), which keeps pensioners' incomes very close to the poverty line. Since pensioners increasingly supplement their state pension with occupational and private
pensions, poverty is now concentrated amongst older pensioners who only
receive the state pension (Walker *et al.*, 2000).

Income Poverty

Of retired people aged 45 or over, 23 per cent reported incomes below the
poverty line in both 1995 and 1996 (Table 7.11). This was more than a third
higher than the national poverty rate of 15 per cent, but only about half the
level of the official rate of pensioner poverty, which only includes people

*Table 7.11   Income poverty dynamics: retired people, adults over 45 years,
UK, ECHP, 1995–6*

Income poverty	Remained in life course group (%)	Never in life course group (%)	All adults (16+) (%)
Transitions			
Persistence rate	80	68	77
Exit rate	20	32	23
Entrance rate	9	3	6
Avoidance rate	91	97	94
Turnover			
Remained in poverty	23	7	15
Exited poverty	5	3	4
Entered poverty	6	3	5
Never in poverty	67	87	76
Base (unweighted)	1 587	1 363	6 645

over the state pension age (40 per cent; DSS, 2000c). Just over one-third of retired people (34 per cent) experienced income poverty in 1995 or 1996, or in both years, compared to 24 per cent of the total adult population.

The transition rates revealed that retired people suffered an increased risk of becoming poor and a decreased chance of exiting from a state of income poverty. Only 20 per cent of retired people in poverty in 1995 were no longer poor in 1996, compared to 32 per cent who were never retired (and 23 per cent of the all-adult population). Moreover, 9 per cent of retired people who were not poor in 1995 had become poor by 1996, compared to 3 per cent of the non-retired population. Retirement therefore substantially increased the risk of becoming and remaining poor. This was also apparent from turnover and transition statistics for people who retired between 1995 and 1996 (data not shown). Individuals amongst this group who were not poor in 1995 were nearly twice as likely to experience income poverty in 1996 (11 per cent) than people who retired in both years and had not been poor in 1995 (6 per cent). In fact, the inflow into income poverty amongst people retiring between the years almost doubled the poverty rate amongst this group, from 12 per cent to 22 per cent. Aggregate poverty rates amongst people retired in both years, in contrast, remained largely unchanged (1995: 28 per cent; 1996: 29 per cent).

For the majority of retired people in the UK, pensions were the main source of their income (men: 76 per cent; women: 78 per cent). A further 14 per cent of men and 8 per cent of women received the main part of their income from social transfers other than pensions, while other main income sources were private intergenerational and intra-household transfers (men: 4 per cent; women: 6 per cent) and wages or salaries (men: 5 per cent; women: 4 per cent).

Although pensions in the UK, in particular state pensions, tend to be low by international comparison, they nevertheless constituted an important buffer against poverty. Without their public, occupational or private pension incomes, an additional 51 per cent of retired adults would have been in poverty in the UK in 1995. Social transfers other than pensions prevented 19 per cent of retired people from falling below the poverty line.

Deprivation

As for the other three risk groups, income poverty and deprivation often went hand in hand for retired people. Once again, the greatest risk was posed by deprivation of basic household and personal necessities: 25 per cent of people who were retired throughout the period were deprived of necessities during this time, compared to a national all-adult average of 11 per cent

Table 7.12   Deprivation of necessities dynamics: retired adults, adults over 45 years, UK, ECHP, 1995–6

Deprivation of necessities	Remained in life course group (%)	Entered life course group (%)	All adults (16+) (%)
Transitions			
Persistence rate	66	67	64
Exit rate	34	33	36
Entrance rate	7	*	6
Avoidance rate	93	Over 90	94
Turnover			
Remained in deprivation	25	42	11
Exited deprivation	11	*	6
Entered deprivation	12	*	5
Never in deprivation	52	47	78
Base (unweighted)	1527	96	6355

Note: * indicates a cell size of less than 10 unweighted observations.

(Table 7.12). This figure increased to 42 per cent amongst adults over 45 who retired between 1995 and 1996. In other words, a disproportionately large number of people retiring were already deprived (and poor – see above) before they retired. In fact, the incidence of deprivation prior to retirement was considerably higher than the incidence of income poverty (11 per cent) for individuals retiring between 1995 and 1996.

Persistent or emerging income poverty amongst retired people added to the risk of deprivation of necessities. Whereas 12 per cent of retired people who were poor in both years or became poor in 1996 also became deprived of necessities in 1996, this was true for only 3 per cent of retired people who avoided poverty throughout this period. A similar share of retired people who were poor throughout the period or became poor in the second year were deprived of necessities throughout the period (28 per cent and 26 per cent, respectively).

Social Isolation

Finally, income poverty also had an adverse effect on the social interactions of retired adults. Retired people engaged in activities, such as club membership and meeting friends and family and talking to neighbours, to a similar extent to that of the population at large (Table 7.13). In fact, more retired people reported talking to their neighbours (86 per cent) than was the case for the adult population (79 per cent). However, whereas poverty had only a small impact on activities involving clubs and societies, or friends and relatives, it strongly affected interaction with neighbours. Poor retired people were less likely to talk to their neighbours regularly (81 per cent) than were non-poor retirees (88 per cent). In contrast, amongst the all-adult population, the non-poor adults were less likely to be in contact with their neighbours (78 per cent) than poor adults (81 per cent). Although it would only be fair to acknowledge that the level of contact in all four cases remained high, poverty amongst retired people nevertheless exerted a negative effect on contact with neighbours, which did not occur amongst the all-adult population.

Table 7.13   Income poverty and social isolation dynamics (turnover): retired people, UK, ECHP, 1995–6

	Retired adults		All adults (16+)	
Social isolation	Remained in poverty (%)	Never in poverty (%)	Remained in poverty (%)	Never in poverty (%)
Not a member of a club				
Remained in exclusion	57	37	57	39
Exited exclusion	11	8	11	10
Entered exclusion	[8]	8	8	11
Never in exclusion	24	48	24	41
Talking to neighbours				
Remained in exclusion	[5]	4	5	9
Exited exclusion	[5]	4	5	7
Entered exclusion	[9]	3	9	6
Never in exclusion	81	88	81	78
Meeting friends/relatives				
Remained in exclusion	[8]	9	8	8
Exited exclusion	9	7	9	8
Entered exclusion	[9]	7	9	8
Never in exclusion	75	78	75	77
Base (unweighted)	338	1072	891	5156

Notes:
[1] Adults only: 'talks to neighbours less than once a week'.
[2] Adults only: 'meets friends or relatives (not living with the person) at home or elsewhere, less than once a week'.
All adults (16+) means all adults 16 years of age and over, including those above state retirement age; [ ] indicates a cell size of between 10 and 29 unweighted observations.

SUMMARY AND POLICY IMPLICATIONS

This chapter has highlighted the increased risk of income poverty and deprivation, and social isolation that 'risk' and 'life course' groups faced in the UK. Whilst socioeconomic characteristics, such as a person's level of educational achievement or employment status, in many instances contributed to the risk of income poverty and deprivation amongst these groups, the analysis also revealed that life cycle and risk transitions independently added to these risks.

Movements into or out of income poverty were often closely matched by similar movements into or out of deprivation. This association between income poverty and deprivation was particularly true for deprivation of durables, and household and personal necessities. It was universally absent for deprivation of household amenities and of housing, which included features such as the quality of the neighbourhood. For this reason, a discussion of the latter evidence has been omitted from this chapter. However, the distinction between, on the one hand, consumer durables and household and personal necessities and, on the other hand, housing and housing amenities, was an important one. With few exceptions, household amenities and (quality) housing were 'public goods' provided or regulated by the state sector. In contrast, consumer durables and household and personal necessities were private goods, whose provision or acquisition were largely a matter for individuals to decide. The lack of evidence of deprivation concerning public goods suggested that public provision of goods, by and large, met basic needs and contributed to reducing the risk of deprivation. However, social, social security and economic policy failed to ensure that risk groups enjoyed financial security on a par with that of the adult population at large. In the following, the public policy implications of these findings are discussed for each of the groups.

Young Adults

As this analysis has shown, young adults in the UK experienced similar income poverty and deprivation dynamics to that of the all-adult population, but they were more susceptible to transitions into and out of poverty and deprivation, even over a short period. Those who were living alone or in work-poor households, who had poor educational status and who were unemployed or economically inactive were at greatest risk of poverty and deprivation.

Young adults in the UK, especially those below the age of 25, are excluded from a number of key social security benefits, including Income Support and Housing Benefit. In addition, whilst young people are entitled to means-tested Jobseeker's Allowance (JSA), the insurance-based unem-ployment benefit, contributory Jobseeker's Allowance, excludes young people from eligibility until they have met the minimum contribution requirements, based on earnings, which many – even amongst the adult pop-ulation – do not. Moreover, even for those in the labour market, especially with few educational or occupational qualifications, steady earnings at a sufficiently high level to protect them from income poverty and deprivation are often only achieved after several years of continuous employment.

Current government policy seeks to improve the standard of national education and encourage young people to stay on at school or college beyond the school leaving age. Through the 'New Deal' policies, the govern-ment also looks towards moving unemployed young people directly into work, while retaining supplementary options of human resource develop-ment and job skills training. The direct link between income poverty and deprivation for this group suggests that many young adults might be unable to cope with setbacks in their income. Employment policy would benefit from considering ways and means to help young people maintain as well as obtain jobs, and to accelerate improving their earnings potential. Education policy would be well advised to take account of the finding that participation in training or education significantly enhanced the risk of poverty. Although financial incentives as currently piloted under the Educational Maintenance Allowance (a weekly, means-tested allowance paid to students for attendance and achievement in further education) might help to increase participation rates, if the incentives are at too low a level they will fail to address this risk of poverty amongst students and trainees. A long-term view of policy making would aim to improve the material well-being of young adults, by integrating strategies for security and progression in education and work, and from education into work.

Lone Mothers

Lone mothers in the UK faced the highest risk of poverty amongst all four risk and life course groups, and the highest risk amongst the five countries in the comparative study. A high proportion of them relied on social secur-ity benefits as their main source of income. Only a minority of lone mothers was in employment, which, in the UK, typically is low-paid. Together, these substantially increased the risk of income poverty in this group.

The UK government has introduced the New Deal for Lone Parents, a voluntary scheme whereby those who wish to work or train can be helped to obtain placements. It is well established that lone parents frequently would like to work, but many have found it difficult to obtain employment offering sufficient pay for their child care needs. The recently introduced

Childcare Tax Credit, payable to all parents, is designed to do just that, but it is too early to say where it is meeting its objective of helping lone parents to (re-) enter the labour market.

The government is also promoting 'family-friendly working' at the workplace. This campaign is designed to encourage employers to consider the child care needs of their employees, allow flexible working practice or even provide access to child care facilities. The immediate impact of this campaign is likely to be limited, as it incorporates few direct measures to improve working practices to accommodate the needs of parents.

However, access to child care is not the only barrier to employment that lone mothers face. Many prefer to stay with and look after their children rather than go out to work, especially when the children are young (Ford, 1996). Employment is, therefore, unlikely ever entirely to remove the threat of poverty and deprivation amongst lone parents, and paid work does not guarantee their protection from poverty (Finlayson and Marsh, 1998). Even in countries with high employment rates, a core of poor and deprived lone parents persists, many of whom choose not to work, or simply cannot work, because of their parental commitments (Bradshaw *et al.*, 2000). For these lone parents, improved social security and child support may be the most appropriate tools for helping prevent, or at least reduce, the current high levels of poverty.

Sick or Disabled People

After lone parents, sick or disabled people experienced the highest levels of poverty and deprivation in the UK in 1995 and 1996. Sickness or disability particularly affected social relations, decreasing the contact between sick or disabled people and their friends and family. The findings highlighted the limited personal resources, both material and in terms of social networks, at their disposal. The high incidence of poverty was a measure of the added costs of impairment to sick or disabled people. More longitudinal data would be required to assess the impact of social security on protecting sick or disabled people from long-term poverty and deprivation. Further analysis would also benefit our understanding of the causal linkages between social isolation and sickness or disability, and the impact of the former on the life chances of people with impairment.

Government policy for disabled people centres on the New Deal for Disabled People and stricter tests on Incapacity Benefit claimants' ability to work, which both seek to reduce the number of sick or disabled people receiving state benefit and to increase their number in employment. As for other risk groups, employment might reduce the risk of poverty and deprivation amongst sick or disabled people. It might also help re-balance the relative deficit in social networks of many sick or disabled people. The depth of disadvantage that this group experiences, however, should warn against expectations of quick solutions and easy remedies, modelled on those in place for less disadvantaged groups. Work will also only ever be a solution for those who are physically and mentally in a position to pursue some kind of employment. The challenge is to ensure that, for those who cannot, the social security that they receive protects them from poverty and deprivation.

Retired People

In international comparison, the experience of poverty placed the UK's retired population between retirees in the two Latin Rim countries, Portugal and Greece, and the two corporate welfare states, Austria and Germany (Table 7.14). However, the UK's retired people suffered a relatively greater risk of deprivation of household and personal necessities, owing to the high chance of deprivation before retirement and the sharp impact of income poverty during retirement on the risk of deprivation. The UK and Greece were the only two countries in which deprivation rates amongst retired people were higher than their poverty rates.

Table 7.14   Income poverty, deprivation and social isolation rates, UK, ECHP, 1995–6

	Poverty rank and (%)	Necessities deprivation rank and (%)	Friends & family exclusion rank[1] and (%)
Germany	8 (1)	10 (2)	82 (2)
Austria	14 (2)	7 (1)	108 (4)
Britain	28(3)	36 (4)	106 (3)
Portugal	38 (5)	25 (3)	133 (5)
Greece	33(4)	44 (5)	73 (1)

Note: [1]Exclusion rate of those who 'remained in income poverty' over those 'never in poverty'.

The average income poverty rate of retired people of 24 per cent in 1995 and 1996 masked considerable variation in income poverty rates between 'younger' and 'older' retired people, that is, people retired who are below or above the retirement age. Poverty and deprivation during retirement often result from low earnings and low insurance contributions during a person's working life, which may ultimately lead to exclusion from pension rights.

Small pensions and low supplementary benefits can exacerbate the risk of poverty and deprivation.

The New Deal for the Over 50s offers financial incentives to encourage and help older workers who are unemployed for six months or more to return to employment, including part-time work. The policy seeks to increase income from earnings amongst older people, but should ultimately also increase national insurance contributions and might thus positively affect older people's entitlement to a state pension. However, it is unlikely to redress the gender imbalance of pension provisions in the UK. Moving the over-50s back into frequently low-paid or part-time work, as it does at present, might also do little to increase pension entitlement in the long term.

Those aged between 50 and the retirement age accounted for about a fifth of the retired population in the UK in 1995–6. Income poverty was less severe amongst this group, who were only approximately half as likely to be experiencing incomes below the poverty line (16 per cent) than were adults above the retirement age (28 per cent). Government policy places considerable emphasis on assisting working-age people approaching retirement in and into work, including legislating for new, third-tier pension provisions. However, policy aimed at securing current pensioners' incomes and standard of living has been more haphazard. Suggestions that increases in pensions might once again be linked to wages, rather than prices, as has been the case since 1986, have not been followed up. The replacement of the pension–wages link by the pensions–retail price index link was originally blamed for the relative decline in the value of pensions in recent decades. However, a Minimum Income Guarantee (MIG) for pensioners has been introduced, but this only ensures that state pensions equal the current level of Income Support, which is unlikely to greatly reduce pensioners' risk of poverty. Moreover, the adjustment is not automatic, and pensioners whose state pensions are below Income Support must apply for the increase.

Finally, as this analysis has shown, for many people in these four risk groups access to the labour market is difficult and often completely out of their reach. This is most obvious for retired people, many sick or disabled people, and lone mothers, but also applies to young adults, be they in education or training, or in low-waged entry jobs. But the government's anti-poverty strategy largely rests on increasing the labour market attachment of poor people and benefit recipients in particular. This is important – paid work, and progression in work, may for some or many be the way out of poverty or deprivation – but financial security must remain available at adequate levels to those for whom employment is not the answer. The UK's flat-rate, residual benefit system rarely succeeds in moving people of any age or households of any composition above the poverty line (Mitchell,

1991; Behrendt, 2000). Moreover, between 15 and 20 per cent of those eligible do not take up their benefit entitlements, lower than in many other European countries (van Oorschot, 1991). Britain's social security system is cost-efficient, achieving redistribution of market incomes with limited tax and benefit resources, but has limited effectiveness in reducing poverty. This must be considered alongside policies to promote employment.

8. Tackling poverty and social exclusion

Christopher Heady and Graham Room

This chapter brings together the analysis in the preceding chapters and draws policy conclusions. As most of the analysis has been organized by country, a first step is to look for patterns across countries, and this is the subject of the first section below. This is followed by a discussion of the policy implications of the results, at the national and the European levels. Finally, some of the methodological issues that arose in our research are summarized.

CROSS-COUNTRY PATTERNS

This section proceeds by first looking at the results for each life course and risk group, in terms of both static and dynamic measures of poverty and deprivation. The links between the static and dynamic measures, and their policy relevance, are then discussed.

Retired People

On a static headcount basis, retired people experienced greater poverty than all adults in every country except Germany. Their poverty rates were even further above those of adults near to retirement: non-retired adults over 45. At the same time, their chances of poverty exit were slightly lower than for all adults and (with the exception of Portugal) non-retired adults over 45. These observations combined to produce a situation where retired people had a higher probability than both all adults and (even for Portugal) non-retired adults over 45 of experiencing poverty in two successive years, even in Germany. This contrast between the static and dynamic results for Germany provides an illustration of the importance of dynamic analysis in analysing the effectiveness of social policy. The higher incidence of persistent poverty amongst Germany's retired was particularly acute amongst women who were living alone and had low levels of educational attainment.

Although the reduced poverty exit rates for retired people resulted in higher persistent poverty, the fact that they were not even lower was surprising, given that retired people often have few opportunities for increasing their income. Although in Greece and Portugal some retired people had returned to work to supplement their pension incomes, for most this barely improved their financial situation. In Portugal, those who did work and receive a pension were more likely to have low education levels and be self-employed. Women in general, and widowed or single men or women, were most likely to have been working while drawing a pension or other social benefits. Pensions remained in most cases the retired person's main source of income. In other words, additional earnings tended to be low and insufficient to lift people out of poverty.

The factors that were most strongly associated with movements into poverty were changing from living with a partner to living alone and (with the exception of Greece) moving from all other household members working to no household members working. There was not such a clear pattern of factors associated with moving out of poverty but the movement from other household members working to no household members working reduced the probability of escaping poverty in Austria, Germany and Greece.

These findings suggest that the movement into retirement is likely to be associated with an increased risk of moving into poverty. However, it is not conclusive proof, as the people we observe in retirement are different from those that we observe before retirement. For example, people who are now just before retirement may have better pension entitlements than people who retired several years ago. What is really required is the observation of particular individuals moving from work into retirement. Unfortunately, the ECHP samples for most of the study countries do not include a sufficient number of people moving into retirement between wave 2 and wave 3 to draw any statistically reliable conclusions. However, the data for Greece are, at least, consistent with the hypothesis: people entering retirement were more likely to enter poverty and less likely to escape poverty than either those who had been retired in both years or those who had not been retired in either year. Also people over 45 who move into retirement have twice the probability of entering poverty as other adults.

As one would expect from the poverty figures, retired people generally experienced greater material deprivation than all adults and, particularly, non-retired people over 45. This was clearest for deprivation of necessities, where all countries showed a lower exit rate and a higher rate of two-year deprivation for retired people. For deprivation of durables, all countries but Germany showed a comparatively high exit rate for retired people as compared to all adults, but they still suffered a higher rate of two-year deprivation in all countries apart from Austria. Finally, both Austria and Germany showed a lower rate of two-year deprivation of amenities for retired people than for all adults, although only Austria maintained this when the comparison was with non-retired people over 45.

Sick or Disabled People

In all the study countries, sick or disabled people suffered a higher rate of poverty than both all adults and all adults under state retirement age, on a static headcount basis. Strikingly, the transitions out of poverty of sick or disabled people, across all countries, put this group at a disadvantage over its comparison group (adults below retirement age and not sick). Even in comparison to all adults, only in Portugal did the exit chances of sick or disabled people match those of other healthy adults. Clearly, sickness and disability had a strong additional 'inhibiting' impact on people's ability to cope with and escape poverty. In the insurance-based systems this can be explained by their inability to have been in employment and, therefore, to have gained sufficiently substantial contributions. This meant that sick and disabled people were substantially more likely to be poor in two successive years than both all other adults and those adults below retirement age.

There is some evidence that the risk of sick or disabled people becoming or remaining poor was greater for people over 45 and those with low levels of education. As one would expect, the data for Greece show that being out of work increased the chances of entering poverty, while finding a job increased the chance of exit. Unfortunately, small sample sizes meant that it was impossible to tell whether actual movement into sickness or disability increased the risk of falling into poverty.

The greater propensity of sick or disabled people to become, and often also to remain, poor in most countries was probably the result of this group experiencing increased costs of living when their incomes were falling. Sick or disabled people said that they found it more difficult than their comparison group to meet personal needs, and they generally experienced an increased risk of suffering material deprivation and a decreased chance of escaping this deprivation. The only case in which the sick and disabled had a lower probability of material deprivation in two successive years than other adults was amenities deprivation in Austria.

Young Adults

Compared to other transition groups in this study, young adults were at a lower risk of poverty. In all countries apart from Germany, they had a lower headcount ratio than all adults. In addition, they had a higher chance of escaping poverty than other adults. So, except in Germany, young people had a lower chance of being in poverty for two successive years than other adults.

Germany was the notable exception to this pattern of low poverty amongst young adults. As in the other countries, young adults experienced poverty exit rates that were higher than those of the whole adult population. However, Germany was the only country in which the poverty entrance rate was substantially higher than that of the adult population. It is difficult to speculate about the reasons for this difference. It may be the result of young adults in Germany spending comparatively more time in higher education, or the greater incidence of single household living, both of which were found to be associated with increased poverty rates in that country.

Across all countries, unemployment and inactivity were highly correlated with an increased chance of moving into and remaining in poverty. The chances of moving into and out of poverty were also influenced by changes in household composition, but the effects varied widely between countries.

In contrast to their relatively good poverty position, young adults were more likely to suffer material deprivation, in all three categories, than all adults. In the cases of necessities and amenities, this was offset to some extent by a higher exit rate in all countries apart from the UK (and Austria for amenities). The chances of escape were more mixed for deprivation of durables. Generally, Greece and Portugal stood out as countries where young people were able to escape deprivation at a high rate, with the result that (with the exception of durables in Greece) their probability of being deprived in two successive years was lower than for all other adults.

Lone Parents

Lone parents, who were mainly lone mothers, had a higher static headcount poverty rate than all adults and than partnered mothers. Also, with the exception of Greece, they had a lower chance of exiting from poverty than all adults. Thus they had a substantially higher risk of experiencing poverty in two successive years.

It is most instructive to distinguish between lone parents with dependent children and lone parents with only non-dependent children. In Austria, Germany and the UK, lone parents with dependent children experienced higher poverty entrance and lower poverty exit rates than partnered mothers. In the UK, this was most likely a reflection of high levels of economic inactivity and unemployment amongst lone parents. Moreover, even where lone parents were in work, their employment was most likely to be part-time, thus reducing their earnings potential. As a result, many lone parents relied on low-level social assistance to top up their low earnings, or as their only source of income. In contrast, in Germany and Austria, employment rates amongst lone mothers were considerably higher and proportionately more recorded earnings as their main source of income. This was reflected in this group's lower poverty and deprivation rates. However, German and Austrian lone mothers not in work were often only entitled to low-level social assistance. Only in rare instances did their past insurance contributions entitle them to unemployment insurance benefit. For these women, exiting from poverty was particularly difficult perhaps because of attachment to the labour market weakening with time. In all three countries, lone parents also encountered a lack of available and/or affordable child care facilities.

The position of lone mothers with non-dependent children was somewhat different. In the UK, lone mothers with non-dependent children were as likely to exit from poverty as partnered mothers with non-dependent children, and in Germany and Greece their poverty exit rates were higher than those of partnered mothers. This was the result of household members providing an income in addition to that obtained by the lone parent, and perhaps of maintenance payments received from absent parents. In fact, in Germany it appeared that other household members provided additional income that was in excess of that typical for households of partnered mothers.

In Austria, lone mothers with non-dependent children experienced a very much lower poverty exit rate than partnered mothers. In Portugal, the exit rate was slightly lower. This suggests that other household members did not provide, or were not capable of providing, the additional income that would have lifted lone mothers out of poverty.

With the partial exception of Austria, the poor experience of lone parents in terms of poverty was reproduced in terms of material deprivation: they experienced lower rates of exit from all forms of deprivation and had a higher probability of experiencing deprivation in two successive years than the rest of the population and partnered mothers.

Links between Static and Dynamic Poverty and Deprivation Measures

In most cases, the static and dynamic measures of poverty reinforce each other. In most countries, the retired, the sick or disabled and lone mothers experienced both a higher poverty headcount ratio and a lower chance of escaping poverty than the rest of the population. Similarly, young people had a lower headcount ratio and a higher chance of escaping poverty. Thus differences in the chances of suffering poverty in two successive years ('sustained poverty') between a life course group and its comparator simply magnify the differences in the static headcount ratio.

However, there are exceptions. Retired people in Germany had a lower headcount ratio but a lower exit rate, with the result that the chance of sustained poverty was higher than for other adults. Young adults in Germany had a higher headcount ratio despite having a similar exit rate to other adults, because they had a higher entry rate into poverty. Similarly, Greek lone parents had a higher headcount ratio despite a higher exit rate.

Exceptions become much more common when attention is turned from poverty measures to material deprivation measures. For example, young adults in several countries have higher exit rates from material deprivation than other adults, despite the fact that they suffer higher headcount ratios. Retired people also show a mixed pattern in terms of the relationship between headcount ratios and exit rates, especially for durables deprivation. The groups that show the greatest consistency between static and dynamic measures are the sick or disabled and lone parents.

To a considerable extent, this lack of consistency reflects the imperfect correlation between poverty and material deprivation, which results from at least three factors. First, the extent of a person's material deprivation depends on a past history of acquiring goods and housing, and so does not respond immediately to changes in money income. Second, some people learn to cope better with low incomes than others. Third, particularly in the case of sick or disabled people (and arguably in the case of lone parents), the scales that are used to calculate equivalent income do not reflect the additional costs of living that their circumstances involve.

There are two policy implications of these observations. First, as these different measures of financial and material deprivation can differ substantially from each other, they should all be monitored to obtain a complete picture of the effects of policy. Second, it is important in designing policy to decide which indicator, or group of indicators, is the target of the policy. It is not enough simply to address 'deprivation'. In a world of limited resources for social programmes, a choice has to be made between the indicators which represent the most severe aspects of hardship.

NATIONAL POLICY IMPLICATIONS

The pattern across countries and groups suggests that it is unlikely that one policy can address the problem of poverty among a single population group in all countries, or of all groups in a single country. However, these patterns also suggest that there is scope for policy learning between individual countries within, but also between, risk categories. Each country's peculiar circumstances will frequently make policy responses unique and idiosyncratic, and these are discussed in the individual country chapters.

However, this does not mean that policies will be exclusive and that single-country solutions must be the result.

The analysis in this book has highlighted a number of overarching themes or policy issues, which concerned transition groups in all countries, but also the countries' populations in general. These include the following.

- *Gender:* poverty and deprivation disproportionately affect women. Lone mothers and female pensioners are at particular risk of poverty or deprivation. Women often face retirement without the security of an adequate pension, and unemployment without benefit entitlement, because of gaps in their contribution records. These come about as a result of past caring or household management responsibilities and a greater incidence of part-time work. To the present day, women across Europe suffer the consequences of the neglect of their independent welfare rights by social security systems, which assumed that men would go out to work and women would stay at home. The scale of disadvantage experienced by women across countries and transition groups calls for a concerted effort to tackle the gendered nature of poverty and disadvantage, and to address the continued gender inequality in the labour market.

- *Single households:* the proportion of single-person households amongst all households is growing across Europe. This book shows that such households are at increased risk of poverty and deprivation, presumably because of the absence of anybody to contribute resources. Public policy needs to respond to this increased risk.

- *Work and wages:* evidence from this book confirms that people entering full-time employment often also manage to escape or avoid poverty. Part-time employment, by contrast, is less likely an exit route from poverty. The last two decades have seen income inequality and worklessness in households rise in many parts of Europe (Gregg and Wadsworth, 1996). National employment growth can counter growing joblessness unequally distributed across socioeconomic groups. But the link between employment creation and the take-up of work, on the one hand, and poverty, on the other, can be tenuous. A large proportion of people in poverty today are, in fact, employed. Across the northern half of Europe, national governments are implementing new programmes designed to move people off welfare into employment. These governments would be well advised to take account of the possible limits on the sustainability and internal progression to improved pay that welfare-to-work employment may offer. In the southern parts of Europe, the problem may yet be greater where national economies or important sectors of these economies are comparatively weak, perhaps lacking international competitiveness, and where wages are low.

IMPLICATIONS FOR THE EUROPEAN POLICY AGENDA[1]

The research project that has formed the basis of this book and its companion volume (Barnes *et al.*, 2002) was launched in 1997. During the period since then, the EU has steadily strengthened its commitment to combating social exclusion. The Amsterdam Treaty of May 1997 made the combating of exclusion an explicit objective of the Community (Treaty establishing the European Community, Article 136). However, it is not only policies which directly address social exclusion that are relevant. As our research underlines, processes of social exclusion are inextricably linked to other economic, social and political developments: for example, changes in employment opportunities and in social protection systems.

During the Autumn of 1997, the Luxembourg Employment Summit established a new framework for a concerted policy for employment, in part to promote social inclusion through an active employment strategy. During the same period, the European Commission sought to reactivate and organize Community debates on social protection through a series of Communications. Finally, the Lisbon and Nice Summits of March and December 2000 defined a new set of strategic goals for the Union, designed to create a knowledge-based economy, but recognizing the new risks of social exclusion that this might generate and the consequent imperative for policies to promote social inclusion. It is by reference to these important steps that the policy significance of our findings at European level can be viewed.

The Luxembourg Employment Strategy

Indebted to the Delors White Paper on *Growth, Competitiveness and Employment* of 1993, and the Essen Summit of 1994, the Luxembourg Employment Summit of Autumn 1997 established the framework for concerted action under four pillars: employability, adaptability, entrepreneurship and equal opportunities. This framework has subsequently become the basis for an annual cycle of national reporting and multilateral benchmarking. Our research findings illuminate the implications of two of these pillars in particular for measures to combat social exclusion: employability and equal opportunities.

'Employability' includes reference to the transition from school to work, training and lifelong learning. Our research findings similarly give a central place to education and training, and human resource policies in the workplace, as a means of securing the social integration of young people in particular. However, they also highlight the barriers to education and training that are posed by governmental attempts to impose a growing proportion of the costs on the individuals concerned. As noted earlier in this chapter, the dynamic analysis which is presented in this volume reveals that the risks of poverty and deprivation that young people face are not entirely straightforward: a lower risk of poverty than for the adult population in general, and greater chance of a quick escape, but higher rates of material deprivation.

'Equal opportunities' includes measures to reconcile work and family life, something of particular importance for lone mothers. Our findings confirm that everywhere employment is (with re-partnering) the surest route out of poverty for lone parents, with the availability of child care facilities crucial to enabling them to take advantage of opportunities. Our evidence that persistence of poverty is stronger among lone parents than among adults in general underlines the potential importance of policies that build bridges between home and work.

Developments in Social Protection

The modernization of social protection systems has been a further area of concerted debate, if not action, at EU level. These systems grew piecemeal in response to industrialization at a time when individuals' lives tended to be rather static: geographically, relationally and economically. In a postmodern society, all these aspects of life are characterized by rapid change. Our findings confirm the importance of social transfer payments in reducing levels of poverty among elderly and sick or disabled people in particular, although our dynamic analysis confirms that for these groups persistence of poverty remains strong. These are the 'traditional' targets of social protection systems. Our findings are, however, also consistent with the argument that the inherited social protection systems deal less effectively with those groups of the population whose vulnerability is a feature of recent decades – young people and lone parents.

Two Communications from the European Commission, relating to social protection, have appeared during the period of this project (European Commission, 1997, 1999b). Among the issues upon which these Communications focus are three in particular to which our research findings are relevant.

First is the individualization of social rights, with particular reference to women, so that their social protection is no longer subsidiary to that of a male breadwinner, especially given the precarious nature of modern family relationships. As our findings confirm, poverty and deprivation affect women disproportionately: especially lone mothers and female pensioners. As is increasingly recognized, their social insurance contribution records, commonly less complete than their male counterparts' when earnings are interrupted, because of caring and home management responsibilities, can no longer be assumed to be cushioned by those of a partner.

A second issue is combining minimum income benefits with active pathways to enable reintegration into the labour market, as part of a wider strategy to make social protection more employment-friendly. As our findings confirm, full-time employment is the most common route out of poverty. However, much low-paid work remains, and in some countries there is growing polarization between work-rich and work-poor households. Making social protection more employment-friendly may therefore not suffice as a strategy for promoting social inclusion, even among those of working age.

Thirdly measures are needed to secure the sustainability of public pension schemes, as part of the effort to adapt social protection to the demographic ageing of the population. Our findings underline that, while poverty among older people is in general less severe than it was a generation ago, they continue to enjoy a substantially lower standard of living than the rest of the population, notably in the southern countries and the UK. Poverty among the elderly has by no means been abolished and, for those who are poor, persistence is more likely than for the adult population as a whole. During the coming decades, new cohorts of pensioners will include substantial numbers of people with contribution records interrupted by the high unemployment of recent decades; at the same time, we must expect growing political resistance by those of working age to supporting an expanding pensioner generation. The sustainability of public pension schemes in face of this twin challenge must be in doubt; worsening poverty among such pensioners the growing risk.

The Lisbon and Nice Summits: Concertation of National Plans for Social Inclusion

The Lisbon Summit of March 2000 defined a new set of strategic goals for the Union, designed to create a knowledge-based economy, but recognizing the new risks of social exclusion that this might generate and the consequent imperative for policies to promote social inclusion. During 2000, the High Level Group on Social Protection, established under the Finnish presidency the previous Autumn, had the task of agreeing indicators which could then be used as benchmarks for national policies to combat social exclusion. The Nice Summit of December 2000 asked member states to submit by June 2001 national action plans covering a two-year period, with indicators and monitoring mechanisms capable of measuring progress (Presidency Conclusions, 2000, para. 18). The European Commission and the Council have agreed a proposal for a new action programme in this field, a key part of which is to improve understanding of social exclusion (European Commission, 2000c).

The relevance of our own work for these developments is twofold: on the one hand in relation to the indicators that have been proposed, on the other to the portrait of social exclusion that emerges from the national action plans. As far as cross-nationally comparative indicators are concerned, the main focus of the official discussions is upon appropriate monetary and non-monetary indicators (corresponding to what we have here referred to as poverty and non-monetary material deprivation) and upon the persistence of such situations of disadvantage over time (Social Protection Committee, 2001; Atkinson *et al.*, 2002; European Commission, 2001). However, the dynamic analysis presented in the present volume suggests that it is also important to have indicators revealing how many people – and in what types of situation – are at high risk of downward trajectories into long-term exclusion. It has, admittedly, been difficult to produce robust conclusions on the basis of such a small number of waves of the ECHP.

Nevertheless, and taking account also of findings emerging from other studies, it is evident that particular risks and transition situations are disproportionately associated with such negative trajectories. Thus, for example, UK studies reveal that childhood poverty, unwanted teenage pregnancy and lack of qualifications on leaving school are all powerful predictors of adverse outcomes in adulthood (Hobcraft, 1998; Hobcraft and Kiernan, 1999). It is important that indicators adopted for policy monitoring at EU level should not be limited to mapping the distribution of disadvantage across the population, but should also identify situations of prospective cumulative and catastrophic disadvantage.

The National Action Plans for Social Inclusion, to which member states committed themselves at the Lisbon Summit, were submitted in June 2001 and were then the subject of a review by the Commission, as part of the Lisbon process of peer review. The action plans provide a portrait of social exclusion and an assessment of national policies to combat social exclusion not attempted by the EU institutions since the EU Observatory on National Policies to Combat Social Exclusion was wound up in 1994 (European Commission, 1991, 1992, 1994). The national action plans, and the Commission's overview report, are consistent with our own analysis of the major risk factors within the countries of the EU, while lacking the detailed empirical findings which our own work supplies. What the plans also do, however, is to highlight certain new risks that are emerging and that were not anticipated when the ECHP was established and that could not, therefore, be taken into account in our own work: most obviously, the risks of exclusion within the information society (European Commission, 2001, p. 15). Just as new risk groups – for example, young people and lone parents – emerged in the late twentieth century and made evident that social protection systems were oriented to the risks of an earlier period, so now new risks of exclusion are rapidly emerging, that will place new demands not only on our social systems but also on the data systems by means of which such risks can be monitored.

METHODOLOGICAL ISSUES

The EU institutions and the member states have recognized that, for effective policies to be developed and monitored, an improved understanding of social exclusion is first required. We believe that the findings from our research, as set out in the preceding pages and in the companion volume (Barnes *et al.*, 2002), make a significant contribution to this understanding and can thereby help to equip the EU with the means to carry forward its new policy commitments.

Eurostat is already planning the successor to the ECHP (*Statistics on Income and Living Conditions* – EU-SILC: see Eurostat, 2001). We believe that our experience, methodology and findings should be taken into account in deciding the conceptual, methodological and logistical basis for the new generation of data instruments which may be established for the monitoring of social exclusion. Some of our methodological innovations could usefully be incorporated into future work in this field. Thus, for example, our methodology for weighting different elements of multidimensional disadvantage, by reference to the prevalence of the disadvantage in question within the population as a whole, provides an unusual and, we think, defensible method for assessing a particular deprivation relative to the population in which it is found: a precise analogue to the definition of relative financial poverty lines.

The difficulties we faced also provide some lessons. One was connected with the timing of the income data in particular, referring as they did to the year before the interview. Our analysis has also been vitiated by the small numbers of cases to be found in many cells of interest. Social exclusion and poverty are, thankfully, a minority fate in our relatively prosperous societies. This means, however, that, unless an instrument such as ECHP has national samples of more substantial size, the detailed analysis of social exclusion trajectories and transitions which might be hoped for will not be possible.

Our work also allows us to comment on the relative wealth and poverty of the ECHP questions for tapping different variables relevant to the analysis of social exclusion. The ECHP provides a useful array of questions concerned with social benefits and employment but those dealing with social relationships and with experience of education and training are more sparse. One of the gaps to which we have pointed concerns the role of parents in supporting their children's educational and employment development, something which appears to be crucial. It may be difficult to collect data on this, but additional questions could be included on the extent to which parents contribute (directly or indirectly) to the costs of education for post-school leaving age children, and on the constraints that people feel that they face in gaining access to education and training.

Finally, it is worth taking stock of the limitations of data instruments and indicators which focus on individuals and households, if social exclusion is to be monitored and understood. Such is of course the focus of the ECHP, on which our own work has relied. Such seems also to be the principal focus of the various attempts in official EU circles to define indicators which can be used as benchmarks for national policies to combat social exclusion (Social Protection Committee, 2001; Atkinson *et al.*, 2002; European Commission, 2001). This focus is too limited, in at least two respects.

First, the focus upon individuals and households means that no direct attention is given to the wider communities within which people live: communities whose collective quality of life can reinforce or moderate the deprivation which people experience at the individual or household level.[2] This collective quality of life includes the amenities that are available in these local communities, the collective organizations and social networks, the extent of environmental decay, pollution and crime. Even within national statistical systems, these factors are in general neglected, and poorly connected to statistical information about households:[3] it is therefore hardly surprising that at a European level the same reticence is evident. Nevertheless, this neglect can have important policy implications, if it diverts attention from policies which involve investments in local communities and if it encourages policy makers to think in terms of actions focused on individuals and households alone. There is, of course, every sign that policy makers are alert to this danger, and that they recognize that, in order to tackle social exclusion, community- and neighbourhood-based policies are also needed. This is evident, for example, in the criteria used by the EU structural funds to channel assistance to regions in difficulties and their use of community support frameworks, and in the neighbourhood-focused programmes instituted by many national governments. However, the available data instruments have yet to catch up.

Second, while the focus upon individuals and households enables the arithmetic of their misery to be monitored, it hardly suffices to illuminate the processes involved and it is therefore of only limited use in informing policy. To understand the processes involved would require information also in relation to the social and economic institutions which mediate these individual and household fates and which thereby shape the trajectories along which people go. The ECHP data can tell us that particular individuals were made redundant by their employers and that they descended into poverty; it casts no light on the decisions made by those employers, and the labour market regulations in regard to redundancy within which employers acted. The ECHP data can tell us that particular young people moved into further education and training, but tell us nothing about the selection mechanisms involved, filtering out some youngsters and opening up opportunities for others. In the preceding chapters we have sought at various points to suggest what policy implications may follow from our analysis of household situations, but they are no more than this – suggestions. Only with a fuller picture, bringing together information about institutional strategies, administrative processes, policy context and household-level experience, can the policy maker make informed decisions about policy reform.

As far as statistical methods are concerned, what this is likely to require is a certain pragmatism, matching household survey data (including panel data of the sort which the ECHP offers) with a variety of survey and administrative data from the wide range of agencies which shape the lives of those households. In terms of European data systems, a modest first step would be to secure better concertation than has existed in the past between, for example, the statistical work of Eurostat, the policy-driven information gathering of DG Employment and the social research sponsored by DG Research, all of which include substantial reference to social exclusion.

NOTES

1. This section builds on, and expands, the corresponding discussion in the final chapter of Barnes *et al.* (2002).
2. This was an important but neglected conclusion emerging from the European seminar organized under the auspices of the European Commission and the UK Department of Social Security in 1994, to inform European work on the Measurement and Analysis of Social Exclusion: see Room (1995, final chapter).
3. In the UK, the most recent Index of Local Conditions adopted by the Department for the Environment, Transport and the Regions, on the advice of a research team at the University of Oxford, seeks to incorporate some of these factors: see DETR (2000).

Bibliography

Adamy, Wilhelm and Johannes Steffen (1998), *Abseits des Wohlstands: Arbeitslosigkeit und neue Armut*, Darmstadt: Primus.

Almeida, J., L. Capucha, A. Costa, F. Machado, I. Nicolau and E. Reis (1992), *Exclusão Social – Factores e Tipos de Pobreza em Portugal*, Oeiras: Celta Editora.

Andreß, Hans-Jürgen (1999), *Leben in Armut: Analysen der Verhaltensweisen armer Haushalte mit Umfragedaten*, Opladen: Westdeutscher Verlag.

Apospori E. (1998), 'Analysis of data of 1996 Labour Force Survey and 1991 Census', in M. Liapi and K. Kylakou (eds), *First Scientific Report for the TSER-Project 'Self-employment activities concerning women and minorities'*, Athens: Diotima, Centre of Research in Women's Issues.

Atkinson A.B. (1998) 'Social exclusion, poverty and unemployment', in A.B. Atkinson and J. Hills (eds), *Exclusion, Employment and Opportunity*, Centre for the Analysis of Social Exclusion, paper no 4, LSE, pp. 1–20.

Atkinson, A.B., B. Cantillon, E. Marlier and B. Nolan (2002), *Social indicators: The EU and social inclusion*, Oxford: Oxford University Press.

Badelt, Christoph and Karin Heitzmann (1998), 'Policy Analysis Of Transitions – The Case of Austria', working paper for the EU T.S.E.R. research project on 'Family Structure, Labour Market Participation and the Dynamics of Social Exclusion', Vienna University of Economics and Business Administration.

Badelt, Christoph and August Österle (2001), *Grundzüge der Sozialpolitik: Spezieller Teil*, Vienna: Manz.

Badelt, Christoph, Andrea Holzmann-Jenkins, Christian Matul and August Österle (1997), *Analyse der Auswirkungen des Pflegevorsorgesystems*, Vienna: BMAGS.

Barnes, M., C. Heady, S. Middleton, J. Millar, F. Papadopoulos and P. Tsakloglou (2002), *Poverty and Social Exclusion in Europe*, Cheltenham, UK and Northampton, MA, USA: Edward Elgar.

Barreiros, L. (2000), 'Pobreza e Desigualdade: Portugal no contexto europeu', in CESIS *Pobreza e Exclusão Social – Percursos e Perspectivas da Investigação em Portugal*, Lisbon: CESIS.

Becker, Irene (1997), 'Die Entwicklung von Einkommensverteilung und Einkommensarmut in den alten Bundesländern von 1962 bis 1988', in

Irene Becker and Richard Hauser (eds), *Einkommensverteilung und Armut*, Frankfurt/M. and New York: Campus, pp. 43–62.

Becker, Irene and Richard Hauser (eds) (1997), *Einkommensverteilung und Armut. Deutschland auf dem Weg zur Vierfünftel-Gesellschaft*, Frankfurt/M. and New York: Campus.

Behrendt, C. (2000), 'Holes in the safety net? Social security and the alleviation of poverty in a comparative perspective', paper presented at the Year 2000 International Research Conference on Social Security, International Social Security Association, Helsinki, 25–7 September.

Bennett, F. and R. Walker (1998), *Working with work*, York: York Publishing Service for the Joseph Rowntree Foundation.

Berghman, J. (1995), 'Social exclusion in Europe: policy context and analytical framework', in Graham Room (ed.), *Beyond the Threshold: The Measurement and Analysis of Social Exclusion*, Bristol: Policy Press, pp.10–28.

Berthoud, R., J. Lakey and S. McKay (1993), *The economic problems of disabled people*, London: Policy Studies Institute.

Böhnke, Petra and Jan Delhey (1999), 'Lebensstandard und Armut im vereinten Deutschland', WZB-Diskussionspapier FS III 99–408, Wissenschaftszentrum Berlin für Sozialforschung.

Bradshaw, J. (1999), 'Child poverty in comparative perspective', *European Journal of Social Security*, 1(4), 383–404.

Bradshaw, J. and J. Millar (1991), *Lone parent families in the UK*, Department of Social Security Research Report no.6, London: HMSO.

Bradshaw, J., L.I. Terum and A. Skevik (2000), 'Lone Parenthood in the 1990s: New challenges, new responses?', paper presented at the Year 2000 International Research Conference on Social Security, International Social Security Association, Helsinki, 25–7 September.

Bruto da Costa, A. and M. Silva (eds) (1985), *A Pobreza em Portugal*, Lisbon: Cáritas.

Buhmann B., L. Rainwater, G. Schmaus and T. Smeeding (1988), 'Equivalence scales, well-being, inequality and poverty: Estimates across ten countries using the LIS database', *Review of Income and Wealth*, 34, 115–42.

Buhr, Petra (1995), *Dynamik von Armut – Dauer und biographische Bedeutung von Sozialhilfebezug*, Opladen: Westdeutscher Verlag.

Buhr, Petra and Wolfgang Voges (1998), 'Akten als Datenquelle. Die Bremer Längsschnitt-Stichprobe von Sozialhilfeakten (LSA)', in Wolfgang Voges (ed.), *Kommunale Sozialberichterstattung*, Leverkusen: Leske and Budrich, pp. 142–61.

Buhr, Petra, Markus Gangl and Doris Rentzsch (1998), 'Wege aus der Sozialhilfe – Wege in den Arbeitsmarkt? Chancen der Überwindung des

Sozialhilfebezuges in Ost- und Westdeutschland', in Walter R. Heinz, Werner Dressel, Dieter Blaschke and Gerhard Engelbrech (eds), *Was prägt Berufsbiographien? Lebenslaufdynamik und Institutionenpolitik*, Nürnberg: Institut für Arbeitsmarkt- und Berufsforschung, pp. 219–316 (BeitrAB 215).

Bundesministerium für Soziale Sicherheit und Generationen (BMSG) (2001), *Bericht über die soziale Lage: Analysen und Ressortaktivitäten*, Vienna: BMSG.

Craig, P. and M. Greenslade (1998), *First Findings from the Disability Follow-up to the Family Resources Survey*, DSS In-house Research Summary no. 5, London: Department of Social Security.

DETR (2000), *Measuring Multiple Deprivation at the Small Area Level: The Indices of Deprivation 2000*, London: Department of Environment, Transport and the Regions.

DSS (1999) *The Changing Welfare State – Opportunity for All – Tackling Poverty and Social Exclusion*, First Annual Report, Cm 4445, London: Department of Social Security.

DSS (2000a), *Households below average income, 1994/5–1998/9*, London: Department of Social Security.

DSS (2000b), *Incapacity Benefit and Severe Disablement Allowance. Quarterly summary statistics May 2000*, London: Department of Social Security.

DSS (2000c), *The Changing Welfare State – Pensioner Incomes*, London: Department of Social Security Paper.

Duncan, Greg and Wolfgang Voges (1995), 'Do Generous Social Assistance Programs Lead to Dependence?', Poverty Working Paper WP-95-1, Northwestern University, Evanston.

Eckardt, Thomas (1997), *Arm in Deutschland: eine sozialpolitische Bestandsaufnahme*, Munich: Olzog.

Ehlers, Karen (1997), *Armut in der Bundesrepublik Deutschland: die Entwicklung von Armutsdominanzrelationen ausgewaehlter Risikogruppen in den alten Bundeslaendern im Zeitraum 1984–1994*, Frankfurt/M: Lang.

EKKE (National Centre of Social Research) (1996), *Dimensions of social exclusion in Greece* (in Greek) Athens: EKKE.

Endean, R. (1999), 'Work, low pay and poverty, evidence from the BHPS and LLMDB', in H. Finch and G. Elam (eds) (1995), *Managing money in later life – Qualitative research among retirement pensioners*, DSS Research report no. 38, London: Department of Social Security.

Esping-Andersen, Gøsta (1991), *The Three Worlds of Welfare Capitalism*, Cambridge: Polity Press.

Esping-Andersen, Gøsta (1996), *Welfare States at the End of the Century:*

The Impact of Labour Market, Family and Demographic Change, OECD Working Papers on Social Policy, Paris: OECD.

European Commission (1984), *Council Decision of December 19, 1984*, Brussels: European Commission.

European Commission (1991), *National Policies to Combat Social Exclusion*, report published by the University of Bath on behalf of the European Commission.

European Commission (1992), *Second Annual Report of the European Community Observatory on National Policies to Combat Social Exclusion*, Brussels: European Commission.

European Commission (1993), *Growth, Competitiveness and Employment*, Luxembourg: Office for Official Publications of the European Communities.

European Commission (1994), *Third Annual Report of the European Community Observatory on National Policies to Combat Social Exclusion*, Brussels: European Commission.

European Commission (1996), *Employment in Europe*, Luxembourg: Office for Official Publications of the European Communities.

European Commission (1997), *Modernising and Improving Social Protection in the European Union*, Communication, Brussels: European Commission.

European Commission (1999a), *European Community Household Panel (ECHP): Selected indicators from the 1995 wave*, Luxembourg: Office for Official Publications of the European Communities.

European Commission (1999b), *A Concerted Strategy for Modernising Social Protection*, Communication, Brussels: European Commission.

European Commission (2000a), *Building an inclusive Europe*, COM (2000) 79 Final, Brussels: European Commission.

European Commission (2000b), *European social statistics – Income, poverty and social exclusion*, Luxembourg: Office for Official Publications of the European Communities.

European Commission (2000c), *Decision of the European Parliament and of the Council establishing a programme of Community action to encourage co-operation between Member States to combat social exclusion*, COM(2000) 368, Brussels: European Commission.

European Commission (2001), *Communication from the Commission to the Council, the European Parliament, the Economic and Social Committee and the Committee of the Regions: Draft Joint Report on Social Inclusion, Annex 1: Social Inclusion Indicators*, Brussels: European Commission.

European Commission (2002), *Joint Report on Social Inclusion*, Luxembourg: Office for Official Publications of the European Communities.

Eurostat (1996), *The European Community Household Panel (ECHP): Survey methodology and implementation, Theme 3, Series E*, Luxembourg: Eurostat.

Eurostat (1998), *Recommendations on poverty and social exclusion statistics*, Luxembourg: Eurostat.

Eurostat (1999), *ECHP data quality*, DOC.PAN 119/99, Luxembourg: Eurostat.

Eurostat (2000), *European social statistics. Income, poverty and social exclusion*, Luxembourg: Eurostat.

Eurostat (2001), *EC Household Panel Newsletter* (1/01), Luxembourg: Eurostat.

Ferreira, A.F. (1987), *Por uma Política de Habitação*, Oporto: Ed. Afrontamento.

Ferreira, L. (1993), *Pobreza em Portugal – Variação e Decomposição de Medidas de Pobreza a partir de Orçamentos Familiares de 1980/81 e 1989/90*, Lisbon: CISEP.

Finlayson, L. and A. Marsh (1998), *Lone parents on the margins of work*, DSS Research Report No. 80, Leeds: Corporate Document Services.

Ford, R. (1996), *Childcare in the Balance*, London: Policy Studies Institute.

Förster, Michael (2001), 'Armutsgefährdete und arme Personen', in BM für Soziale Sicherheit und Generationen (ed.), *Bericht über die soziale Lage*, Vienna: BMSG, pp. 197–215.

Gallie, D. and S. Paugam (eds) (2000), *Welfare regimes and the experience of unemployment in Europe*, Oxford: Oxford University Press.

Goodin, R.E., B. Headey, R. Muffels and H.D. Dirven (1999), *The real worlds of welfare capitalism*, Cambridge: Cambridge University Press.

Gordon, D. L. Adelman, K. Ashworth, J. Bradshaw, R. Levitas, S. Middleton, C. Pantazis, D. Patsios, S. Payne, P. Townsend and J. Williams (2000), *Poverty and social exclusion in Britain*, York: Joseph Rowntree Foundation.

Grácio, S. (n.d.), 'Crise juvenil e invenção da juventude: notas para um programa de pesquisa', unpublished.

Gregg, P. (1999), 'Scarring effects of unemployment', in HM Treasury and CASE (eds), *Persistent poverty and lifetime inequality: the evidence*, CASE report 5/ HM Treasury Occasional Paper no. 10, London: Centre for Analysis of Social Exclusion/HM Treasury, pp.89–96.

Gregg, P. and J. Wadsworth (1996), 'It takes two: employment polarisation in the OECD', discussion paper no. 304, Centre for Economic Performance, London School of Economics.

Gustafsson, Bjørn and Wolfgang Voges (1998), 'Contrasting Welfare Dynamics: Germany and Sweden', in Lutz Leisering and Robert Walker (eds), *The Dynamics of Modern Society: Policy, Poverty and Welfare*, Bristol: Policy Press, pp. 243–61.

Habich, Roland and Peter Krause (1997), 'Armut', in Statistisches Bundesamt (ed.), *Datenreport 1997*, Bonn: Bundeszentrale für politische Bildung.

Hagenaars, A.J.M., K. de Vos and M.A. Zaidi (1994), *Poverty statistics in the late 1980s: Research based on micro-data, Theme 3, Series C*, Luxembourg: Eurostat.

Hanesch, Walter, Wilhelm Adamy and Rudolf Martens (eds) (1994), *Armut in Deutschland. Der Armutsbericht des DGB und des Paritätischen Wohlfahrtsverbands*, Reinbek: Rowohlt.

Hauptverband der österreichischen Sozialversicherungsträger (2001), *Handbuch der österreichischen Sozialversicherung – 2001*, Vienna: HV der österreichischen Sozialversicherungsträger.

Hauser, Richard (1995), 'Das empirische Bild der Armut in der Bundesrepublik Deutschland – ein Überblick', in *Aus Politik und Zeitgeschichte, Beilage zur Wochenzeitung Das Parlament*, B 31–32/95, pp.3–13.

Hauser, Richard (1997), 'Vergleichende Analyse der Einkommensverteilung und der Einkommensarmut in den alten und neuen Bundesländern 1990 bis 1995', in Irene Becker and Richard Hauser (eds), *Einkommensverteilung und Armut*, Frankfurt/M. and New York: Campus, pp. 63–82.

Hauser, Richard and Irene Becker (2001), *Einkommensverteilung im Querschnitt und im Zeitverlauf 1973 bis 1998. Studie im Auftrag des Bundesministeriums für Arbeit und Sozialordnung*, Bonn: BMA.

Hauser, Richard and Werner Hübinger (1993), *Arme unter uns, Teil 1: Ergebnisse und Konsequenzen der Caritas-Armutsuntersuchung*, edited by Deutscher Caritasverband, Freiburg: Lambertus.

Hauser, Richard, Wolfgang Glatzer, Stefan Hradil, Günther Kleinhenz, Thomas Olk and Eckart Pankoke (1996), *Ungleichheit und Sozialpolitik*, Opladen: Leske + Budrich.

Hawlik, Johannes (1981), *Armut in Wien, Kommunalpolitische Schriftenreihe des Dr. Karl-Lueger Instituts der Wiener Volkspartei*, Vienna: Dr. Karl Lueger-Institut.

Heady C. (1997) 'Labour market transitions and social exclusion', *Journal of European Social Policy* (7), 119–28.

Heitzmann, Karin (2000), 'The Dynamics of Poverty and Social Exclusion: The Case of Austria', working paper for the EU T.S.E.R. research project on 'Family Structure, Labour Market Participation and the Dynamics of Social Exclusion', Vienna University of Economics and Business Administration.

Heitzmann, Karin (2001), 'Armut ist weiblich ! – Ist Armut weiblich?', in Karin Heitzmann and Angelika Schmidt (eds), *Frauenarmut: Hintergründe, Facetten, Perspektiven*, Vienna: Peter-Lang.

Hills, J. (1998), 'Thatcherism, New Labour and the Welfare State', CASE paper 13, Centre for Analysis of Social Exclusion, London School of Economics.

Hills, J. (1999), *Social exclusion, income dynamics and public policy*, Annual Sir Charles Carter lecture, Belfast: Northern Ireland Economic Development Office.

Hills, J., J. Le Grand and D. Piachaud (eds) (2002), *Understanding Social Exclusion*, Oxford: Oxford University Press.

Hobcraft, J. (1998), 'Intergenerational and Life Course Transmission of Social Exclusion: Influences of Childhood Poverty, Family Disruption and Contact with the Police', London: LSE Centre for the Analysis of Social Exclusion (CASE Paper 15).

Hobcraft, J. and K. Kiernan (1999), 'Childhood Poverty, Early Motherhood and Adult Social Exclusion', CASE paper 28, Centre for the Analysis of Social Exclusion, London School of Economics.

Hobson, B. (1994), 'Solo mothers, social policy regimes and the logics of gender', in D. Sainsbury (ed.) *Gendering welfare states*, London: Sage, pp. 170–87.

IDS (1999), *Relatório de Execução da Medida e Caracterização dos Beneficiários*, Lisbon: Instituto para o Desenvolvimento Social.

ISSAS (1990), *Poverty in figures: Europe in the early 1980s, Theme 3, Series C*, Luxembourg: Eurostat.

Jenkins, Stephen (1991), 'Poverty Measurement and the Within-Household Distribution: Agenda for Social Action', *Journal of Social Policy*, 20(4), 457–83.

Kass, Gordon V. (1975), 'Significance testing in automatic interaction detecting (A.I.D.)', *Applied Statistics*, 24, 178–89.

Kass, Gordon V. (1980), 'An exploratory technique for investigating large quantities of categorical data', *Applied Statistics*, 29, 119–27.

Katrougalos, G.S. (1996), 'The South European Welfare Model: The Greek Welfare State in Search of Identity', *Journal of European Social Policy*, 6(1), 39–60.

Kilkey, M. and J. Bradshaw (1999), 'Lone mothers, economic well being and policies' in D. Sainsbury (ed.), *Gender and Welfare Regimes*, Oxford: Oxford University Press, pp.147–84.

Krause, Peter, Joachim Frick, Jan Goebel, Markus Grabka, Birgit Otto and Gert Wagner (2001), *Einkommensverteilung und Einkommensmobilität (Endbericht). Beitrag zur Armuts- und Reichtumsberichterstattung der Bundesregierung im Auftrag des Bundesministeriums für Arbeit und Sozialordnung*, Berlin: Deutsches Institut für Wirtschaftsforschung.

Kronauer, Martin (1998), 'Social Exclusion and Increasing Uncertainty of the Middle Classes: The West German Case', in Bram Steijn, Jan Berting and Mart-Jan de Jong (eds), *Economic Restructuring and the Growing Uncertainty of the Middle Class*, Boston and London: Kluwer Academic, pp. 61–72.

Lamnek, Siegfried and Jens Luedtke (1999), *Der Sozialstaat zwischen Markt und Hedonismus?*, Opladen: Leske + Budrich.

Langan, Mary and Ilona Ostner (1991), 'Gender and Welfare: Towards a Comparative Framework', in Graham Room (ed.), *Towards a European Welfare State?*, Bristol: Policy Press, pp.127–50.

Leibfried, S. (1992), 'Towards a European welfare state: on integrating poverty regimes into the European Community', in S. Ferge and J. Kohlberg (eds), *Social Policy in a Changing Europe*, Boulder: Westview Press.

Levitas, R. (1998), *The inclusive society? Social exclusion and New Labour*, Basingstoke: Macmillan.

Lewis, Jane (2001), 'The decline of the male breadwinner model: implications for work and care', *Social Politics*, 8(2), 152–69.

Lutz, Burkart (1984), *Der kurze Traum immerwährender Prosperität. Eine Neuinterpretation der industriell-kapitalistischen Entwicklung in Europa des 20. Jahrhunderts*, Frankfurt/M. and New York: Campus.

Lutz, Hedwig, Michael Wagner and Walter, Wolf (1993), *Von Ausgrenzung bedroht: Struktur und Umfang der materiellen Armutsgefährdung im österreichischen Wohlfahrtsstaat der achtziger Jahre*, Vienna: BMAS.

Lutz, Ronald and Matthias Zeng (eds) (1998), *Armutsforschung und Sozialberichterstattung in den neuen Bundeslaendern*, Opladen: Leske + Budrich.

Mansel, Jürgen and Klaus-Peter Brinkhoff (eds) (1998), *Armut im Jugendalter: soziale Ungleichheit, Gettoisierung und die psychosozialen Folgen*, Weinheim: Juventa.

Micklewright, J. (2002), 'Social exclusion and children: A European view for a US debate', CASE paper 54, Centre for Analysis of Social Exclusion, London School of Economics.

Middleton, Sue, Karl Ashworth and Ian Braithwaite (1997), *Small Fortunes: Spending on Children, Childhood Poverty and Parental Sacrifice*, York: York Publishing Services for the Joseph Rowntree Foundation.

Millar, J. (1989), *Poverty and the lone-parent: the challenge to social policy*, Aldershot: Avebury.

Millar, Jane and Caroline Glendinning (1989), 'Gender and Poverty', *Journal of Social Policy*, 3(18), 363–81.

Mitchell, D. (1991), *Income Transfers in Ten Welfare States*, Aldershot: Avebury.

Müller, Siegfried and Ulrich Otto (1997), *Armut im Sozialstaat*, Neuwied: Luchterhand.

Neuhäuser, J. (1995), 'Sozialhilfeempfänger 1993', *Wirtschaft und Statistik*, 5, 704–18.

O'Higgins M. and S.P. Jenkins (1990), 'Poverty in EC: Estimates for 1975, 1980 and 1985', in R. Teekens and B.M.S. van Praag (eds), *Analysing poverty in the European Community*, Luxembourg: Eurostat News Special Edition.

Olk, Thomas and Doris Rentzsch (1997), 'Armutsverläufe – erste Ergebnisse einer Kohortenanalyse Hallenser Sozialhilfe-empfänger(innen)', in Irene Becker and Richard Hauser (eds), *Einkommensverteilung und Armut*, Frankfurt/M. and New York: Campus, pp. 135–60.

Olk, Thomas and Doris Rentzsch (1998), 'Kinder in ostdeutschen Armutshaushalten', in A. Klocke and Klaus Hurrelmann (eds), *Kinder und Jugendliche in Armut*, Opladen: Westdeutscher Verlag, pp. 87–111.

Organisation for Economic Co-operation and Development (OECD) (1995a), *Main economic indicators*, Geneva: OECD.

Organisation for Economic Co-operation and Development (OECD) (1995b), *Employment Outlook 1995*, Geneva: OECD.

Organisation for Economic Co-operation and Development (OECD) (1996), *Social expenditure statistics of OECD member countries*, Geneva: OECD.

Otto, Ulrich (1997), *Aufwachsen in Armut: Erfahrungswelten und soziale Lagen von Kindern armer Familien*, Opladen: Leske + Budrich.

Paugam, S. (1996), 'Poverty and social disqualification: A comparative analysis of cumulative social disadvantage in Europe', *Journal of European Social Policy*, 6, 287–303.

Perista, H., M. Silva and M. Gomes (1993), *A pobreza no feminino na cidade de Lisboa*, Lisbon: ONG's do Conselho Consultivo da CIDM.

Presidency Conclusions (2000), *Nice European Council Meeting*, 7–9 December.

Reinl, Heidi (1997), 'Ist die Armut weiblich? Über die Ungleichheit der Geschlechter im Sozialstaat', in Siegfried Müller and Ulrich Otto (eds), *Armut im Sozialstaat: Gesellschaftliche Analysen und sozialpolitische Konsequenzen,* Berlin: Luchterhand, pp.113–33.

Rentzsch, Doris and Petra Buhr (1996), 'Im Osten nichts Neues? Sozialhilfe in Ost- und Westdeutschland im Vergleich', working paper No. 41 of the Special Collaborative Programme No. 186 at the University of Bremen.

Rodrigues, C.F. (1999), 'Income distribution and poverty in Portugal: 1994/95', Lisbon: Technical University of Lisbon, Department of Economics Discussion Paper 4/1999.

Room, G. (ed.) (1995), *Beyond the Threshold: The Measurement and Analysis of Social Exclusion*, Bristol: Policy Press.

Room G. (1999) 'Social exclusion, solidarity and the challenge of globalization', *International Journal of Social Welfare*, 8, 166–74.

Sachverständigenrat zur Begutachtung der gesamtwirtschaftlichen Entwicklung (1996), *Jahresgutachten 1996/97*, Bundestagsdrucksache 13/6200 v. 18.11.96.

Schneidewind, Peter (1985), *Mindestlebensstandards in Österreich*, Vienna: Bundesministerium für soziale Verwaltung.

Schupp, J. and G. Wagner (1991), 'Die Ost-Stichprobe des Sozioökonomischen Panels', in Projektgruppe Das Sozio-ökonomische Panel (eds), *Lebenslagen im Wandel: Basisdaten und -analysen zur Entwicklung in den Neuen Bundesländern*, Frankfurt/M. pp.25–41.

Seifert, Wolfgang (1994), 'Am Rande der Gesellschaft? Zur Entwicklung von Haushaltseinkommen und Armut unter Ausländern', in *Informationsdienst zur Ausländerarbeit*, pp. 16–23.

Silva, M. and A. Bruto da Costa (eds) (1989), *Pobreza Urbana em Portugal*, Lisbon: Cáritas.

Silva, M. and A. Bruto da Costa (eds) (1991), *Crianças Pobres em Lisboa – implicações para a intervenção social*, Lisbon: DPS/CRC.

Smeeding T.M., P. Saunders, J. Coder, S. Jenkins, J. Fritzell, A.J.M. Hagenaars, R. Hauser and M. Wolfson (1993), 'Poverty, inequality and living standard impacts across seven nations: the effects of non-cash subsidies for health, education and housing', *Review of Income and Wealth*, 39, 229–56.

Social Protection Committee (2001), *Report from the Chairman of the Indicators Sub-Group to the SPC* (SPC/2001/June/01_EN), Brussels: European Commission.

Sopp, Peter (1994), 'Das Ende der Zwei-Drittel-Gesellschaft? Zur Einkommensmobilität in Westdeutschland', in Michael Zwick (ed.), *Einmal arm, immer arm? Neue Befunde zur Armut in Deutschland*, Frankfurt/M. and New York: Campus, pp.47–74.

Spinellis C., E. Apospori, M. Kranidioti, P. Simiyanni and K. Angelopoulou (1994), 'Key-Findings of a Preliminary Self-Report Delinquency Study in Athens, Greece', in Josine Junger-Tas, Gert-Jan Terlouw and Malcolm W. Klein (eds), *Delinquent Behavior Among Young People in the Western World*, a series from the Dutch Research and Documentation Centre, Amsterdam: Studies on Crime and Justice, pp.288–388.

Standing, G. (2000), *Unemployment and Income Security*, Geneva: International Labour Organization.

Statistisches Bundesamt (2000), *Datenreport 1999*, Bonn: Bundeszentrale für politische Bildung.

Steiner, Hans and Liana Giorgi (1997), 'Armut und Armutsbekämpfung in Österreich', in Bundesministerium für Arbeit, Gesundheit und Soziales, BMAGS (ed.), *Bericht über die soziale Lage: Analysen und Ressortaktivitäten*, Vienna: BMAGS, pp.177–205.

Steiner, Hans and Walter Wolf (1996), *Armutsgefährdung in Österreich, Schriftenreihe Soziales Europa*, Vienna: BMAS.

Strengmann-Kuhn, Wolfgang (1997), 'Erwerbs- und Arbeitsmarkt-beteiligung der Armutsbevölkerung in Deutschland' in Irene Becker and Richard Hauser (eds), *Einkommensverteilung und Armut*, Frankfurt/M. and New York: Campus, pp.113–33.

Tálos, Emmerich (1999), 'Atypische Beschäftigung: Verbreitung – Konsequenzen – sozialstaatliche Regelungen. Ein vergleichendes Resümee', in Emmerich Tálos (ed.), *Atypische Beschäftigung – internationale Trends und sozialstaatliche Regelungen*, Vienna: Manz, pp.417–68.

Till, Matthias and Hans Steiner (2000), 'Zur sozialen Lage der Haushalte in Österreich – Ergebnisse des Europäischen Haushaltspanels', in Bundesministerium für Arbeit, Gesundheit und Soziales, BMAGS (ed.), *Bericht über die soziale Lage: Analysen und Ressortaktivitäten – 1998*, Vienna: BMAGS, pp.87–105.

Trickey, H. and R. Walker (2000), 'Steps to compulsion within British labour market policies', in I. Lødemel and H. Trickey (eds), *'An offer you can't refuse': Workfare in international perspective*, Bristol: Policy Press, pp.181–213.

Tsakloglou P. and F. Papadopoulos (2002), 'Poverty, material deprivation and multidimensional disadvantage during four life stages: Evidence from the ECHP', in M. Barnes, C. Heady, S. Middleton, J. Millar, F. Papadopoulos and P. Tsakloglou, (eds), *Poverty and Social Exclusion in Europe*, Cheltenham, UK and Northampton, MA, USA: Edward Elgar.

Tsakloglou, P. and Papadopoulos F. (2003), 'Identifying population groups at high risk of social exclusion' in R. Muffels, P. Tsakloglou and D. Mayes (eds), *Social Exclusion in European Welfare States,* Cheltenham, UK and Northampton, MA, USA: Edward Elgar.

Van Oorschot, W. (1991), 'Non-take up of social security benefits in Europe', *Journal of European Social Policy*, 1(1), 15–30.

Venieris, D.N. (1997), 'Dimensions of Social Policy in Greece', in M. Rhodes (ed.), *Southern European Welfare States: Between Crisis and Reform*, Florence: European University Institute, pp. 260

Voges, Wolfgang (2001), *Pflege alter Menschen als Beruf*, Opladen: Westdeutscher Verlag.

Voges, Wolfgang and Andreas Weber (1998), 'Neue Zuwanderergruppen in der Sozialhilfe', in Wolfgang Voges (ed.), *Kommunale Sozialberichterstattung*, Opladen: Leske + Budrich, pp. 367–97.

Voges, Wolfgang and Yuri Kazepov (1998), 'Welfare Regimes and Welfare Use. Social Assistance Patterns as an Outcome of Minimum Income Support Policies in German and Italian Cities', Working Paper no. 52 of the Special Collaborative Programme 186 at the University of Bremen: Bremen.

Voges, Wolfgang, Jürgen Frick and Felix Büchel (1998), 'The Integration of Immigrants into West German Society. The Impact of Social Assistance', in Hermann Kurthen, Jürgen Fijalkowski and Gert Wagner (eds), *Immigration, Citizenship, and the Welfare State: Germany and the U.S. in Comparison*, Stamford and London: JAI Press, pp. 159–74.

Voges, Wolfgang, Bjørn Gustafsson, and Nikolei Steinhage (1999), 'Immigration and Welfare Use. Social Assistance as Integration Support in Germany and Sweden', Working Paper no. 54 of the Special Collaborative Programme 186 at the University of Bremen.

Walker, Robert (1995), *Poverty Dynamics: Issues and Examples*, Aldershot: Avebury.

Walker, R. with M. Howard (2000), *The Making of a Welfare Class? Benefit receipt in Britain*, Bristol: Policy Press.

Walker, R., C. Heaver and S. McKay (2000), *Building Up Pension Rights*, DSS Research Report no. 114. London: Department of Social Security.

Wall, K. (1997), 'Famílias monoparentais em Portugal', *Actas do 3º Congresso de Sociologia*, Oeiras: Celta Editora.

Weick, Stefan (1999), 'Relative Einkommensarmut bei Kindern: Untersuchung zu Lebensbedingungen und Lebensqualität', in *Deutschland von 1984 bis 1996*, dissertation, Justus-Liebig-Universität, Gießen.

Whelan, C.T., R. Layte and B. Maitre (2001), 'What is the scale of multiple deprivation in the European Union?', EPAG working paper 19, University of Essex, Colchester, UK.

Whelan, C.T., R. Layte and B. Maitre (2002), 'Multiple deprivation and persistant poverty in the European Union', *Journal of European Social Policy*, 12, 91–105.

Index